SEEDS OF HOPE

ALSO BY JANE GOODALL

Books for Adults

Hope for Animals and Their World
(with Thane Maynard and Gail Hudson)

Harvest for Hope
(with Gary McAvoy and Gail Hudson)

The Ten Trusts
(with Marc Bekoff)

Reason for Hope
(with Phillip Berman)

The Chimpanzees of Gombe: Patterns of Behavior

In the Shadow of Man

Innocent Killers
(with Hugo van Lawick)

Through a Window

Visions of Caliban: On Chimpanzees and People
(with Dale Peterson)

Books for Children

The Chimpanzee Family

The Chimpanzee Family Book

Grub the Bush Baby

My Friends the Wild Chimpanzees

My Life with the Chimpanzees

With Love

SEEDS OF HOPE

Wisdom and Wonder from the World of Plants

JANE GOODALL

with

GAIL HUDSON

GRAND CENTRAL PUBLISHING

NEW YORK BOSTON

Grand Central Publishing
Hachette Book Group
237 Park Avenue
New York, NY 10017

HachetteBookGroup.com

Printed in the United States of America

RRD-C

First Edition: April 2013
10 9 8 7 6 5 4 3 2 1

Grand Central Publishing is a division of Hachette Book Group, Inc. The Grand Central Publishing name and logo is a trademark of Hachette Book Group, Inc.

The Hachette Speakers Bureau provides a wide range of authors for speaking events. To find out more, go to www.hachettespeakersbureau.com or call (866) 376-6591.

The publisher is not responsible for websites (or their content) that are not owned by the publisher.

Library of Congress Cataloging-in-Publication data has been applied for.

This book was printed on Domtar's EarthChoice Tradebook. The paper contains fiber from well-managed environmentally sound forests that are independently certified to the standards of the Forest Stewardship Council. This paper also contains 30% recycled paper, which was recovered from post-consumer waste.

This book is dedicated to Danny, Olly, and Uncle Eric, who created a magic garden during my childhood; and to Judy, Pip, and Wayne, who keep it alive today; to the scientists, naturalists and traditional healers whose fascination with the Green Kingdom has helped me to understand many of its mysteries; to all those who dare to speak out against "conventional" farming and genetically modified plants and the poisoning of our planet; and to the glorious diversity and resilience of the plants and trees themselves.

Contents

PART FOUR

The Way Forward

Foreword by Michael Pollan

My first reaction upon learning that Jane Goodall was taking a break from animals to write a book about plants was that this was very good news indeed for the plants. Plants don't get nearly as much ink or respect as the animals do, something I've always felt was deeply unfair, if entirely understandable. Animals are much easier for humans to identify with, sharing with us as they do such traits as consciousness, emotion, locomotion, and communication skills. You can tell stories about animals that have the same dramatic shape as stories about people, with heroes and villains, journeys and conflicts. That's not so easily done with plants, which seem simple by comparison and rather opaque.

Though it is worth remembering that, before Jane Goodall came along and introduced us to a society of chimpanzees at Gombe, in Tanzania, even the primates seemed much simpler and more opaque to us—much more difficult for us to identify with. It was her meticulous observation and chronicling of the lives of Mike and Humphrey, of Flo and Gigi and Frodo—all of them chimpanzees—that demonstrated once and for all that animals were far more like us than we had imagined or cared to admit. They too made and used tools, learned and passed on cultural information, and formed communities of individuals with distinct "personalities"—a word that in light of her work needs some rethinking. More than any other scientist or writer I can think of, Jane Goodall expanded the circle of human empathy to take in the emotional lives of other creatures.

I'm not sure whether plants have emotional lives, exactly, but anyone who reads *Seeds of Hope* cannot fail to come away thinking that they are far more complicated and interesting creatures than we give them credit for. I suspect the habit of underestimating them has its roots in our self-centered definition of what constitutes complexity or sophistication. We prize things like self-consciousness or abstract reasoning or language simply because these have been the destinations of our own evolutionary journey—the particular tools we evolved to help us cope with living on this earth. Yet the plants have been evolving even longer than we have, evolving their own tools for living, and these are easily as sophisticated as ours, just different. So while we were working hard on locomotion and consciousness, they were getting really, really good at biochemistry, up to and including their mastery of the astonishing trick of eating sunlight and turning it into food. Photosynthesis might be a skill hard for us to identify with, but—you've got to admit—it puts something like the opposable thumb, or even trigonometry, right in its place. The world could get by just fine without those little tricks, but without photosynthesis it would be a much, much duller place, lacking, among a great many other things, *us*.

In the pages of *Seeds of Hope*, Goodall introduces us to plants capable of the most extraordinary biochemical feats. There are the trees that alert one another to the arrival of an insect pest, causing the entire forest to produce compounds that render the flavor of its leaves unappetizing to the bug. (Who said plants don't have communication skills?) And though plants may not themselves possess consciousness, at least as we understand it, they do know how to manipulate the consciousness of other supposedly "higher" creatures, manufacturing chemical compounds that can change animal minds in the most striking ways—and thereby get the animals to do the bidding of the plants. We meet plants in this book that are masters of metaphor and simulation: "carrion plants" that mimic the stench of rotten meat to lure insects, and orchids that adorn themselves so as to resemble the hindquarters of female bees. Why? To trick credulous male bees into performing acts of "pseudocopulation" that, unbeknownst to them, are actually acts of pollination. In fact there are so many stories in this book of plants getting the better of animals that you really have to wonder which kingdom of creatures is really calling the shots, even in an enterprise as seemingly humanocentric as "agriculture." To read *Seeds of Hope* as a member of the animal kingdom is, among other things, a humbling experience.

In writing about plants, Goodall combines the cozy traditions of English garden writing—the epistolary ease and familiarity with horticulture—with the authority of an intrepid scientist who has spent not just days or weeks but years living in the forest among the trees. She has cultivated that way of being in (and with) nature E.O. Wilson had in mind when he coined the word "biophilia." Though the book is steeped in science, Goodall's feelings for the plants are spiritual—and her concern for their fate in the modern world is forthrightly political.

Seeds of Hope is not just a love letter to the plant world, though it is certainly that. It's also a call to arms, sounding the alarm about habitat destruction, the violence of industrial agriculture, and the risks of genetic engineering. In our own time, the long, beautiful, and mutually beneficial co-evolutionary journey of plants and animals has arrived at a critical new juncture, Goodall suggests, and this gives *Seeds of Hope* its sense of urgency. Jane Goodall wants nothing less than to expand the circle of human affection once again, make it wide enough to take in the sunlight eaters. For both their sake and our own, let us hope she succeeds.

PART ONE

My Love for the Natural World

Chapter 1

A Childhood Rooted in Nature

Me, about three years old, setting out to explore the forest.
(CREDIT: W. E. JOSEPH, "UNCLE ERIC")

"Jane Goodall has written a book about plants? Surely not—isn't she the one who studied chimpanzees in Africa?" I can hear the comments. Indeed, I have been hearing them for the past couple of years as I collected information for this book. Of course I am best known—thanks especially to *National Geographic*'s magazine articles and documentaries—for the study of the Gombe chimpanzees. In 2010 we celebrated fifty years of research there. But there would be no chimpanzees without plants—nor human beings either, for that matter. And the chimpanzee might never have materialized for me had I not been obsessed, as a child, with stories of the wilderness areas of the planet and most especially, the forests of Africa.

From my window, as I write in my house in Bournemouth, England, I can see the trees that I used to climb as a child. Up in the branches of one of them, a beech tree, I would read about Doctor Dolittle and Tarzan, and dream about the time when I, too, would live in the forest.

When war broke out in Europe, my father went off to fight for his country against Hitler and the Nazi scourge. This is when I came with my sister and my mother to live with her two sisters, Olly and Audrey, and her mother—known by all as "Danny" (as I could not say "Granny" when I was small)—in this 1872 red-brick Victorian house, with huge sash windows and high ceilings. *The Birches.*

We had little money between us—and anyway, it was wartime rationing, tightened belts, and so on. But we had a big garden (or yard) with a lawn where moss insisted on growing, and a good many trees. There was my beech and three magnificent silver birch trees, with their smooth, silvery trunks and graceful branches. There was a mountain ash, or rowan, glorious with red berries in autumn, and two Spanish chestnut trees—one of which produced minute chestnuts each year, hardly worth the bother of opening the prickly cases, while the other—which we named "Nooky"—had been maimed. The upper half of his trunk and branches had been sawed off so that he was, in effect, little more than a twenty-foot-tall stump. A stump that sprouted prolific branches that reached up to the sky for another twenty feet or more, as though to compensate for the missing trunk. Nooky never produced a flower, let alone a chestnut.

All around the garden was a tall hedge of privet interspersed with the occasional trimmed holly tree. It was not a "bright" garden because it was shaded by two big fir trees and five pines, and there were rhododendron bushes and ivy all over the place. And so, although Danny and Olly worked hard trying to grow vegetables for the war effort, what with the shade and the sandy soil (we are just a ten-minute walk from the ocean), and the acidity caused by the rhododendrons and pines, it was only runner beans and Danny's parsley and mint that really flourished.

But some things grew. All year-round, except in the very cold months, there were daisies all over the lawn. I wonder how many daisy chains we made each year. And dandelions appeared everywhere—almost impossible to dig up with their long, long roots. Every spring we watched for the first snowdrops pushing through soil still hard from winter frosts. They were followed by crocus and then, as the ground warmed, the primroses, foxgloves, bluebells, buttercups, and Wordsworth's "cloud of dancing daffodils." And all the time the buds on the trees were growing fat and bursting into tiny infant leaves. Then came the glorious awakening of the white blossom on the hawthorn, the rich pink red of the may, the bright yellow of the laburnum, and the purple of the lilac. And, best of all for me, lilies of the valley with their heady fragrance that, today, poignantly reminds me of those childhood days.

Later, as spring changed to summer, Olly's roses began to bloom, one after the other, as did her azalea that grew beside her beloved rhubarb plant, and Danny's special dark-red peonies surrounded by her precious runner beans. And the leaves on the trees, fed by the rising sap, reached their full maturity and worked each day to change sunlight into food for the tree or shrub that had nurtured their growing.

My love of plants and trees was heightened by hours of roaming, together with my dog Rusty, the wild cliffs that drop down to the sandy beach below. They are intersected by a series of dry streambeds that are known, in these parts, by an archaic French word—*chine.* Our house stands on Durley Chine Road. Every spring gorse bushes blossom into a blaze of yellow on the lower slopes of our chine, and tiny sweet-scented violets appear in one spot. I used to try to find the very first tiny purple flowers to take to Olly. Violets were her passion.

When the rhododendrons bloom in the summer, the steep sides of Middle Chine are glorious with the mauve color of their exotic

Rusty and I spent as much time in the garden as we could.
(CREDIT: JANE GOODALL)

flowers—they grew thickly in our school grounds, as well. Danny had a favorite outside the kitchen window that had rich-red blooms.

Autumn was a time I loved. The verdant green of summer changed to soft yellows and gold, and here and there a splash of red leaves. Gradually the leaves fell and the ground was carpeted with their glowing colors until they rotted into rich loam, or were swept from the lawn and burned on a bonfire at the bottom of the garden and we baked potatoes in the hot ashes.

On the cliffs there were a few oak and beech trees, but mostly a host of pine trees (Scots, Maritime, and Caledonian) that were planted on the original heath land in the massive landscaping project that started early in the nineteenth century. There were a couple of ancient Spanish chestnuts which, while they did not produce the large chestnuts sold commercially, were two or three times the size of those in our garden, and we loved to roast them around the grate of our small sitting-room fire.

During my childhood, Danny's one son, my uncle Eric, would bring us nuts from the huge and ancient walnut tree in his garden, and he brought apples too. We would pick blackberries on the cliff and Danny would make blackberry-and-apple pies. She also made elderberry wine from the clusters of black fruits from our own elder. It was nonalcoholic, but the very fact that it was called "wine" gave us children a sense of being grown up when we drank it at Christmas time in grown-up wineglasses.

I have no doubt that growing up in this idyllic home and landscape of England was the foundation of my lifelong love of the plant kingdom and the natural world. The other day, when I was looking through a box of childhood treasures that had been lovingly preserved by my mother, I came across a "Nature Notebook" in which the twelve-year-old Jane, with great attention to detail, had sketched and painted a number of local plants and flowers. Beside each drawing or watercolor I had handwritten a detailed description of the plant, based on my careful observations and probably a bit of book research.

A painting from my childhood, "Nature Notebook." This is a primrose, one of my favorite flowers from our garden. (CREDIT: JANE GOODALL)

This was not a schoolbook. This wasn't done for an assignment. I just loved to draw and paint and write about the plant world. In a sense, I began writing *Seeds of Hope* over sixty years ago!

Of course, even as I was becoming increasingly aware of plants—well, trees really—as individual beings, I was, at the same time, learning ever more about the animals. I especially loved the barn owls that would punctuate the night with their eerie calls, the bullfinches with their glowing red-pink breast feathers, and the herring and black-headed gulls who flew low over the garden, screaming and waiting for one of us to go out and throw them bread crusts. Blackbirds, song thrushes, robins, and many kinds of tits nested in our tall, tangled hedges and in the trees. There were still one or two red squirrels left on the cliff back then, but the gray invaders were rapidly taking over the real estate. Occasionally we took a bus to the New Forest, woods interspersed with moors covered in heather, where there were New Forest ponies and deer, and if we were lucky, we might glimpse a fox.

And let me not forget the insects. In those days there were buzzings and hummings and chirpings of bugs of all sorts. In the daytime there were the shimmering, fluttering wings of butterflies (surely they were originally "flutterbys" until some medieval scholar got his *f*'s and *b*'s confused?). Then in the evening came the irritating high-pitched whine of the mosquitoes, and at night the moths arrived, attracted by the white blossoms and night fragrance of the syringa and white lilac—and, unfortunately, by our lights.

There were Olly and Danny's enemies, the slugs and snails. My sister, Judy, and I loved snails and often kept them so that we could race them. Years later I learned that snail racing was at one time a popular pastime among elderly gentlemen in France! Our garden had its full quota of those invaluable little helpers, the earthworms, eating their way through the soil, aerating it, an important part of the ecosystem. I once took a whole handful to bed with me when I was just eighteen months old. My wise mother, instead of scolding, told me they would die, for they needed the earth, and together we took them back to a flowerbed.

And then there were the bees, the pollinators so absolutely essential to the gardener. I watched them for hours—honeybees flying busily from flower to flower, the "breadbaskets" on their legs gradually filling with bright yellow pollen as they performed that all-important task of pollination. The big, furry-coated bumblebees, jet black with one or two bright-yellow stripes on the abdomen—who really did "bumble" from flower to flower—seemed almost lazy by comparison with the honeybees. It was fascinating to see them push their way into the foxglove flowers and watch as the blooms trembled while the invisible visitor probed for nectar.

When I got my first job—as a secretary—in Oxford, I was able to explore a different part of England. Every weekend I set off on my bicycle into the surrounding countryside, exploring lanes and hedgerows, which, in those halcyon days of the mid-1950s, were a riot of wildflowers. I would leave my bike and wander through the fields, past grazing cows (keeping a wary eye out for the occasional bull), and getting familiar with cow parsley (or Queen Anne's lace), campion, speedwell, ragged robin, and the mauve sweet-scented clover that was so beloved by bees—and cattle and horses too.

Sometimes in the evening I would hire a little canoe for an hour and paddle, silently, past bulrushes and reed beds, nosing in toward the bank where I could be hidden in a cave of green under the trailing branches of a huge weeping willow to watch the mallard ducks. I remember that a couple of verses of a very different sort of poem would sometimes repeat themselves in my mind in a somewhat annoying way—they came from one of my favorite childhood books, *The Wind in the Willows.*

All along the backwater,
Through the rushes tall,
Ducks are a-dabbling,
Up tails all!
Ducks' tails, drakes' tails,
Yellow feet a-quiver,
Yellow bills all out of sight
Busy in the river!

I could only paddle about a mile upriver—partly because I could only afford the canoe for an hour, but also because one then came to a stretch of river that was forbidden to women—named Parson's Pleasure, it was reserved for gentlemen who desired to disport themselves in their "birthday suits." I knew of girls who would hide for hours in thick undergrowth to get a glimpse of certain body parts, and I suspect the men were well aware of those immodest eyes!

Not only did my mother preserve my "Nature Notebooks," she also saved the only three copies ever produced of "The Alligator Magazine," written at about the same time as I was painting local wildflowers. They were put together for the benefit of the four members of "The Alligator Club"—me and Judy, and the two friends who came to stay almost every holiday, Sally and Susie. I was the eldest, and bossed the others around, and planned the games we would play and the things we would do.

Sally (a year my junior) and I were the real tomboys. Sue and Judy—the "Little Ones" (three and four years younger than me, respectively)—were not quite as keen on climbing trees and pretending to be Robin Hood and his men. But we got on well together—and, when I was about eleven, I started the Alligator Club. Why I picked the name *alligator* I have absolutely no idea!

It was a club for nature lovers. We watched the plants and animals and wrote little stories in our nature notebooks about them. Well, to be really truthful, I did those things and did my best to persuade the others to do the same. This was easier when we were together, but when Sally and Sue went home after the holidays, it was hard.

So I put together a magazine. I wrote—by hand as there was no other option at the time—articles about all sorts of things, and asked the others to make contributions. Of course, there was only one copy, so after they read it, Sally and Sue had to return it. In the next edition I asked questions about the articles I had written in the one before. The members were supposed to put their answers in the "letter box"—an envelope glued to the inside of the cardboard cover at the back. After four "editions" I tired of producing this magazine, since it was almost impossible to get the others to contribute, and only Judy answered the questions, and only because I bullied her into doing so! But it taught me a lot.

In fact it may well have been my experience with the Alligator Club that enabled me to persevere in developing what is, today, a movement for young people from kindergarten through university, now in over 130 countries—Jane Goodall's Roots & Shoots (R&S). The Alligator Club had only four members, including myself. Roots & Shoots is encouraging hundreds of thousands of young people to take action and try to make this a better world for all living things.

Looking at my nature notebook with the carefully drawn and painted flowers, and looking through those magazines, preserved from a time long gone, brought those magical days of childhood alive. I found myself thinking about cold, wet winter days when I used to read, curled up in front of the fire, on winter evenings. Then I traveled in my imagination to *The Secret Garden* with Mary and Colin and Dickon. I was entranced by C. S. Lewis's *Voyage to Venus*, in which he describes, so brilliantly, flowers and fruits, tastes and colors and scents, unknown on Planet Earth. I raced through the skies with little Diamond, who was curled up in the flowing hair of the Lady North Wind, as she showed him what was going on in the world, the beauty and the sadness and the joy (*At the Back of the North Wind*). And of course I was utterly in love with Mole and Ratty and Mr. Badger in *The Wind in the Willows*. If *The Lord of the Rings* had been written when I was a child, there is no doubt I would have been entranced by Treebeard and the ancient forest of Fangorn, and Lothlorien, the enchanted forest of the elves.

Of course at the same time I was reading more and more about the animals who lived in the wild places of the world. I am so glad TV had not been invented then—it meant I had to, and most certainly did, exercise and develop my powers of imagination.

Those two worlds of my childhood—that of the imagination, and that of nature—were I think equally important in shaping the person I have become. But although the memories are beautiful and precious, they are bittersweet. Today, most of the fields where I roamed have been sold to the developers, and those that remain have been destroyed by chemical pesticides and fertilizers and herbicides and fungicides and the hedges hacked down to provide more land for more growing. The wildflowers have disappeared from the fields, and many of the songbirds that sang to my young ears are in steep decline. Of course there was always war between the farmers and the animals that sought to share the bounty of their labors, the shooting of rabbits and pigeons, but the mass destruction of wildlife caused by the introduction of chemicals in agriculture did not happen until after World War II. Since then our wildflowers (along with so much wildlife) have been decreasing, becoming extinct in place after place.

And it is the same in so many parts of the world. The health of the soil has gradually been weakened, sometimes altogether destroyed. These days there are acres and acres of farmland where no crops will grow without massive doses of chemical fertilizer. And the chemical poison is contaminating the groundwater, the streams and rivers, bringing death to animals and plants alike. Tropical and old-growth forests, those magical places to which I had traveled in imagination, are disappearing at a terrifying rate. The same goes for other types of landscape—woodlands, wetlands, prairies and grasslands, moors and heaths. Indeed, the list is limited only by the types of environments found on Planet Earth.

Everywhere the natural world with its rich diversity of living things is under attack from human population growth, development, industrial agriculture, pollution, and shrinking water supplies of freshwater. Habitat loss is a theme that comes up again and again, diminishing the biodiversity and causing local extinctions in place after place. And, over and above everything else, looms the reality of climate change. The ice is disappearing from the North and South Poles and from the mountaintops.

Yet here in Bournemouth some things have changed but little. The garden at The Birches has continued to provide a magical playground for children—first Judy and me, then our children, and now our grandchildren. Judy has taken on the role of gardener, helped by her daughter, Pip, and our good friend Wayne Caswell. More species of flowers and vegetables are growing—the answer was to acquire better soil and grow a lot of plants in tubs. So today we have sweet peas and morning glory, geraniums and pansies, and many more. And they grow in between peas, tomatoes, spinach, potatoes, and courgettes (zucchinis). The bright-red flowers of the runner beans still brighten the garden on a dull day, and now there are the glossy black flowers of the broad bean, as exotic as the white fur that you find inside the seedpod when you open it. Danny's parsley still grows outside the kitchen window, and the little pink flowers on which she waged war have obstinately remained, though not in their original profusion. My precious lilies of the valley have all but gone—the hens we rescued from a battery farm, thrilled with their new freedom to forage in a garden, ate all but a few bulbs! Olly's greenhouse overflows with cucumbers and little seedlings of all sorts waiting to be planted outside. The pines and firs and Spanish chestnuts are still here, but our birch trees died in the 1975–76 drought, and only one of the three we planted to take their place survived a recent very dry summer. Nooky was trimmed by a tree surgeon—the branches from the old trunk were getting too big and heavy. And amazingly this produced, for the very first time, a massive crop of chestnuts—tiny ones of course.

The neighborhood—the streets, the cliffs, and the chines—is much as it was in my childhood. There has been some "manicuring"—the vegetation growing up the sides of the chines has been thinned out in some places, mainly because it provided an environment for winos and people doing drugs. Branches have been trimmed and some trees felled lest a passerby should be hurt by a falling limb and the city council sued. But the whole area is a conservation area. No one can cut down a tree without permission from the city council, and so the gardens are still green and leafy. When I am here, between my endless lecture tours around the world, there is always a dog to accompany me when, each day, I return to the haunts of my childhood. The current one is Charlie, a boxer cross—before her was Astro, who followed Whiskey, who was preceded by Cida—there have always been dogs at The Birches.

As I reflect on my early life and the experiences that shaped my thinking, I realize that it is not strange at all that I have written this book. What *is* strange is that this is not the book I first planned to write—that was to be simply a companion to *Hope for Animals and their World*, for which I had written a whole section on the kingdom of the plants. But the manuscript for *Hope for Animals* was too long, and almost all of the plant section had to be cut. I was sad about that—many of those who had contributed their plant stories had been so generous and so pleased for me to write about their work. So I planned to write a short book, simply adding a little to that original plant section. It was to have been about plant species rescued from the brink of extinction. But it has not worked out that way.

It was as though the plants wanted me to write a different kind of book and sent gentle roots deep into my brain. They wanted me to fully acknowledge their importance in human history, their amazing powers of healing, the nourishment they provide, their ability to harm if we misused them, and, ultimately, our dependence on the plant kingdom. The plants seemed to want me to share with the world my own understanding of their *beingness*, so that people might better honor them as important partners in so many of our endeavors.

The more I followed these promptings, the more avenues of thought I pursued, the more I talked with botanists and horticulturists and conservationists, the more fascinated I became and the more horrified at all that we are harming and destroying.

At the same time I was learning so much about the efforts that are being made, all around the globe, to protect and restore the natural world. The plant species that have been saved, in the nick of time, from extinction and given another chance. The work of the botanical gardens, introducing millions of people to the wonder of the plant world while, at the same time, carrying out cutting-edge research on the best ways of propagating endangered species. The people who are growing native plants in their gardens, creating havens for wildlife and insects. The increasing number of those who are prepared to fight for the plants and trees, the grasslands and the forests. That is the hope.

And so I have written a book to acknowledge the enormous debt we owe to the plants and to celebrate the beauty, mystery, and complexity of their world. That we may save this world before it is too late.

Chapter 2

The Kingdom of the Plants

This Strangler Fig's roots are now an integral part of the ancient temple at Angkor Watt in Cambodia. I shall never forget the feeling of stepping back in time, the sense of wonder at these extraordinary ruins deep in the forest.
(CREDIT: © JANE GOODALL INSTITUTE / BY MARY LEWIS)

Science divides the natural world into two main kingdoms—the animal kingdom and the plant kingdom. And in both we find huge diversity of form and size and color, and so many fascinating and complex societies. Most people are more familiar with the inhabitants of the plant kingdom, for they are all around us, just about all the time. I have spent a lifetime loving plants, even though I have never studied them as a scientist. And over the years, people have given me marvelous books—collections of photographs of various habitats, and of exotic fruits and seeds and flowers that might have been drawn from the imagination of artists high on psychedelic drugs.

I have walked through forests in many parts of the world and marveled at ancient trees festooned with vines, ferns spreading their graceful fronds beside fast-flowing streams, and rocks clothed in mosses. I have a special love for old-growth forests with their wealth of interconnected life-forms—I always feel that I belong there. But there is so much more to marvel at in the kingdom of the plants. I often use the zoom setting of my camera to photograph the exquisite flowering of tiny plants that most people walk past, or trample on, not noticing.

The first time I visited the tundra, in Greenland, I was humbled to see small plants that had sprung into life after enduring eight months under snow and ice. And amazed to learn that they were actually trees—but although they had managed to survive in those bleak conditions they could never attain the typical height of their species. How different that arctic habitat is from the exotic riot of color, the sheer enchantment, of an alpine meadow in spring, with its myriad of flowers, the humming and buzzing and droning as a host of insects feast on nectar, pollinating the flowers so that they will reappear next year.

When I first saw the spring flowers blanketing the California hillsides, I wanted to walk out among the lupines and poppies and wild mustard, and simply lie among them, looking up into the blue, blue sky. But I was restrained, warned of snakes among the flowers, and had to be content just to feast my eyes on their colors and inhale their sweet fragrance.

The plants of the arid parts of the world—the dry plains and the desert—are also fascinating. These are the places where succulents and cacti have adapted to survive long periods without water, storing it in their leaves and stems and roots. Just this past spring I spent a couple of hours wandering in the semidesert of Santa Fe, in

New Mexico, utterly captivated by the strange shapes of the cacti. I was lucky, for most of them were in bloom, their yellow and red and deep-purple flowers like gifts from Mother Nature in the dry landscape. And I have marveled to see how, after a long period of drought, the first rains will carpet the Serengeti Plain of East Africa with white and golden flowers shining through the dry, trampled grass. Here and there the vivid coral-colored flowers of the aloe plants peek through.

Recently, as I drove from Johannesburg to Nelspruit, in South Africa, I desperately wished there was time to stop off and find an *E. elephantine* tree, which, presumably able to withstand the cold, dry winters of its harsh upland habitat, lives almost entirely under the ground. If you walk among the branches of what seem like small bushes, rising only some three feet above the ground, you will actually be walking on the canopy of a very large and very ancient tree that is mostly out of sight beneath you.

It would be absurd in a book like this to try to describe the fantastic variety of plants, from the tiny mosses to the mighty redwoods. A recent inventory lists 298,000 different plant species (and 611,000 species of mushrooms, molds, and other fungi). And the authors reckon that 86 percent of all plants have yet to be named! All I can do here is to share some of what I find particularly compelling about this vast and wondrous kingdom of the plants.

Roots

Wouldn't it be fantastic if we had eyes that could see underground? So that we could observe everything down there in the same way we can look up through the skies to the stars. When I look at a giant tree I marvel at the gnarled trunk, the spreading branches, the multitude of leaves. Yet that is only half of the tree-being—the rest is far, far down, penetrating deep beneath the ground. The roots. Bit by bit they work their way through the substrate, pushing aside small pebbles, growing around big rocks, coiling around one another, taking from the soil the water and minerals needed by the partner up above, and creating a firm anchor for it. In many trees, the roots go as deep below the ground as the height of the tree above the ground, and spread out about three times farther than the spread of the branches. One root system, recorded during excavation of a building site in Arizona, had grown down some two hundred feet.

Some of the so-called "weeds" that colonize our gardens as unwanted guests have very deep roots. The dandelion goes down so far it is almost impossible to get the whole thing out of the ground. I can see my grandmother Danny now, kneeling on her little rubber pad, digging down around the roots of one dandelion plant after another, then trying to yank them out of the ground with that tool that looks like the end of the hammer that you use to pull out old nails. But she never got the whole root out.

There are so many kinds of roots. Aerial roots grow above the ground, such as those on epiphytes—which are plants growing on trees or sometimes buildings, taking water and nutrients from the air and rain—including many orchids, ferns, mosses, and so on. Aerial roots are almost always adventitious (I called them "adventurous" when I was a child), roots that can grow from branches, especially where they have been wounded, or from the tips of stems. Taproots, like those of carrots, act as storage organs. The small, tough adventitious roots of some climbing plants, such as ivy and Virginia creeper, enable the stems to cling to tree trunks—or the walls of our houses—with a viselike grip.

In the coastal mangrove swamps of Africa and Asia I have seen how the trees live with their roots totally submerged in water. Because these roots are able to exclude salt, they can survive in brackish water, even water that is twice as saline as the ocean. Some mangrove trees send down "stilt roots" from their lowest branches, others have roots that send tubelike structures upward through the mud and water and into the air, for breathing.

Then there are those plants, such as the well-known mistletoe, beloved by young lovers at Christmas time but hated by foresters, that are parasitic, sending roots deep into the host tree to steal its sap. The most advanced of the parasitic plants have long ago given up any attempt at working for their own food—their leaves have become like scales, or are missing altogether.

The strangler fig is even more sinister. Its seeds germinate in the branches of other trees and send out roots that slowly grow down toward the ground. Once the end touches the soil, it takes root. The roots hanging down all around the support tree grow into saplings that will eventually strangle the host. I was awestruck when I saw the famed temple at Angkor Wat in Cambodia, utterly embraced by the gnarled roots of a giant and ancient strangler fig. Tree and building are now so entwined that each would collapse without the support of the other. I noticed that strangler figs have been at work on many of the Mayan ruins in Mexico as well.

The so-called clonal trees have remarkable root systems that seem capable of growing over hundreds of thousands of years. The most famous of them—"Pando," or "The Trembling Giant"—has a root system that spreads out beneath more than one hundred acres in Utah and has been there, we are told, for eighty thousand to one million years! The multiple "stems" (meaning the tree trunks) of this colony age and die, but new ones keep coming up. It is the roots that are so ancient.

One of the most important things about roots is that they hold the soil in place. When the early settler farmers moved onto the American prairies, they cut down the trees that grew there and plowed up the land, destroying the native grasses so that they could grow agricultural crops. Over countless thousands of years those native grasses had developed root systems that delved deep, deep into the ground, holding the soil together so that it could withstand the constant stress of the wind. Human interference in this ancient system led to the Dust Bowl of the 1930s, when the soil was blown away in great clouds, much of it ending up in far-off oceans. Something similar happens in China today when clouds of dust are blown from the deforested center of the country and darken the skies over faraway Beijing for days on end.

Leaves

I always love to walk through the trees in the evening, when the sun is low and the leaves are backlit. And each single leaf, so beautiful with all its veins etched so clearly, some with an incredibly intricate branching pattern. These veins are the end point of the system that carries water and nutrients up, up from root to leaf. And they are the start of the system that carries the sap, with its dissolved sucrose, back out of the leaf to provide nutrients to the mother tree.

When I was a child, I used to spend hours searching under the trees, looking for the skeletons of leaves—when all the soft material has rotted away and only the veins remain. It is rare to find a perfect one, without tear or holes, but it is worth searching diligently—for the one that is without blemish is truly a work of art. I still search when I am walking through the Gombe forests.

The variety of leaves seems almost infinite. They are typically green from the chlorophyll that captures sunlight, and many are large and flat so as to catch the maximum amount. Indeed, some tropical leaves are so huge that people use them for umbrellas—and they are very effective, as I discovered during an aboriginal ceremony in Taiwan, when we were caught in a tropical downpour.

Orangutans have also learned to use large leaves during heavy rain. My favorite story concerns an infant, who was rescued from a poacher and was being looked after in a sanctuary. During one rainstorm she was sitting under the shelter provided but, after staring out, rushed into the rain, picked a huge leaf, and ran back to hold it over herself as she sat back in the dry shelter!

Some leaves are delicate, some are tough and armed with prickles, yet others are long and stiff, like needles. The often-vicious spines of the cactus are actually modified leaves—in these plants it is the stems that capture the energy from the sun. I used to think that the brilliant red of the poinsettia and the varied colors of bougainvillea were flowers, but of course they are leaves adapted to attract pollinating insects to the very small insignificant-looking flowers in the center. And there are those leaves adapted to capturing insects, some covered with resin-tipped glands that curl over and imprison the prey, others able to snap shut in an instant when an insect touches the hairs, which act as triggers.

And then there are the most extraordinary leaves of that bizarre plant, *Welwitschia mirabilis.* Each plant has only two leaves. On younger plants they look like quite ordinary long-shaped leaves, but they continue to grow, those exact same two leaves, for as long as the plant lives—which can be more than a thousand years.

The Welwitschia was first discovered in Africa's Namib Desert by Dr. Friedrich Welwitsch in 1859, and it is said that he fell to his knees and stared and stared, in silence. He sent a specimen to Sir Joseph Hooker, at Kew Royal Botanic Gardens—and Sir Joseph for several months became obsessed with it, devoting hours at a time to studying, writing about, and lecturing about the botanical oddity. It is, indeed, one of the most amazing plants on Earth, a living fossil, a relict of the cone-bearing plants that dominated the world during the Jurassic age. Imagine—this gangly plant, which Darwin called "the duckbill of the vegetable kingdom," has survived as a species, unchanged, for 135 to 205 million years. Originally its habitat was lush, moist forest, yet it has now adapted to a very different environment—the harsh Namib Desert.

The photograph in the color insert shows what looks like many untidy leaves, but they are really only the two. They first appear as the seed germinates—and as the years pass, they become increasingly leathery and tattered, nibbled by animals and buffeted by the wind—but they are never replaced. The tallest plant known is only five feet high; most are no more than twenty inches. Some Welwitschia plants growing in the wild have been carbon-dated and are between five hundred and six hundred years old, but it is thought that some of the largest could be two thousand years old.

Capturing Sunlight

At school I had to learn in my biology lessons about photosynthesis—which literally means "synthesis with the help of light." When I looked at my son's biology textbook some thirty years later I was amazed—and shocked actually—by the complex chemical process that he was supposed to learn as a schoolboy. It was the sort of information that was once reserved for university students specializing in botany—the kind of stuff that would have totally disenchanted me from the wonder of plants. And, indeed, it is pure chemistry.

The point is that plants can capture energy from sunlight. I love how this was described by the German surgeon Julius Robert Mayer in the 1800s. Nature, he said, has solved "the problem of how to catch in flight light streaming to the Earth; and to store this most elusive of all powers in rigid form."

Plants do this through extremely complex chemical reactions, which can, however, be described quite simply. There are special cells, usually in the leaves, that store molecules of chlorophyll, which is what gives them their green color. These molecules interact with nearby carbon dioxide (CO_2) (which they absorb from the atmosphere) and water (delivered by the plant's roots) to synthesize glucose and a "waste" product—oxygen. The glucose is either used at once, for energy needed by the plant, or it is changed (by another complex chemical process) into starch, which can be stored till needed. The "waste" product is excreted into the atmosphere—where it is used for respiration by plant and animal alike. It amused me, when I read about this, to think of our so-precious oxygen as a "waste" product—that is chemistry talking. The small amount of CO_2 produced by the plants during *their* respiration (basically their exhalations) is quickly used up by the ongoing photosynthesis process.

Think about all this for a moment. Our exhalations are nourishing the plants as they capture CO_2, and the plants' exhalations allow us (and them) to breathe. How utterly amazing—awe inspiring really. *One cupful of CO_2, a few tablespoons of water, mix with a beam of sunlight.* The ultimate and only recipe for the food that supports all plant life, including algae and other such forms. And since we depend on plants, either directly, by eating them, or indirectly, by eating animals that themselves depend on plants, the process of photosynthesis supports almost all life on Earth.

Carnivorous Plants

I am not a devotee of science fiction books, but John Wyndham's *The Day of the Triffids*, published in 1951, utterly captivated my imagination. "Triffids" are seven to ten feet tall, have three leg-like appendages that can be rooted into the ground, a sort of trunk, and a funnel-like head containing a sticky substance that attracts and captures insects that are then digested. Within this funnel there is also a stinger that, when fully extended, can measure up to ten feet. Sometimes a triffid will shuffle along the ground on its "legs" and, when it contacts a person, will aim at the face with its stinger. The victim dies quickly, and the triffid roots itself near the body, which it can digest as the flesh decomposes.

Science fiction, yes, but Mother Nature has designed monsters too—they are smaller, they cannot harm people, but the behavior of some of the carnivorous plants would make terrifying bedside reading for the tiny prey they capture. Take the Darlingtonia pitcher plant, also known as the cobra pitcher or cobra lily. It has a well-developed forked protrusion on the end of the modified leaf that forms the lip of the pitcher, which is designed to capture insects. This protrusion offers a convenient platform on which a flying insect can land, attracted to the nasty smell from inside the pitcher—well, nasty to us but obviously irresistible to the insect.

The hapless prey then slips down the walls, helped on its way by both lubricating secretions and downward-pointing hairs, and falls into the water and enzyme soup. The small exit is cunningly curled downward and thus hidden from the trapped insect, which exhausts itself by repeatedly crawling up the many translucent false exits. Eventually it will drown, and as it gradually decomposes, it will be absorbed by the plant. Unlike other pitcher plants, this one does not trap rainwater in its pitcher, but pumps up water from its roots, reabsorbing it if the level gets too high.

This is just one of the plants that have become carnivorous, capturing flies and other insects in a whole variety of ingenious ways and then slowly digesting them in special juices. There are about 630 species in six genera with five different kinds of traps, known as pitfall, flypaper, snap, bladder, and lobster traps. Scientists estimate that they first appeared some 200 million years ago in marshy, infertile soils that were lacking in essential minerals, especially nitrogen. Only by devising a novel way of getting the necessary nutrients could these plants survive. I get so carried away, reading about these cunning plants—it would not be difficult to write a whole chapter about them.

The best known are the pitcher plants, sundews, Venus flytraps, and the bladderworts. I remember our biology teacher bringing a sundew to school for us to see. Somehow my imagination had created a much more impressive being, and I was disappointed to see such a tiny plant, though fascinated by its behavior. Each leaf has a number of resin-tipped glands that serve to attract and capture small insects. Our biology teacher placed an unfortunate fly on this trap and we watched as the leaf curled slowly over it.

There are plants that have some but not all of the adaptations of the genuine carnivorous plants and are known as "borderline carnivorous." One of these has developed a pitfall trap, a sort of urn with a slippery waxed lip. It successfully catches insects—but does not digest them itself. Instead, it is hunting on behalf of a species of assassin bug. The bug eats the prey, and the plant lives on the bug's decomposed dung! Just one more example of the complex animal-plant relationships that make the natural world endlessly fascinating.

Seeds and Fruits

If plants could be credited with reasoning powers, we would marvel at the imaginative ways they bribe or ensnare other creatures into carrying out their wishes. And no more so than when we consider the strategies devised for the dispersal of their seeds. One such involves coating their seeds in delicious fruit and hoping that they will be carried in the bellies of animals to be deposited, in feces, at a suitable distance from the parent.

Charles Darwin was fascinated by seed dispersal (well, of course—he was fascinated by everything) and he once recorded, in his diary, "Hurrah! A seed has germinated after twenty-one and a half hours in an owl's stomach." Indeed, some seeds will not germinate unless they have first passed through the stomach and gut of some animal, relying on the digestive juices to weaken their hard coating. The antelopes on the Serengeti Plain perform this service for the seeds of the acacia.

In Gombe the chimpanzees, baboons, and monkeys are marvelous dispersers of seeds. When I first began my study, the chimpanzees were often too far away for me to be sure what they were eating, so in addition to my hours of direct observation I would search for food remains—seeds, leaves, parts of insects or other animals—in their dung. Many field biologists around the world do the same.

Some seeds are covered in Velcro-like burs (where do you think the idea of Velcro came from, anyway?) or armed with ferocious hooks so that a passing animal, willy-nilly, is drafted into servitude. Gombe is thick with seeds like this and I have spent hours plucking them from my hair and clothes. Sometimes my socks have been so snarled with barbs that, by the time they are plucked out, the socks are all but useless. Some seeds are caught up in the mud that waterbirds carry from place to place on their feet and legs.

I wonder how many dandelion "clocks" are picked and blown by lovesick adolescent girls: "He loves me, he loves me not. He loves me, he loves me not," and calculating the strength of the last breaths so that they can end, triumphantly, "He loves me!" Those little seeds, each suspended from a perfect parachute, are carried away in their thousands by the summer and autumn winds, colonizing gardens and parks—almost anywhere that plants can grow—and often where they are most definitely not wanted.

The kapok seed floats through the air attached to the softest white fluff. I watched one chimpanzee infant as he gazed, as though entranced at this spectacle, then reached out to try to catch some. I sometimes do the same! Sycamore seeds set off on their journey in pairs, fastened between two propeller-shaped wings that spin around and around like the blades of a miniature helicopter as they spiral down toward the ground.

Other seeds, lacking such convenient mechanisms, rely on their pods to shoot them as far away as possible. From my window, at school, I could hear the little *pops* of the broom pods as they burst open when the seeds were ripe inside and the sun was warm. They were carried several feet—and sometimes ants then carried them farther—which was an advantage only for those that were not eaten. The pods of some plants reach such a state of tension when their seeds are ripe that they seem literally to explode at the slightest touch—like the touch-me-not balsam. And there is a plant in Gombe that splits open, with a loud crack, at the first drop of rain, sending out seeds in all directions. I used to collect these pods and take them to my son, when he was little, and arrange a show for him.

Seeds come in all shapes and sizes. Most are quite small, but not so the coconut. This giant can be carried for miles across the ocean and, in this way, has enabled coconut palms to colonize almost every tropical island.

Sex Education

Plants reproduce both sexually and asexually. Every gardener knows how a cutting, given by a friend, can grow roots and survive. This is how my second husband, Derek Bryceson, and I built up our garden in Dar es Salaam. Some plants, such as the blackberry, form adventitious roots when the tip of a stem arches over and touches the ground. At this place a new plant will grow. Then there are those that send out special stems that are called runners when they grow *over* the ground, like strawberries, or rhizomes when they grow *under* the ground, like buttercups. When the runner, or rhizome, is far enough away from the parent plant, the tip puts out roots from which new plants can grow.

There is no doubt whatsoever that this kind of asexual, or "vegetative," reproduction can be an immensely efficient strategy. And when plants are introduced to new environments, it can also be very destructive. The water hyacinth is a free-floating aquatic plant with attractive lavender or pink flowers. It originated in South America, but has been introduced widely in tropical and subtropical areas of North America, Asia, Africa, Australia, and New Zealand. It reproduces asexually by runners and is one of the fastest-growing known plants—it can double its population in just two weeks. It clogs waterways and lakes. It starves water of oxygen, killing fish, turtles, and other wildlife. It was actually grown on lakes in World War II to fool Japanese pilots into thinking they could land. Governments have spent a great deal of money in their efforts to control the water hyacinth.

However, while reproduction without sex may be efficient, it doesn't allow for genetic diversity, and so almost all plants can reproduce sexually as well. We know all about human sex (way too much, in some instances). Most of us are familiar with the couplings of dogs (cats are far more discreet and usually do their thing at night). Country people know about farm animals, and naturalists have found out a great deal about the mating behavior of countless wild mammals, birds, and insects. Much of all the above involves courtship, which may be elaborate. And we have come to realize, with all this private life exposed by patience, binoculars, and DNA analysis, how much cheating goes on.

What about plants? We can hardly suppose that plants could *enjoy* sex—but who knows? Maybe, one day, a scientist will detect something akin to the endorphins that are produced in humans during pleasurable experiences (including excitement, love, and orgasm) in some part of a plant when bees are tickling its stamens or brushing against the pistil while it is being pollinated. Nothing in the plant world would really surprise me—but it does seem unlikely. So for now I will stick to the plain and obvious facts.

The bladder wrack, a common seaweed, was well known by us as children. We loved to walk along the beach at low tide when a storm had cast lots of seaweed onto the beach. We would seek out the strands of bladder wrack and stamp on the partially dried bladders, which made a marvelously satisfying popping sound (the same as when you pop the air bubbles of Bubble Wrap). It is at the tips of these bladders that the sperm and eggs are stored. There are male and female bladder wracks, and reproduction takes place only once a year, when both sperm and eggs are released into the water at the same time. Fertilized eggs sink to the bottom of the sea and soon attach themselves to some hard surface.

Flowering plants, of course, have the most complex reproduction. And it is the love of flowers, of the blossoms with their staggering variety of shape, color, and size, that have so bewitched people over the ages. The largest single bloom in the world is that of the "corpse flower" (*Rafflesia arnoldii*) of Sumatra—it may measure a yard across and weigh as much as fifteen pounds. The flowers actually look and smell like rotting flesh, which is why it's commonly known as the corpse flower. The smallest, by contrast, is that of the tiny water weed *Wolffia*, which measures a mere .01 inch across. And, too, there are the perfumes, the sometimes-intoxicating scents produced by flowers, especially those that are put out at night to attract moths and other night pollinators. Even bats.

Flowers are equipped with female and male organs, the pistil and the stamen. The stamen produces the pollen, which must somehow reach the pistil so that the waiting undeveloped seeds can be fertilized. This happens when pollen grains pass through little openings (stigma) at the tip of the pistil and travel down a tube (the style) to the ovum at its base.

The Swedish botanist Carl Linnaeus discussed this in his famous work on the classification of plants. He was dismayed when he learned that one of his articles, translated into English, was banned because it was "lewd and salacious"—"stamen" and "style" had been translated with the words *husband* and *wife*. One plant was thus described as having four husbands, two taller than the others; another had twenty husbands or so in the same marriage! At any rate, irrespective of the number of husbands, successful pollination results in the development of a seed.

The countless and cunning ways that plants have devised to get the pollen grains with their live sperm from stamens to pistils are absolutely awesome. Some release their pollen in large quantities, sometimes explosively, into air or water with the hope that it will be transported by the currents of air or water to the waiting pistils. As I write this, the pollen from the pine trees in our garden is being carried by the breeze in yellow clouds. The ground, the cars, our clothes—everything is covered with fine yellow dust. Bad luck for those who suffer from allergies.

Other plants have opted to have their pollen transported by a variety of animals, who are lured into service by enticing fragrances, delicious nectars, and attractive colors. Many kinds of insects serve as pollinators—and so do birds such as hummingbirds, occasionally bats, and even, it has been suggested, small amphibians. Some plants, including many orchids, have very specific needs—only one species of wasp pollinator will do.

Probably the first pollinating insect that springs to mind is the bee. I already described how I loved to watch the bees in the glorious summer days of childhood as they buzzed from flower to flower, probing for nectar and gathering golden pollen on their back legs in what we called their "bread basket." This was the bee benefiting from the flower, obtaining the ingredients for making honey and "bee bread" to feed the young back in the hive. But at the same time, as the bees moved from one bloom to the next, pollen was repeatedly brushed off onto the outstretched pistils. So the flowers were achieving their goal as well.

Not all insects are attracted by glorious scent or alluring nectar—certain plants cater to the preference of those that prefer a "fragrance" most horrid to our senses. The titan arum, which stands about six feet tall, and the corpse flower (*Rafflesia arnoldii*) of Sumatra, which, as mentioned, has the biggest single bloom in the world, both emit a stench that is irresistible to those flies and beetles that eat or lay their eggs on rotting flesh. I well remember when a titan arum was in bloom at Kew Botanic Gardens and lines of people gathered for the dubious thrill of experiencing its vile smell.

Defense Strategies

The other day I watched a cow feeding in a field. She was chewing her way through grass and a whole lot of herbs. There was clearly nothing the plants could do about it. Or was there? There were a few clumps of ragwort in the field, and I noticed how the cow avoided them. She clearly knew, somehow or other (from a bad experience or instinctive reaction to the toxins in its scent), that this plant was poisonous.

Plants are unable to run away or fly, so unless they develop some kind of defense, such as poison, they are liable to become someone's breakfast, lunch, or dinner. In fact, plants have developed a whole host of ways to protect themselves. Some simply taste nasty, and some of the nasty ones are actually as poisonous as the ragwort is to cows. Deadly nightshade, so often mentioned in the old storybooks, is even more poisonous to us than is the ragwort—children can die from eating as few as three berries—but many birds eat it without any ill effect.

Unfortunately for the ragwort, the caterpillars of the cinnabar moth have become resistant to this poison and live on the leaves. This is, of course, what happens when we spray pesticide on farms or gardens—some insects become resistant, so other forms of poison must be concocted. In nature there is usually a balance so that if an insect predator proliferates unduly, its plant food will diminish to the point where the insect numbers cannot be sustained. And when the predators are then reduced, the plants can make a comeback. Then the whole predator/plant cycle can start again.

Poison is not the only defense—plants have evolved a great variety of other weapons, many of which I learned about as a child as a result of personal experience. Holly trees have leaves with sharp prickles, as we realized each Christmas when collecting some for decorating the rooms, placing sprigs with their bright-red berries behind every picture—and one on the Christmas pudding. When we went picking blackberries in the summer, we returned with arms and legs scratched and bleeding from the thorns on the stems—and it was the same when I picked wild roses, desperate to capture their fragrance and take it home with me.

Nettle leaves are covered with fine stinging hairs. And they are vicious—my mother told me about her time as a schoolgirl when a bullying gang of older girls, which included, I regret to say, her older sister Olly, threw her into a bed of stinging nettles. Fifty years later she still remembered the pain with horror. Even the traditional remedy—pressing dock leaves onto the affected area—did not help such widely tortured skin.

My childhood was free of the two scourges of the American woodlands—poison ivy and poison oak. I have only once had a close encounter with poison ivy—I was fortunate, for it hardly bothered me, although the person I was with was badly affected. I have, however, had many unpleasant experiences with a small and very inconspicuous plant at Gombe that has tiny leaves covered, like those of a nettle, in stinging hairs. And when, intent on watching a chimpanzee, you inadvertently sit on one of these plants in the wet season, the burning itching lasts for well over a day—it is extremely painful. How on earth the minute stinging hairs can attack through two layers of cloth I simply cannot imagine.

Plants have evolved a variety of impressive defenses. How on earth can this infant vervet monkey move about in this Acacia tree with its formidable thorns?! It's even more incredible to see giraffes eating them. The photo was taken in Lake Manyara National Park in Tanzania.
(CREDIT: © THOMAS D. MANGELSEN/WWW.MANGELSEN.COM)

I learned a lot about the defenses of the plants that flourished in the Olduvai (or Oldupai) Gorge in Tanzania when I worked there for three weeks in the dry season of 1957. In the daytime I was digging for fossils, along with Mary and Louis Leakey. But every evening Gillian (the other English girl on the expedition) and I were allowed to wander in the gorge and onto the plains. And there we learned to know and respect the vicious thorns of the acacia trees—and marvel at the sight of a giraffe munching on the spiky foliage with impunity.

We also encountered the wild sisal (*Sansevieria ehrenbergii*). Indeed, it grows there so prolifically that the Masai, who call it "oldupai," named the gorge in its honor. A close encounter with those strong spiked leaves, so beloved by the rhino who lived there then, left wounds in our skin that hurt and itched for hours, though soothed a little if they were smeared with the sap from a cut leaf. There were euphorbia there too, and one evening, as we sat around the campfire, Louis told us how baboons can chew the leaves of the euphorbia for moisture—but that one man, desperately thirsty, almost died when he thought it would be okay for him to do the same. His throat and tongue swelled up so that he could hardly breathe, and he was lucky to survive, for the milky sap, or latex, can be deadly.

Some plants have another extraordinary adaptation to protect not only themselves, but also each other, from attack by predators—they communicate with each other.

Communication Between Plants

The very idea of plants communicating with each other is normally treated with skepticism. Yet new research is substantiating claims, initially made in the 1980s, that some of them actually can. And in two ways: through airborne chemical molecules released by the leaf, and underground, through their roots.

In 1982 David Rhoades, a scientist from the University of Washington, announced at a conference his belief that trees were able to communicate with each other. If an herbivorous insect attacked a tree, nearby trees were alerted, most probably through airborne chemicals released by damaged leaves. These airborne chemicals, Rhoades suggested, triggered chemical defense mechanisms in neighboring trees. When I heard about this, I was really excited, and included the information in many of my lectures at the time, although the idea was ridiculed by most scientists.

But gradually the notion of tree-to-tree communication gained credence. In 1983, Dartmouth biologist Jack Schultz and his research assistant Ian Baldwin, published a paper in *Science* that provided evidence of this type of communication between poplar trees and between maples. Rhoades was able to pronounce, triumphantly, "Trees have a few tricks up their leaves—they aren't static things just waiting to be eaten."

Meanwhile another research team from Ben-Gurion University, in Israel, led by biologist Ariel Novoplansky, has shown that plants can transmit distress signals to each other through their roots (although the exact mechanism had not yet been worked out). In this study, published in the spring of 2012, five domestic pea plants were subjected to stressful drought conditions. This caused the plants to close their leaves to prevent water loss. At the same time signals were sent out, through their roots, and were picked up by neighboring unstressed plants—which then reacted as though they, too, were suffering drought conditions.

The fact that information of this sort can be sent, received, and stored by plants has profound implications. Novoplansky explained it this way: the discovery "demonstrates the ability of plants and other 'simple' organisms to learn, remember and respond to environmental challenges in ways so far known only in complex creatures with a central nervous system."

Amazingly, the scientists found that the nonstressed plants that had nevertheless reacted in the same way as their water-deprived neighbors subsequently coped better, when exposed to the stress, than naïve plants.

It reminds me, in a way, of the impact of some of my early discoveries about chimpanzee behavior. In the 1960s science (and religion) believed that humans were the only beings on Planet Earth with personalities, minds capable of thought, and emotions. In other words, we were the only sapient, sentient beings. Research on the chimpanzees at Gombe showed that this was not true, and that humans were indeed part of the animal kingdom. Plants have their own magical kingdom, and it certainly does not surprise me that they are capable of communicating in ways once thought unique to complex animals.

Another recent study is revealing a different kind of communication through roots—which also has far-reaching implications. Millions of years ago a fascinating partnership was forged between plants and a unique group of organisms living in the soil, the mycorrhizal fungi. Today, the roots of about 95 percent of all plant species are coated with these threadlike fungi that act as a kind of secondary root system, creeping way out into the ground, extracting water and minerals. They share these vital resources with their host plant, which, in turn, provides the fungi with sugars.

Suzanne Simard, a forest ecologist from the University of British Columbia, heads a team that is finding ways to "see" under the ground, and this cutting-edge research shows that the mycorrhizal fungi serve to connect the roots of one tree to another, creating an underground network deep down under the forest floor.

Their study site is a Douglas fir forest, and here graduate student Kevin Beiler used a new DNA-reading technology to distinguish between different individual fungi and the roots of different individual trees. It is now clear not only that all the trees in the forest are interconnected below the ground but also that each of the largest and oldest trees serves as a "mother tree," with younger trees growing within her root-fungi network.

What I find absolutely fascinating is the fact that the "mother tree" sends carbon, nitrogen, and water along her roots, and while these nutrients are absorbed by the fungi, some are passed on, through the fungi's interconnected threadlike strands, to the roots of seedlings that, living in the gloom of the forest floor, desperately need them. When a mother tree is cut down, this is likely to have an adverse effect on the development of the young, replacement seedling, and thus the regeneration of the entire forest may be compromised.

It seems there is no end to the plant marvels that are taking place around us.

Plants and Humans—A Love Affair

It is hardly surprising, given the endless variety of plants, their beauty, and their fragrance, that they have captured the imaginations of people through the ages. Indeed, our love affair with plants has been interwoven into human history for centuries. Just recently archaeologists discovered that a Bronze Age grave, located south of Perth in Australia, contained a bunch of meadowsweet blossoms. Dr. Kenneth Brophy of Glasgow University commented that while the dried flowers were nothing much to look it, they represent the

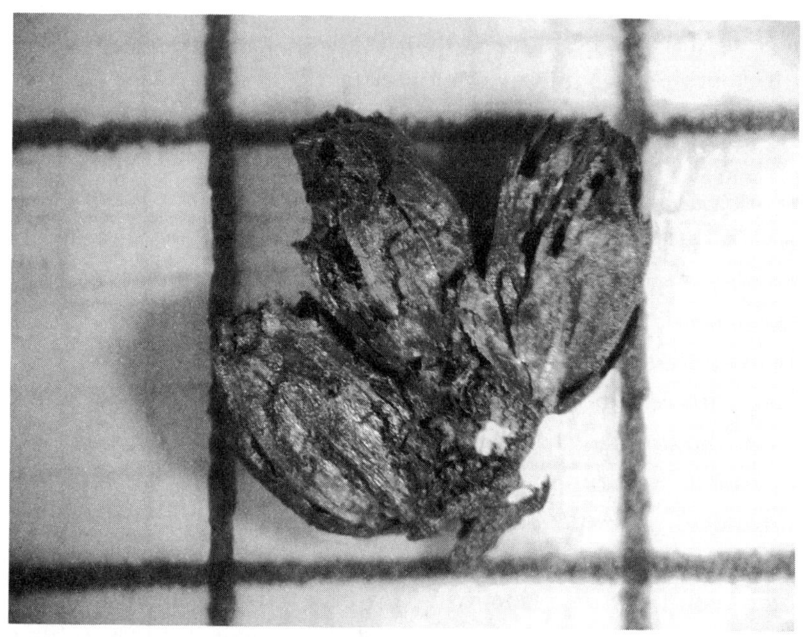

How exciting it must have been to find the dried remains of a bouquet of meadowsweet blossoms in a Bronze Age grave, indicating that the people back then were placing flowers with their dead.

(CREDIT: UNIVERSITY OF GLASGOW)

first indication that people in the Bronze Age were actually placing flowers with their dead. And of course they would have looked much better when they were freshly picked.

"To find these very human touches is something very rare," he said, and he suddenly felt that what he was looking at was "not just a series of abstract remains."

Why were the flowers there? Did those Bronze Age people want to ensure that the dead would have flowers in the afterworld? Were the meadowsweets a favorite flower, something the deceased would enjoy in another world?

In ancient Rome the ground around a grave was sometimes laid out like a garden so that the soul of the departed might enjoy the flowers. Today the custom of leaving flowers on the graves of our loved ones is widespread so that many graveyards do, indeed, look like gardens. And it is common practice to throw flowers or petals onto the coffin before the earth is shoveled over it. I have not been able to discover how this custom originated—I suppose it means different things to different mourners.

I was enchanted to learn that in Victorian Britain, when some feelings could not be openly spoken of, the "language of flowers" (floriography) was highly developed. By sending particular flowers, or combinations of flowers, it was possible to send almost any message—and many floriography dictionaries were published. This language of flowers apparently originated in Turkey and spread to many different countries. Even today some flowers are still associated with certain feelings—any woman receiving a bouquet of red roses knows exactly what a man is telling her!

When I was running the research center at Gombe, Derek was director of Tanzania's national parks. He regularly visited each of them, including Gombe, flying the parks' single-engine plane. One afternoon I saw the plane flying low over the lake. As it drew level with my house on the beach, it waggled its wings, and Derek threw something out of the window, enclosed in a plastic bag. I waded out into the water to retrieve it. A single red rose! This was shortly before he asked me to marry him.

Plants offer so much to so many. For the scientist there are endless new questions to ponder as modern technologies reveal more facts about plant biology. For the naturalist there is constant opportunity to gain an ever-growing appreciation of the miracles of nature—a simple magnifying glass can open up a whole new world. For the artist—what a richness of material for pen or paintbrush or camera. And for a child there is the magic of a beautiful flower springing from a bulb planted in the soil.

We can all be cheered by the natural beauty that is around us, if only we will look. Even in the busy city streets small plants push bravely up through cracks in the paving. Pause and look at the next one you see, marvel at its determination, its will to live. And give thanks that we live in such a wonderful, magical, and endlessly fascinating kingdom. The kingdom of the plants.

Chapter 3

Trees

I spent hours in Beech, reading books about Africa and doing my homework. Here I am about thirteen years old. (CREDIT: SALLY PUGH)

I have always loved trees. I remember once, when I was about six years old, bursting into tears and frantically hitting an older cousin (with my little hands only) because he was stamping on a small sapling at the bottom of the garden. He told me he hated trees because they "made wind"! Even at six years I knew how wrong he was. I have already mentioned the trees in my childhood garden—the most special was a beech tree. I persuaded Danny to leave

DECLARATION
This States Briefly
that
ELIZABETH
JOSEPH
Hereby Presents "BEECH"
to
V. J. M.–GOODALL, ON APRIL 3, 1948
E. H. Joseph. March 17th 1948

I loved Beech so much I persuaded my grandmother Danny to give me Beech on my fourteenth birthday. (CREDIT: JANE GOODALL)

"Beech" to me in a "Last Will and Testament" that I drew up, making it look as legal as I could, and she signed it for me on my eleventh birthday.

I spent hours up that tree, perched in my special place. I had a little basket on the end of a long piece of string that was tied to my branch: I would load it before I climbed, then haul up the contents—a Tarzan book, a saved piece of cake, sometimes my homework. I talked to Beech, telling him my secrets. I often placed my hands or my cheek against the slightly rough texture of his bark. And how I loved the sound of his leaves in summertime: the gentle whispering as the breeze played with them; the joyous, abandoned dancing and rustling as the breeze quickened; and the wild tossing and swishing sounds, for which I have no words, when the wind was strong and the branches swayed. And I was part of it all.

During the first four months at Gombe I was with my mother—for the authorities would not allow a young woman to be on her own in such a remote area. But when she had to return to England, people had gotten to know me and considered I would be fine staying on with my two staff. And, as weeks became months, I gradually felt ever more at home in my new world.

Often, when I walked alone up to the Peak—the observation point from which, using my binoculars, I could usually locate the chimpanzees—I would pause to talk to some of the trees I passed each day. There was the huge old fig tree, with great wide branches, laden with fruit and feasting chimpanzees, monkeys, birds, and insects in the summer, and the very tall and upright mvule, or "dudu" tree, which attracted chimpanzees to feed on white galls made by a lace bug in the spring. Then there were the groves of the mgwiza, or "plum tree," that grew near the streams, and the mbula and msiloti of the open woodlands, all of which provide, in their seasons, plentiful food for the chimpanzees—and other creatures too.

I became increasingly aware of these trees, and many, many more, as *beings*. I loved the feeling of the rough sun-warmed bark of my old fig, and the cool, smooth skin of my *dudu* tree. I seemed to know the movement of the sap as it was sucked up by unseen roots and drawn up to the leaves high overhead where it mixed with CO_2 and sunlight to provide the trees with their nourishment.

I had a special bond with some of the young eager saplings, thrusting determinedly toward the canopy seeking their share of the good light and life up there. They reminded me of myself and I wished them luck.

Of all the trees at Gombe, it was the gnarled old fig tree that I loved best. How long had he stood there? How many rains had he known and how many wild storms had tossed his branches? With modern technology we could answer that question. We even know, today, when the first trees appeared on Planet Earth.

When Trees Began

From the fossil record it has been suggested that trees appeared about 370 million years ago, about 100 million years after the first plants had gained a foothold on the land. I can well imagine the excitement of the scientists working at a site in Gilboa, New York, who, in 2004,

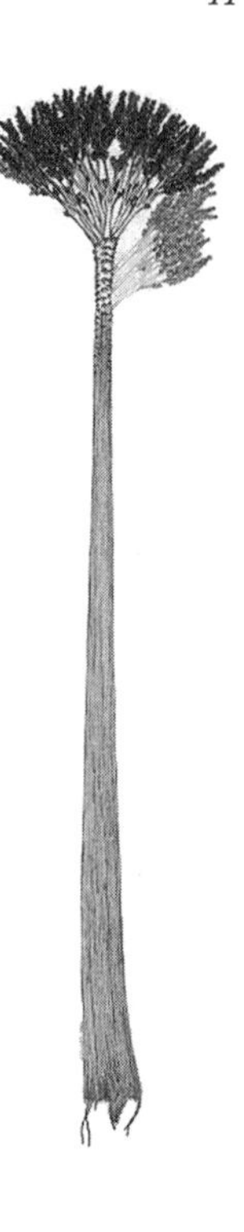

This is a reconstruction of the fernlike tree, known as Wattieza, which appeared 140 million years before the first dinosaurs. The Wattieza forests sent roots into the hard surface, preparing the way for the proliferation of land animals that followed.
(CREDIT: FRANK MANNOLINI/NEW YORK STATE MUSEUM)

discovered a four-hundred-pound fossil that was the crown of a fernlike tree. The following year they found fragments of a twenty-eight-foot-high trunk. And suddenly they realized the significance of the hundreds of upright fossil tree stumps that had been exposed during a flash flood over a century earlier. Those tree stumps were just ten miles away from their site and were estimated to be 385 million years old—the crown and the new trunk fragments were the same age. The newly discovered species *Eospermatopteris* is commonly known as Wattieza, which actually refers to the type of foliage.

It seems that these treelike plants spread across the land, and began the work of sending roots down into the ground, breaking up the hard surface, and eventually forming the first forests. And as their numbers increased, they played an increasingly important role in removing CO_2 from the atmosphere and cooling Devonian temperatures. Thus they prepared things for the proliferation of land animals across the barren landscape of the early Devonian.

The *Archaeopteris*, which flourished in the late Devonian period, is the most likely candidate so far for the ancestor of modern trees. It was a woody tree with a branched trunk, but it reproduced by means of spores, like a fern. It could reach thirty feet in height, and trunks have been found with diameters of up to three feet. It seems to have spread rather fast, occupying areas around the globe wherever there were wet soils, and soon became the dominant tree in the spreading early forests, continuing to remove CO_2 from the atmosphere.

And then there are the "living fossils," the cycads. They look like palms but are in fact most closely related to the evergreen conifers, pines, firs, and spruces. They were widespread throughout the Mesozoic era, 250 to 65 million years ago—most commonly referred to as the "Age of the Reptiles," but some botanists call it the "Age of the Cycads." I remember Louis Leakey talking about them as we sat around the fire at Olduvai Gorge, and imagining myself back in that strange prehistoric era. Today there are about two hundred species throughout the tropical and semitropical zones of the planet.

Once the first forests were established, both plant and animal species took off, conquering more and more habitats, adapting to the changing environment through sometimes quite extraordinary adaptations. Throughout the millennia new tree species have appeared, others have become extinct due to competition or changing environments. Today there are an estimated 100,000 species of trees on Planet Earth.

The Living Ancients

Certain trees, the so-called "big trees," have been on this planet for several thousand years. A few years ago I unexpectedly came upon an ancient olive tree, at least eight hundred years old, in the center of one of the open squares in the city of Palma, Majorca. It was strange to see this ancient being, surrounded by the bustle of the town, and I found myself wondering about the hundreds of thousands of people who must have eaten its fruits, sat in its shade, exchanged words of love or anger. And I wondered, too, if this tree, surrounded only by buildings and some introduced grass and flowers, missed those other trees that, at one time, must have grown around it in a shady and peaceful grove.

One time, when I was fortunate to explore the pristine unlogged Goualougo Triangle in northern Congo, I found myself mesmerized by the ancient giant hardwoods. I had no way of knowing how old they were, but standing at the base of one of the huge trunks—so wide that it would take at least four people holding hands to encircle it—and gazing up and up to the canopy where monkeys looked down chattering, I was humbled by the thought of the thousands of years it had stood there. And I imagined the generations of animals—even of the long-lived elephants—that had come and gone beneath their boughs.

And then there were the towering redwoods and Douglas firs and Scotch pines of North America's West Coast, where I walked, full of wonder, through the forest of giants. I have yet to meet the almost-unreal bristlecone pines that cling to rugged cliffs, their trunks stunted and their limbs twisted into strange contorted shapes by the relentless buffeting of the winds during the past four to five thousand years.

Just last week, out of the blue, I had a letter from Tim Mills, an old friend of mine with whom I had lost touch. As though he knew I was writing about trees (he did not), he told me that one of the things on his "bucket list" had been to meet "Methuselah," the ancient bristlecone who lived at ten thousand feet in the White Mountains of the Sierra Nevada range in California.

The location is kept secret—the ranger told Tim that he thought only four people know where it is. Somehow Tim and his son managed to find that secret place from an old photo. They confirmed that it was indeed Methuselah when they found that the bore holes on the trunk, made when taking samples for carbon dating, matched those shown on the photo. I wrote back and asked him how he had felt in the presence of a tree said to be 4,843 years old.

Tim replied, "Being among the trees in the Forest of the Ancients was awe inspiring. I walked slower, was very quiet and my senses came awake. There was a reverence akin to being in an ancient church. Finding the Methuselah Tree was an unexpected privilege and we bound ourselves by an oath never to share its location."

He told me the only bark on the trunk was an eight- to ten-inch strip of cambium layer that spirals up the tree, carrying needed nutrients from the soil up to the leaves above. It is only because of this thin strip of bark that the tree can stay alive.

"Methuselah," carbon dated at 4,843 years old. After the destruction of an even older tree, this Methuselah is believed to be the oldest known bristlecone pine. This photo was taken by a friend of mine. (CREDIT: T.J. MILLS)

Carbon-dating technologies have greatly improved over the past twenty years or so, and we have increasingly accurate knowledge as to just how old some of the "big trees" actually are. But many cannot be so easily aged, because a great deal of their wood has rotted away, sometimes hollowing out the whole center of the tree. In these cases ages must be estimated by counting and cross-referencing tree rings, calculating growth rate and present size.

The oldest trees in the United Kingdom are English yews. Many of them are thought to be at least two thousand years old—and it is quite possible that some individuals may have been on Planet Earth for four thousand years, the very oldest being the Fortingall Yew in Scotland. Yew trees were often planted in graveyards—they were thought to help people face death, and early churches were often built close to one of these dark, and to me mysterious, trees.

Almost every part of the Yew is poisonous—only the bright-red flesh around the highly toxic seed is innocent and delicious. It was my mother, Vanne, who taught Judy and me that we could join the birds in feasting on this delicacy. How well I remember her telling us this as we stood in the dark, cool shade of a huge yew tree, whose thickly leaved branches cut out the brilliant sunshine outside. The tree grew outside an old church, but, the churchwarden told Vanne, the tree was far older than the church. We plucked the low-growing berries, separating out the soft flesh in our mouths and spitting out the deadly seed.

A "Living Ancient." Some kinds of oak trees can live for over two thousand years, and they are among my favorite trees. This one, in the Valley of the Wolves Deer Park in Denmark, is estimated to be a thousand years old. Two of my friends were actually married inside the hollow interior.
(CREDIT: ILKE PEDERSEN-BEYST)

When we think of ancient trees, we tend to think of them as large, but they are sometimes quite small. When trees live in harsh settings, such as arctic cold or desert conditions, they tend to grow very slowly, so it's hard for people to realize how very special and ancient these trees might be. A friend of mine, the botanist Robin Kobaly, told me that when she was a child, she would pass a wild plum tree every day on her way to and from school in Morongo Valley, a desert area of southern California. It was only about fifteen feet tall, and its trunk was about two feet across.

"I sort of befriended that plant," Robin told me, "and the California Thrasher that always sang from its upper branches as I walked by." When she went off to college, she lost touch with her special tree. Forty years later she moved back to the same neighborhood. "And there, waiting to greet me," said Robin, "was that same wild plum." It was in one of the few lots that had not yet been developed. She had aged during their separation, but the tree had not changed at all, and she wondered how old it was.

"The way I found out," Robin told me, "broke my heart." One morning she awoke to the sound of a bulldozer. She looked out to see her wild plum being ripped from the earth. "I ran down the street to see what remained of that majestic plant. I ended up salvaging the uprooted trunk, and realized I could count the annual growth rings exposed in the split wood—over 350 rings. It amazed me, even after studying desert plants for my master's degree. How much longer might this ancient plant have lived? Even the bulldozer operator felt bad, and said he could have easily gone around it, as it was in a location that they couldn't build on anyway. He said he wished he had known."

After that, Robin began hunting for the trunks of other trees in her area that were being killed. She found junipers over a thousand years old, ironwood trees over eight hundred years old, oaks over five hundred years old, wild plums over four hundred years old, and even the smaller creosote bushes several hundred years old. "But because, in order to survive the extremes of our arid climate, these plants remain small," she said, "no one realizes how old they are." Robin has now dedicated her life's work to educating people about these ancients and protecting them from senseless assaults and destruction that come from ignorance.

Of all the trees in the world, the one I would most like to meet, whose location is top secret, is the Wollemi pine. It was discovered by David Noble, a New South Wales parks and wildlife officer, who was leading an exploration group in 1994, about a hundred miles northwest of Sydney. They were searching for new canyons, when they came across a particularly wild and gloomy one that David couldn't resist exploring. After rappeling down beside a waterfall and trekking through the remote forest below, David and his group came upon a tree with an unusual-looking bark. David picked a few leaves, stuck them in his backpack, and showed them to some botanists after he got home. For several weeks the excitement grew, as the leaves could not be identified by any of the experts. The mystery was solved when it was discovered that the leaves matched the imprint of an identical leaf on an ancient rock. They realized the newly discovered tree was a relative of a tree that had flourished 200 million years ago. What an amazing find—a species that has weathered no less than seventeen ice ages!

The Wisdom of Trees

Many people, it seems, feel deep respect when they encounter ancient trees. A few years ago I was in Bamberg, Germany, attending an event to celebrate the one hundredth anniversary of a hospital where I was giving a talk. They were anxious to have a tree-planting ceremony to mark the event—but it was the wrong time of year, and the ground was covered in snow. So we had a ceremony at the place where a walnut tree would eventually be planted. The nut was handed to me in a basket, and I handed it over to the head of the hospital to plant on my behalf in the spring. And then came a reading, in German, of some inspired lines by Herman Hesse from his book *Bäume. Betrachtungen und Gedichte.* It was icy cold with a blue sky and a chill, chill wind, and we got colder and colder as each sentence was translated for my benefit, but I was spellbound by the words. Later my hosts gave me an English translation of their reading:

> For me, trees have always been the most penetrating preachers. I revere them when they live in tribes and families, in forests and groves. And even more I revere them when they stand alone. They are like lonely persons. Not like hermits who have stolen away out of some weakness, but like great, solitary men, like Beethoven and Nietzsche. In their highest boughs the world rustles, their roots rest in infinity; but they do not lose themselves there, they struggle with all the force of their lives for one thing only: to fulfill themselves according to their own laws, to build up their own form, to represent themselves.
>
> —*Herman Hesse, 1918*

When the last word died away, the lead player of the orchestra, who had been keeping his hands warm under a thick anorak, produced a flute. With his hands losing their warmth and his fingers stiffening, with the spit freezing in the pipe, he nevertheless played a beautiful piece of music, also inspired by trees. I can never forget that occasion—standing in the clean, cold air and listening to the haunting sounds of the flute, sounding for all the world like the singing of trees as they endure the winter, knowing the spring will come. I was in a trancelike state when the music ended, slowly awakening to frozen hands and feet, hastening inside for hot mulled wine.

It is hardly surprising that trees were worshiped, venerated for their age and endurance. Cults of tree worship have existed almost everywhere, and there are still sacred woods in India, Bali, Japan, Africa, and undoubtedly other places too. A number of different species have inspired awe throughout the ages. In ancient Egypt, the sycamore was especially revered—twin sycamores were believed to stand at the eastern gate of heaven through which Ra, the sun god, came each day. These trees were often planted near tombs, and coffins were made of their wood.

In ancient Greece and Rome there were many sacred groves of olive, ash, and oak, and the Celtic tribes in ancient Britain also revered oak trees that were thought, by some, to be the source of sacred wisdom. Perhaps they are, these old trees. Perhaps we simply need to find a way to understand their message, to hear their voices.

In Nepal, in both the Hindu and the Buddhist religions, the two most sacred trees are the bar or banyan (*Ficus benghalensis L.*) and the peepal (*Ficus religiosa*). Brahma, Vishnu, and Shiva, the highest gods in Hinduism, are all thought to be present in the peaceful shade of these trees, and in ancient times people would gather under their shade for discussion—often the king and his ministers would administer justice in the presence of the holy trees. It was under a famous *Ficus religiosa*, also known as the Bodhi Tree, that Buddha received enlightenment. Seedlings from the sacred Bodhi Tree have been transported to many Buddhist nations throughout the world.

A Tree Wedding

I have seen, on several occasions, when driving through Nepal, small clearings at the side of the road that were underneath bar and peepal trees. These are known, I was told, as *chautaras*, or resting places, for weary travelers. When a bar and a peepal are planted side by side, a symbolic wedding may take place, and the trees are referred to as the bride (peepal) and groom (bar). The marriage is performed with the same sort of enthusiasm, music, and rituals that are observed at a human wedding. Once the trees are married and planted together, it is believed they will bring good fortune.

During one of my visits to Nepal, I was privileged to witness such a ceremony, arranged by one of my friends, Narayan Pahari. He wanted to ensure good fortune for a small weekend cabin that was being built for visitors and Roots & Shoots leaders to escape the terribly polluted air of Kathmandu. We climbed to the building site—

a lovely place, nestled on a very steep hillside with a view across the Himalayas.

The "bride" and "groom" were waiting for us, standing there in their earthen pots decked out in their wedding finery of white and yellow silk ribbons. The holes to receive them had been decorated with intricate geometric patterns around the rim, crafted from red and yellow pastes made from crushed flower petals. And amazingly, down in the bottom of each hole, which was perfectly round with straight walls like a well, the same pattern was repeated. An array of symbolic objects was laid out ready for the ceremony—marigold petals, special seeds, and a jar of orange-red vermilion.

The Hindu priest and his five acolytes arrived and began their chanting. One of the plant pots was ritually smashed and bar was placed into his waiting hole. I approached. The senior priest dabbed a vermilion *bindi* in the center of my forehead, then placed a small amount of the same red paste in my outstretched hands, which I smeared on bar's leaves. Next he gave me red and yellow petals: after holding them briefly between my hands, pressed together in prayer, I scattered them over the tree.

Next peepal was released and planted in her hole, about eight yards away. The priest blew a conch shell, the acolytes chanted. And then it was over.

By then it had turned very cold, and we returned to the lodge where we were staying, to a lovely warm wood fire and supper. We talked about the ceremony and the way trees can help us connect to the spiritual world. And I dreamed, that night, of how I stood in a forest and one graceful tree bowed down and encircled me with its branches.

Special Friendships with Trees

No one is surprised to hear about close and loving relationships between a human being and an animal such as a dog or cat. But a person and a tree? Surely that is a stretch of the imagination? Or perhaps not. I have described the closeness I felt with Beech when I was a child—it was something over and above my love for other trees. It was up Beech that I climbed when I was sad, and in the long hours I spent among his branches I came to think of him almost as a person with whom I shared my most-secret thoughts. And I listened to his voice in the wind, and even if I could not understand his actual words, who knows what I may have learned?

I think perhaps many people, especially children, develop close feelings for a particular tree. One of my heroes, Richard St. Barbe Baker, whom I shall mention later, devoted his life to protecting and restoring forests. He grew up close to a British oak-and-beech-wood forest. When he was a very small child, about five years old, he went off into the forest alone, and thus began a special relationship with one particular beech tree. She became, he says, a mother confessor to him, his "Madonna of the Forest." He would stand close to her and imagine he had roots digging deep down into Mother Earth, and that up above were his branches, reaching up to the sky. After such an experience he believed he was imbued with "the strength of the tree."

And a friend of mine, Myron Eshowsky, who developed shamanic powers later in life, had a dream as an eight-year-old child in which a tree told him it was his brother and they would grow old together. Myron went out searching for that tree until he seemed to hear a young maple, taller than him, calling to him, "I'm here." Myron managed to dig up the tree, and replanted it at home. But he had damaged the roots, and the leaves began to droop. *If my brother dies,* he thought, *I shall die too.* And he would creep out each night crying, praying, and begging the tree to live.

Fortunately his tree brother survived and grew strong, and every so often during the past fifty years, Myron goes to visit that so-special tree.

It is not only as children that we form special bonds with trees. There was, for example, the intense relationship between Julia Butterfly Hill and a redwood called Luna, who was 180 feet tall and approximately 1,500 years old. It all started when Julia joined a group that was protesting the clear-cutting of the redwoods in California in 1997. They were taking turns staying up in Luna—Julia was not initially affiliated with the group, and only went up the first time because no one else was volunteering. And she was both scared and exhausted by that first climb. But she soon fell under the spell of the magnificent tree and she stayed up there for a total of 738 days.

Some people form special bonds with trees. Hoping to prevent the clear-cutting of the ancient redwoods, Julia Butterfly Hill spent 738 days living up in the branches of Luna, a 180-foot-tall redwood. Luna, photographed in May 1999, is located in Stafford, California. (CREDIT: SHAUN WALKER)

She defied harassment from the lumber company, who buzzed her with helicopters. She endured torrents of rain, terrifying gale-force winds, and freezing temperatures that gave her frostbite during the coldest winter in northern California's recorded history. She did not leave until the loggers agreed to spare Luna and her grove of companions.

When Julia finally set foot on the ground again, she felt joy for having saved Luna, but she also felt an inner sadness. Leaving Luna, she said, was like leaving the best friend and teacher she'd ever had. And when, years later, a vandal wounded Luna, she felt deep pain as well as anger.

I recently read an interview with Julia in the January 2012 *Sun* magazine, where she said she goes back once or twice a year to visit Luna. "The experience taught me that every living thing can communicate," she told the interviewer. "So I return to let Luna know that I still care."

Communicating with Trees

I have already written about the ways trees communicate with one another through leaves and their root systems. But can trees communicate with us? It seems absurd to even ask the question—but maybe not.

A couple of years ago I was spending the night in a friend's house, and picked a book at random from the shelves for bedside reading. It was *Under the Greenwood Tree* by the British novelist Thomas Hardy, published in 1872. And this is how it begins:

> To dwellers in a wood almost every species of tree has its voice as well as its feature. At the passing of the breeze the fir-trees sob and moan no less distinctly than they rock; the holly whistles as it battles with itself; the ash hisses amid its quiverings; the beech rustles while its flat boughs rise and fall. And winter, which modifies the note of such trees as shed their leaves, does not destroy its individuality.

Hardy knew what many people living close to nature, especially the indigenous people, have always known. My friend the songwriter Dana Lyons told me how, after spending a few days under an ancient tree in an old-growth forest of the Pacific Northwest, he was suddenly filled with a song, which is called, simply, "The Tree."

Shortly after this he was asked to play the song at a Native American powwow. At the end he said how it had seemed as though the tree had "given" him the song—music, words, and all. "Of course," said the chief, and not only told Dana the species of tree but that he recognized the individual tree and told him its exact location. "We know all their voices," said one of the elders.

Tuck is another good friend of mine who is familiar with tree voices. He works for the Kadoorie Farm and Botanic Garden in Hong Kong. There is a little bungalow hidden away in the forest that clothes the slopes of a mountain rising up above the polluted air of the city below. When I have time, I like to walk along the steep trails, to visit the hidden waterfalls and other secret places. It is open to the public in daylight hours, and many people come—to photograph the diversity of trees and plants, or just to breathe clean air for a few hours. But it closes at sunset.

After dark Tuck sometimes drives me around to look for porcupines, barking deer, wild boar, and the little leopard cat. The trees seem to acquire a new presence at night: they are stripped of color, and it is their shapes that one notices. Strange, gnarled, their branches reaching out over the road like arms.

During one such drive Tuck stopped the car beside a large tree whose roots were helping to hold the soil in place on the almost-perpendicular slope from which he grew.

"This old tree has something to say to you," said Tuck.

I was not surprised by his remark, for I knew that he had attended seminars on listening to trees. When it was first proposed, he had thought the whole idea quite crazy, but he had gradually become a believer. He finds he can receive energy from certain trees when he stands near them and meditates.

We sat in the silence that followed the cutting of the engine. There was the call of an owl. After some moments of deep attention to that old tree, I seemed to feel or sense a message—a sort of thinking that urged patience, endurance. I should not expect that the world could change quickly. I should just carry on, do all I could, and never lose hope.

Perhaps I imagined it. Perhaps it was what I expected to hear from an old tree. But it left me with a tranquillity of spirit, and I was grateful. It was not the tranquillity that may come with fatalism. The old tree, most surely, was not suggesting we stop our efforts to prevent the felling of the forests, and the extinction of species. No, rather we must work harder, knowing it will take time, and never give up.

Chapter 4

Forests

There is a spiritual energy at the waterfall in Kakombe Valley at Gombe. This is where the chimpanzees sometimes perform their spectacular "waterfall displays," swaying rhythmically from side to side, stamping and splashing in the water. It can also be a very peaceful place, and I sometimes sit here quietly for hours. (CREDIT: © JANE GOODALL INSTITUTE / CHASE PICKERING)

As a child, when I read the books about Tarzan, I was in love with the forest world in which he grew up as much as I was in love with the Lord of the Jungle himself. I was also entranced by the story of Mowgli in the *Jungle Book*, who was raised by wolves, and the descriptions of the mysterious Indian jungle where he lived with the other animals. I read about other habitats too, of course: the American prairies as they once were, stretching for countless miles over the wild central plains where the vast herds of bison roamed; the wetlands with their teeming bird life; the frozen arctic home of polar bears.

In my imagination I traveled to them all, but it was the forests that I was most in love with. I read voraciously about the jungles of the Amazon Basin, India, Malaya, and Borneo. One book described the Amazonian jungle as a "Green Hell," populated by ferocious wild beasts, snakes that were meters long, a whole array of deadly spiders and insects, fierce Indians, and, of course, rife with all manner of deadly diseases. But the very difficulty of getting to such places, and the dangers that would be encountered, appealed to my adventurous spirit. The fact that I could see no way of attaining my goal made me, despite the fact that people laughed at me, more determined than ever.

I remember, vividly, a childhood visit to the Sherwood Forest, where Robin Hood and his merry men lived in the "greenwood," robbing the rich to give money to the deserving poor. Much nearer home was the New Forest, a place of woods and bogs and wet heath and moors with heather. We went there a few times by train and walked and had picnics.

It was in Bournemouth, however, on the cliffs overlooking the English Channel and in the chines that led down to the seashore, that my real apprenticeship was served. There, with Rusty, I learned to crawl through dense undergrowth, scramble up sheer slopes, and creep silently along narrow trails. In sunshine and rain, heat and cold, those chines were my training ground where I developed the skills that were to stand me in such good stead in the forests of Gombe.

I learned the voices of the different birds—the haunting song of the robin, the sweet liquid notes of the blackbird, and the wild song of the mistle thrush (also known as the "storm cock") as he sang from the very top of a tree when the wind was strong. I knew where many birds had their nests, and one spring I spent an hour most days watching, from behind a screen of bracken and brambles (Rusty lying motionless at my side), as a pair of willow warblers hatched and fledged their chicks. The squirrels gave me endless entertainment as they chased and challenged one another around and around a tree trunk, or sat hurling abuse down at me, their tails jerking with indignation. I loved the sunlight on the pink-gold trunks of the pine trees, and the sighing of the breeze through their leaf needles, and the eerie creaking when two big boughs rubbed against each other in the high wind.

When Dreams Came True

I cannot count the number of times that I have taken the boat from the little town of Kigoma and traveled the twelve miles or so along the eastern shore of Lake Tanganyika to the tiny Gombe National Park. It is only thirty square miles as the crow flies, but if you ironed out the rugged terrain, it would be more than double the size. The beach that fringes the lake has been formed by the endless movement of the waters of the great lake into a series of bays between rocky headlands. The mountains rise up to the peaks of the Rift Escarpment—Lake Tanganyika is the flooded western branch of the great Rift Valley.

The lower slopes along the shore are covered with deciduous woodlands intersected by narrow valleys supporting dense tangles of riverine forest that is almost impossible to move through unless one follows the trails used by bushbuck and bushpigs, baboons and chimpanzees. In the rich, fertile soil of the lower valleys, giant forest trees have found a foothold, and here, where the canopy overhead inhibits the undergrowth, it is possible to make use of our bipedal posture. The upper slopes, often very steep and treacherous, are covered by open woodland interspersed with stretches of grassland that become pale and brittle during dry season. Up high the trees are mostly small, save where the hills are bisected by the upper reaches of the valleys. Where the Rift Escarpment is highest, around five thousand feet, the trees are sometimes festooned with lichens that hang like beards from the branches.

These days my crazy travel schedule only allows me to get to Gombe's forests twice a year, and only for a few days at a time, but one of those days is always set aside for me to be quite alone in the forest, and it is those precious hours that, more than anything else, replenish my energy.

I love to sit by the small, fast-flowing streams and listen to the sound of their gurgling as they tumble past on their way to the lake. Or to lie on my back and gaze up at the canopy, where little specks of captured sky twinkle like stars as the wind stirs the branches and leaves high overhead. I become deeply aware of the voices of the forest—the soft rustling of small creatures going about their business, the buzzing and whirring of insect flight, the shrilling of the cicadas, the calls of birds, the distant bark of a male baboon—and all the other sounds that are as familiar to the forest dweller as the squealing of tires skidding around a corner, the revving of engines, and the drunken shoutings are to those who live in the city. And there are those times when it is raining and I can sit and listen to the pattering of the drops on the leaves and feel utterly enclosed in a dim, twilight world of greens and browns and soft-gray air.

When I am alone and quiet and still, animals will sometimes come very close, especially birds and squirrels feeding in the trees. Very rarely I have been able to watch a checkered "sengi" or elephant shrew (which is not a shrew at all) hunting insects on the forest floor. It has a long snout and squirrel-like body and is very shy. I have never seen one except in thick undergrowth, given away by the rustling of dead leaves. Every so often it slaps the ground with its ratlike tail—I cannot find reference to this, but I wonder if it startles insects so that the sengi can more easily detect them.

Life and Death in a Forest

During all my years in Gombe, I came to realize, in the most vivid way, that the forest is a living, breathing entity of intertwining, interdependent life-forms. It is perfect, complete, a powerful presence, so much more—so very much more—than the sum of its parts. One comes to understand the inevitability of the ancient cycles, life gradually giving place to death, and death in turn leading to new life. It is illustrated every time a tree falls. I was once caught in a sudden and violent thunderstorm during the rainy season. Huge tree trunks bowed before the force of the wind as whole branches were torn off. And I actually witnessed the event as one of them, a species of fig, lost its grip on the rain-softened earth of the forest floor and, with a great rending sound, crashed to the ground. I can never forget that experience, for I was almost crushed by one of the outstretched limbs.

Over the following years I went to visit that tree each time I returned to Gombe. It was not long before the first mosses and lichens and fungi appeared, growing on the fallen trunk. And then came the ferns and small flowering plants. Later, young seedlings sprouted close by, growing up from fruits that had been produced before the tree's death, making the most of the sunlight that shone down through the recently created gap in the canopy. One or more of them would take the place of their decaying parent. Not surprising that these fallen trees are known as "nurse trees."

Year after year, the variety of life around my fallen tree increased, as more and more plant species appeared, as well as all manner of invertebrates. Small mammals made their homes there. And eventually it was difficult to see that it had ever been, so perfectly had it dissolved into the forest floor—"ashes to ashes, dust to dust"—where the "ashes and dust" were the rich loam that helped to ensure the future of the forest.

It was to the forest that I went after my second husband, Derek, lost his painful fight with cancer in 1981. I knew that I would be calmed and find a way to cope with grief, for it is in the forest that I sense most strongly a spiritual power greater than myself. A power in which I, and the forest, and the creatures who make their home there, "live and move and have our being" (Acts 17:28). The sorrows and problems of life take their proper place in the grand scheme of things. Indeed, with reality suspended by the timelessness of the forest world, I gradually came to terms with my loss and discovered that "peace that passes all understanding" (Isaiah 26:3). And I knew my task was to go on fighting to save the places and animals that Derek and I had both loved.

As I travel around the world, people are always telling me that I have an aura of peace—even when I am surrounded by chaos, by people jostling for signatures, or wanting to ask questions, or worrying about logistics. "How can you seem so peaceful?" they ask. The answer, I think, is that the peace of the forest has become part of my being. Indeed, if I close my eyes, I can sometimes transform the noise of loud talking or traffic in the street into the shouting of baboons or chimpanzees, the roaring of the wind through the branches or of the waves crashing onto the shore. That I have this power is a gift that I have taken from the forest for which I am deeply, endlessly grateful, for it helps me to survive the hectic pace of my endless lecture tours.

Forest Challenges

How amazingly fortunate I was that Louis Leakey picked Gombe as my study site—working there, beside the shores of a great lake, with its fast-running, clear, sweet streams and scarcity of dangerous animals, is as close to paradise as it gets. Life is not so easy for many of those who choose to do their research in a tropical forest. Indeed, working in some forests can be challenging for a human from the Western world.

Even in Gombe it is not all plain sailing. There are some trees that can give you a painful surprise until you get to know them and the vicious thorns they grow in unexpected places—on branches and trunks. And there is that little plant with stinging hairs that I have already mentioned—but if you watch where you are sitting, you are fine. There are some biting and stinging insects, but Gombe has far fewer than in many other forests. Probably the nastiest of these are the army, or driver, ants that march through the undergrowth in wide columns, fanning out if disturbed. Their bite is extremely painful—and once they get a grip, they hang on like little bulldogs and must be pulled off. The worst thing about these ants is that they have the sneaky habit of moving undetected up your legs and then, in response to some secret signal, all biting at once—but only when the leaders have got high enough to do real damage!

Of course, the Gombe terrain is rugged, so that, when working in the forest, you spend most of the day climbing up and down steep slopes, often having to crawl—or even wriggle on your tummy—through very dense undergrowth. But that is a small price to pay for the fact that you can lie on your back on the forest floor to watch chimpanzees or monkeys or birds in the canopy above. Other field researchers are less fortunate.

Dian Fossey persuaded Louis Leakey to help her fulfill her passion—to go and study the mountain gorilla in Rwanda. She endured far greater hardships than I had. She had to wear several layers of clothes to protect her from the giant stinging nettles, and endure days and days of mist, pouring rain, and deadly chill. Everywhere was the danger of bumping into forest elephants and buffalo—one of her research assistants (Dr. Sandy Harcourt) was really badly gored by a buffalo during his time at her research station. And she had terrifying encounters with poachers.

Birutė Galdikas was the third of "Leakey's angels," as we were sometimes called. Unlike Dian and me, she already had a degree in anthropology when she first approached Louis, begging him to help her fulfill her dream—to study the orangutan, the "red ape." I think her study site in Indonesia provided the toughest challenges of all. We have often talked about the many difficulties she had to overcome in the forest of Kalimantan. One time she sat on a fallen tree trunk and received second-degree acid burns—through her tough trousers. And, she said, there were ants—vicious, biting, stinging ants—everywhere. Worst of all were the thousands of leeches waiting to attach themselves to her as she walked through the moist undergrowth. And her encounters with the perpetrators of the illegal logging were scary—once she was seized and badly beaten up.

A World of Unique Forests

There are so many different kinds of forests—tropical, temperate, boreal, montane, and cloud forests—and within each category, many different types. There are the riverine forests, belts of dark green that snake across the country, following the rivers, such as those I have known in Tanzania, Uganda, Burundi. In these forests, as mentioned, the undergrowth tends to be dense and tangled, making it difficult for us bipedal apes to move about.

Then there are those that I call the "secret forests" in the western coastal area of Congo-Brazzaville: one moment you are walking across a flat flood plain with its tall grass and stunted trees, and then suddenly you come to the edge of a very steep, narrow gorge. At the bottom, tall trees grow, their canopies barely showing above the gorge, and when you climb down, you are in a completely different atmosphere, cool and dim after the burning sun.

And there are the great forests of the Congo Basin, the Amazon, and the wild forests of Asia, some still unexplored, that are home to such a staggering variety of different species of plants and animals, all forming part of the intricate web of life. If we want to sound knowledgeable, we say that they are "biodiversity hot spots"—it means the same thing. Because the canopy is high and dense, much of the forest floor is deprived of light, the undergrowth is sparse, and often one can walk upright, especially when following elephant "highways."

I have been lucky enough to experience life in the treetops from three different canopy walkways—in Panama, in Ghana, and in a dry forest in America. It is a whole new world up there, populated by countless creatures that know no other existence, that come into being, live, and die in the treetops. It is a world created by those plants that have succeeded in their desperate struggle to escape from the eternal gloom of the forest floor and reached the life-giving sunlight high above.

"Canopy Meg," Margaret Lowman, pioneered the exploration of the forest canopy. Her writings have taught us about a new and previously undreamed of world, high above the ground, where almost half of the world's biodiversity is found. (CREDIT: MEG LOWMAN)

It was from Margaret Lowman, best known as "Canopy Meg," that I learned about this world. She pioneered the study of life high up in the trees, experimenting on the different ways of getting up there. And it was she who told me of the difficulties that must be overcome by every tree that makes it. How incredible to realize that what looks like a "seedling" because it is only four inches high may, in fact, be fifty years old! It is patiently waiting, hoping to avoid being trampled or eaten, for a big tree to fall and create a gap in the canopy, letting some sunlight fall to the ground. Only then can it start to grow up toward the sky. Research in the canopies around the globe, conducted by "Canopy Meg" and her colleagues, has shown that almost half of the world's biodiversity is found up there in the tops of trees—for many species it is the only habitat they know.

Africa's Last Eden

I have vivid memories of the various forests around the world that I have been privileged to visit, but of all my forest experiences, outside Gombe, one was particularly exciting, wonderful—and awe inspiring. That was when I visited the Goualougo Triangle in the Republic of the Congo, a forest that, for thousands of years, was totally protected from human interference. I was invited on this memorable expedition by the scientist, explorer, and conservationist Dr. Mike Fay. Mike discovered the hidden forest, which became known as the "Last Eden," in 1999 when he undertook a marathon eighteen-month walk across Africa to explore the virtually unknown forests spanning the countries of Congo and Gabon. His two-thousand-mile route was mapped out very precisely before he began the expedition, and in the Republic of the Congo it took him straight through a series of great swamps that encircled—and protected—one hundred square miles of ancient, pristine rain forest. Even the indigenous Pygmies had not ventured through those swamps.

Mike was accompanied on much of his trek by my old friend, photographer Mike "Nick" Nichols. Together they struggled through the swamps, coped with insects, leeches, and other parasites, and survived sometimes-terrifying encounters with suspicious and angry elephants and gorillas. These and the other animals had not learned to fear Man—but that did not mean they always welcomed the intrusion of the strange creatures that they had never seen before.

The illustrated story of the "Last Place on Earth," with Nick's fabulous photography, is published by the National Geographic Society.

Since Mike first pioneered the way, an established route has been worked out, and a few lucky people have been privileged to visit. I was one of them. A National Geographic film team, along with writer David Quammen, accompanied Mike, Nick, and me. We flew from Brazzaville in a small plane, landing and spending the night in a field station that had been built for loggers. We left very early the next morning, and as we drove through the old, regenerating logging concession, we could watch the black nighttime silhouette of the branches against the sky gradually acquire depth and color as the sun rose.

After three quarters of an hour or so we arrived at the swamps, not far from a small settlement of Pygmies. Some of them, who would act as our porters, were waiting for us with their canoes. The little boats, propelled forward by powerful thrusts of long poles, glided swiftly and silently through a maze of channels in the bright-green vegetation. There were all manner of birds, including flocks of African gray parrots with their loud, penetrating voices and arrow-swift flight. I was overjoyed to see these highly intelligent animals, so often imprisoned in tiny cages, free in the wild.

Once we had crossed the swamps, it was walking—for me, and for the TV crew with heavy equipment, it seemed a long, long way. The Pygmies with our camping gear went on ahead, women carrying similar loads to the men—as they insisted.

We stopped once for about an hour to watch a group of gorillas emerge from the forest, walk carefully across the bright-green grass of a water meadow, then sit waist-deep in water feeding on great handfuls of waterweed. After that interlude we followed elephant trails for miles beneath the towering and ancient trees. Many kinds of monkeys called down to us as they leapt through the branches high above, and always we were surrounded by bird life. Tiny, stingless bees buzzed so thickly around our heads every time we paused, crawling into eyes and ears—and mouths if they could—that I was glad to wear a hat with mosquito netting hanging down from the brim.

Sharing stories round the campfire during my magical days in "The Last Eden" – the forest of the Goualougo Triangle in the Republic of Congo. I am talking with chimpanzee researcher Crickette Sanz and a group of indigenous Pygmies, one of whom is demonstrating how the chimpanzees from this forest use tools to feed on termites. (CREDIT: MICHAEL NICHOLS / NATIONAL GEOGRAPHIC)

Night had fallen and I was utterly exhausted, with blistered feet, when we finally reached the camp of the two scientists studying chimpanzees there, Dave Morgan and Crickette Sanz. For three days they introduced me to their study site. Their work was not easy, for the chimpanzees were mostly really high in the trees, silhouetted against the sky—and standing peering up through binoculars is neck-breaking, backbreaking work. At Gombe I would have lain flat on my back to watch them—but in that forest I was warned against this because of the small insects that can bite through your clothes and lay eggs under your skin. Later these hatch, producing little bumps that itch and hurt horribly as the developing larvae wriggle about inside, feeding on your flesh. We all carried a little square of tough plastic to sit on, but later I discovered that two had managed to get into my bottom!

As well as the chimpanzees, there are many troops of lowland gorillas in the area, and sometimes as we walked through the forest, we would hear a crashing of branches and the chest thump and heart-stopping roar of a male gorilla protecting his females, just out of sight in the undergrowth. Once Dave Morgan had been severely attacked by a male gorilla and was lucky to have survived. The gorilla had been upset by something—Dave had heard his angry screams before he saw him. It had been a terrifying incident, and I marveled at Dave's courage in continuing his work in the forest—even though that gorilla was far from the study site.

The three days I spent there were among the most memorable of all my forest experiences. I was introduced to some of the individual chimpanzees Crickette and Dave had come to know, and learned about their behavior as we sat around the campfire in the evening. Once, we were joined by three of the Pygmy trackers, and I was fascinated to hear their stories of chimpanzees, especially when they talked about tool using. These men sometimes imitate the call of a duiker as a way of attracting any chimps in the area, for this little antelope is a favorite prey.

And after supper I would lie in my tiny tent, listening to the night sounds of leaves in the wind, and the calls of insects and owls. It was especially wonderful to know that the sound of a chainsaw or ax had never reached this forest, nor had any creature been shot with a gun or arrow.

Mike had organized the whole expedition so that he could introduce me to this magical place—he knew the effect it would have on me, and that I would be an even better advocate for the protection of the rain forest as a result. Once, as we walked through the forest, he stopped to draw my attention to a particularly magnificent tree, towering up and up, its crown lost in the canopy far above.

"It must be at least a thousand years old," he said, gazing up into its branches high above us.

I walked over and laid my hand on the massive trunk of this majestic and venerable individual, sensing its ancient life force. And I thought of the millions of trees, just as old, just as magnificent, that we have cut down and killed over the ages. I closed my eyes and tried to imagine the sound of a chainsaw, the harsh shouting of men, the shuddering, the creaking and groaning, of the assaulted tree. I tried to imagine the horrifying crash it would make as it fell, the harm that would be inflicted on the other trees in its path, and the terror of the countless creatures who had made their homes in its trunk and branches.

And as I visualized the death of that sacred living being who, over hundreds of years, had quietly grown from the forest floor where I stood looking up toward the sky, there were tears in my eyes. Mike must have been thinking similar thoughts, for suddenly he interrupted my musings. "If the trunk of a tree like this is cracked as it falls, then the loggers will just leave it lying in the forest," he said. "And at least half of any large tree is wasted anyway—they only take out the most valuable part of the trunk."

My tears gave way to anger. Someone once wondered why it is that if a work of man is destroyed, it is called vandalism, but if a work of nature, of God, is destroyed it is so often called progress.

The terrifying destruction of the world's forests is one of the greatest ecological disasters of our time. The reason that I left my Gombe paradise to take up my life on the road was that I realized, during a conference in 1986, the speed with which the African forests were disappearing and the shocking decline in the numbers of chimpanzees and gorillas and other wildlife across the continent. Foreign timber companies were operating in the forests of West and Central Africa. Roads to previously inaccessible areas were opening up the forests for the bush-meat trade. Human populations everywhere were expanding, taking more and more land for growing crops and grazing livestock.

Today, a quarter of a century after that conference, the onslaught on the forests continues. It is not only an environmental tragedy but a crime against Mother Nature, and it affects me in the depths of my being. Time was when our ancestors lived in the forest, and I feel an instinctive, primal need to walk among the trees. It is desperately important to influence policy makers and corporate leaders, now more than ever before. The ongoing carnage in our forests is terrifying in its scope—there is not much time left.

Fortunately there are dedicated and passionate people who are fighting desperately to save our last forests, and I shall talk about them and their brave campaigns in a later chapter.

PART TWO

Hunting, Gathering, and Gardening

Chapter 5

The Plant Hunters

Carl Linnaeus (1707–1798) is best known for creating the classification of kingdoms, classes, orders, families, genera, and species that standardized nomenclature. But he was also an intrepid plant hunter. He walked alone for hundreds of miles through unmapped territory in Lapland, discovering over a hundred new plants. This 1853 painting depicts Linnaeus in his traditional Lapland plant-hunting garb. (CREDIT: HEDRIK HOLLANDER)

When I was a child, dreaming about Africa, I read as many books as I could find about the early explorers, those intrepid men who set out on long journeys not knowing what they might find. Not knowing if there would be hostile natives, ferocious wild animals, or the risk of contracting some terrible disease. Not knowing, indeed, if they would ever return. And yet, as I have said, I longed to go on expeditions like that, to explore unknown forests. And back then there were still so many wild places that had not been "tamed," and vast forests and woods, grasslands and wetlands, and all the other kinds of habitats, stretched for miles.

My own adventures have certainly enabled me to go to some places where, perhaps, no one, and certainly no white man, had set foot before—parts of Tanzania's Olduvai Gorge and the Serengeti in 1957, and undoubtedly some parts of Gombe. And I was able to experience my very first encounters with elephants, lions, leopards, rhinos, and hippos (the "big five"), not from the safety of a car, but on foot, and with no gun.

But I have never explored great tracts of unknown territory, nor discovered animals or plants previously unknown to science. My kind of exploration and my kind of discoveries were very different—the exploration of another kind of world, that of the wild chimpanzees, and the discoveries of the secrets of their behavior and way of life.

And while I still envy the early explorers in a way, the more I read of the lives of the plant hunters of the eighteenth and nineteenth centuries, the more I realize that I could not possibly have endured the kind of hardships they endured, at least, not for long. For those plant hunters were, without doubt, among the most fearless—and the most crazy—of all the explorers.

I did not know much about them until I read *The Plant Hunters* by Tyler Whittle and became utterly fascinated by the tales of those extraordinary men of a bygone era, when the mania for collecting plants spread across Europe. Their travels took place during the years when the British empire was being built, when France and Holland, Spain and Portugal, were also sending out expeditions to discover and lay claim to the various islands, territories, and whole countries that would become their colonies overseas.

Those expeditions gave many of the early plant hunters their opportunity to collect (or "hunt") plants abroad, when they were appointed as botanist to some of the great sailing vessels. They went off, for years at a time, to bring some of our best-loved flowers and trees to the gardens of Europe and North America. The accounts of the dangers they faced and overcame seem almost unbelievable to us today, in this era of mechanized transport and sophisticated navigational tools.

No wonder Carl Linnaeus, in 1737, wrote "Good God. When I consider the melancholy fate of so many of botany's votaries, I am tempted to ask whether men are in their right mind who so desperately risk life and everything else through the love of collecting plants."

Linnaeus himself was a plant hunter. He walked, always alone and carrying the minimum of equipment, for hundreds of miles through unmapped territory in Lapland, discovering over one hundred new plants. But he is best known, of course, for the truly mammoth task he set himself—that of sorting out the mess and muddle that prevailed at the time regarding the scientific naming of plant and animal species.

His classification—into kingdoms, classes, orders, families, genera, and species—standardized nomenclature forever. Three hundred and fifty years have gone by since he published the results of his long deliberations in 1753, and his name is still revered. Truly, he was a giant among scientists. He also instilled the love of plants into his students, and took some two hundred of them, from different countries around the world, on his famous field trips.

I am still in awe of the fact that I was honored with one of the special Linnaeus medals given in commemoration of the three-hundredth anniversary of his birth. I felt humbled. We visited the house where he had ended his days, in Upsala, Sweden, and I stood by myself for a short time in one of the small rooms and looked at the plant sketches on the walls, trying to imagine myself back in that long-ago time. Then we walked through some of the countryside where Linnaeus himself had walked, and I marveled, as he had done, at the amazing, inspirational diversity of plant life.

Linnaeus's life and the lives of the other plant hunters inspire me to this day, and I've picked out just a few of their stories to share with you.

John Bartram (1699–1777)—"The Father of American Botany"

A nineteenth-century wood engraving of John Bartram (1699–1777), "The Father of American Botany." Carl Linnaeus himself called him the "greatest natural botanist in the world." (CREDIT: HOWARD PYLE, PUBLISHED IN *HARPER'S NEW MONTHLY MAGAZINE*, FEBRUARY 1880)

One person who was greatly influenced by Linnaeus was John Bartram, a self-taught botanist whose parents had immigrated to America when he was a child and settled to farm in what would become Philadelphia. At the time, theirs was the only house there.

Bartram thus began his life as a farmer, but became increasingly fascinated by plants. So fascinated that he eventually hired a teacher so that he could learn Latin in order to understand Linnaeus's classifications. He went on to become the Father of American Botany and to create the first botanical garden in America—Bartrum's Garden, which is still open in Philadelphia. His name is revered among plant collectors, and Linnaeus himself called Bartrum the "greatest natural botanist in the world."

How fortunate that he was "discovered" by a wealthy British businessman and amateur botanist, Peter Collinson. At Collinson's behest, Bartrum hunted for new plant species over a period of thirty-three years, traveling, always alone, throughout the eastern colonies of North America, where he became a legend, recklessly setting off into "wild Indian country." He was the first white man to go to many of the places he hunted.

"Bartram's Boxes," as they came to be known, were regularly sent to Peter Collinson for distribution to a wide list of European clients. The boxes were mostly filled with seeds, as live plants, at that time, seldom survived overseas travel. With Collinson's help, some two hundred new plants and trees were introduced to the Old World, including witch hazel, magnolia, hydrangea, phlox, iris, and several varieties of lily. Collinson remained enthusiastic to the end, and even became so excited when a specimen of *Lilium superbum* bloomed for the first time in his garden that his family was actually alarmed for his health! Is it not amazing to think that so many of the plants that are so common today in European gardens are actually descendants of seeds from the carefully packed boxes of John Bartrum?

Philibert Commerçon (1727–73)—A Crazed Botomaniac and the Herb Woman He Loved

The French botanist Philibert Commerçon was even more reckless than Bartram. Indeed most people considered him crazy—brilliant but crazy. He himself admitted to "botomania."

As a young man he collected plants in different parts of France.

Again and again he risked his life climbing mountains that others considered inaccessible. He invariably returned from his collecting trips sick, scarred, shaken by falls and accidents, worn out.

Once when he was scrambling down a steep valley, his hair got caught up in a bush (like Absalom). He was able to free himself by cutting off his hair, but then nearly drowned when he crashed down into a swollen stream that raced between steep banks. Another time, plant hunting high in the mountains, he heard the roar of an avalanche above him. He escaped by instantly drawing up his knees to his chin and clasping his legs close, forming himself into a human ball that rolled at breakneck speed down a fiercely steep gradient. He suffered gashes and bruising—but he avoided the avalanche.

Despite these narrow escapes he became increasingly passionate about his collecting—obsessed by it, in fact. He showed scant regard for law and order, and frequently stole bulbs, cuttings, or seeds from small holders in the neighborhood, and even from the botanical garden of his university. Once, he was caught by the professor of botany himself, and temporarily banned from entering the garden. But he had such a strong belief in the importance of his work that he truly considered himself victimized—after all, if he could not obtain the specimens legally, how else was he to acquire them?!

In the mid-1760s the king of France sent out an expedition, the main purpose of which, apparently, was to try to gain the kind of glory already achieved by Great Britain. Commerçon was appointed royal botanist. The ship, *La Boudeuse*, was to sail to the East Indies and from thence to become the first French ship to circumnavigate the globe, giving Commerçon a fantastic opportunity to collect in many different countries.

By this time Commerçon, often in poor health, had secretly developed a liaison with his nurse and housekeeper, Jeanne Baret—a botanist in her own right. According to Glynis Ridley, author of *The Discovery of Jeanne Baret*, the two of them were very passionate lovers. Baret was known as an "herb woman," wise in folk-medicine plant lore. Her extensive wisdom, which had been passed down orally through generations of such women, greatly impressed

Commerçon, whose own botanical knowledge was limited by the restraints of academic teachings. The invitation to go around the world was the opportunity of a lifetime for Commerçon—but he wanted Baret with him, and women were strictly prohibited from traveling on French naval ships. And so they decided that Baret would disguise herself as a man and accompany Commerçon as his

In the mid-1760s Jeanne Baret, a botanist in her own right, disguised herself as a man to accompany plant hunter Philibert Commerçon on his journey around the world. They were traveling on a French naval ship, where women were strictly not allowed. (CREDIT: MITCHELL LIBRARY, STATE LIBRARY OF NSW: 980\C01\22A2)

manservant. For a while the plan was successful, and Baret assisted "her employer" on his plant-collecting expeditions, doing much of the hard work on account of his continuing poor health.

Some members of the crew began to suspect that Baret was not a man, but they respected her for her strength and courage, and not until the expedition reached Tahiti was her secret revealed—for the natives somehow knew immediately that she was a woman. It is said that she confessed to Captain Bougainville, who agreed to arrange a pardon for her from the French government.

In his lifetime, Commerçon identified some sixty new genera of plants and an astonishing three thousand new species. He and Baret never returned to his native France—when the ship left the island of Mauritius, they remained together, collecting there for the rest of his life. Ironically, just one week after his death, at the age of only forty-six, he was unanimously elected to the prestigious Academy of France, the only member to be elected in absentia—and certainly the only one to be elected after his death—though of course the academy did not know he had died.

He is still considered the most prolific of all plant hunters, having collected thousands of specimens, the majority of which are stored in herbariums in France and the United Kingdom. Baret returned to France, where she was publically pardoned, praised for her services to botany, and acclaimed as the first woman to circumnavigate the globe.

Kew's Collectors—Surviving Pirates, Shipwrecks, and Chain Gangs

About a year after Commerçon set off on his expedition, another passionate amateur botanist, Joseph Banks (1743–1820), was appointed naturalist on the British ship *Endeavour* on the first of Captain Cook's great expeditions. For four years they voyaged, first to South America, then via Tahiti to New Zealand, and finally to Australia, where they landed at Botany Bay, so named for its wealth and diversity of plant life. That expedition resulted, among other things, in the British laying claim to eastern Australia.

Banks went on other voyages and discovered many new plants—eighty of which are named for him. He faced many dangers—including occasions when there was the possibility of shipwreck and once when *Endeavour* was actually wrecked crossing the Great Barrier Reef. He commented in his 1769 journal, "The almost certainty of being eaten as soon as you come ashore adds not a little to the terrors of shipwreck."

In the early 1800s his health began to fail. He got gout in the winter, and by 1805 was confined to a wheelchair. Nevertheless, his mind was active and he continued to exert huge influence on science and politics for the rest of his life. And as unofficial director of England's Kew Botanic Gardens, he selected, inspired, and trained a succession of the most successful plant hunters of the time. He always warned them of the hardships and dangers they would face—and they respected him because they knew he had faced and survived the dangers he spoke of. Two of his most successful protégés were David Nelson and Francis Masson.

Banks's protégé David Nelson (birth date unknown–death 1789) actually had to witness a human sacrifice in Tahiti. Moreover, he was in the group attacked by natives on the beach of Kealakekua Bay in Hawaii, and watched, with horror, as Captain Cook, revered as the greatest sailor and navigator of the day, was stabbed to death and cut into small pieces. Somehow he and at least some of the group escaped, and their ship, HMS *Resolution,* made its way home on a long and arduous journey without the guidance of Cook. Nelson was also unfortunate enough to be a botanist on the HMS *Bounty* when the famous mutiny took place.

One of Banks's most famous protégés was Francis Masson (1741–1805). He was sent first to South Africa, where he made many journeys deep into the unknown interior, sending back great quantities of new plants, many of which are now popular gardening plants, including Livingstone daisies, pansies, lobelia, heaths, Cape pelargoniums that gave rise to the garden geraniums, and the spectacular bird-of-paradise flower.

During his expeditions, Masson survived a number of potentially dangerous encounters with wild animals, and he was repeatedly confronted by hostile Africans. One of his most terrifying experiences was when he was almost captured by a chain gang of escaped convicts, who chased him through the African bush, wanting him as hostage to barter for their freedom. He hid all night in some vegetation, fearing for his life. It was fortunate indeed—for him—that they were chained. Yet despite his fear of many of those he encountered, he could never forget—or forgive—the white farmers' ill treatment of the Africans. Much later, when collecting in the West Indies, he was forced into the local militia and then captured as a prisoner of the French army in Grenada, an experience that haunted him for the rest of his life.

Like many of the explorer plant hunters of his day, Masson couldn't simply settle down to a safer job at Kew, preferring to continue his adventurous work until the day he died. All in all Masson offered thirty-three years of courageous service to Kew, and was lauded by Banks as a committed and indefatigable collector—meaningful praise from one who was himself considered indefatigable. It is believed that Masson froze to death in Canada on Christmas Day in 1805.

David Douglas (1799–1834)

The Scotsman David Douglas is legendary among botanists, one of the greatest plant hunters ever known. As a child growing up in the village of Scone, he was a rebel. They did their best to discipline him at school, but he seemed impervious to the typical punishment of the day—severe beating. It appeared to make no difference. When he was ten years old, he was thrown out of school.

How fortunate that on his very doorstep was the Scone Palace, where he managed to get a job tending its magnificent gardens. Suddenly everything changed, and the formerly delinquent boy became passionately interested in plants. Seven years later he was working for Glasgow Botanic Gardens, and there he formed a friendship with one of the most eminent botanists of his time, William Hooker (who would become the first official director of Kew Botanic Gardens). They spent hours talking about plants, and went on many collecting trips together in the Scottish Highland. Hooker recommended his young protégé to the Royal Horticultural Society, and at the age of twenty-four Douglas was sent to collect in North America.

The tales of his travels in what was then a mostly unexplored land, and the courage and stoicism with which he faced and overcame the multitude of dangers along the way, have made him a truly heroic, legendary figure.

He had many encounters with hostile "Indians" in North America, who were, at that time, largely unknown to the white man. Once, he was surrounded by a war party, each brave with a drawn bow. He only escaped because they decided he was obviously crazy, and it was bad luck to kill a crazy man.

There was an occasion when, after falling into a deep gulley, Douglas lay unconscious for over five hours, until he was rescued by friendly Indians. He suffered severe chest pains as a result of the fall—which he treated by bleeding himself, then bathing in an ice-cold river! He was tough as nails, surviving several of the fevers that killed so many Europeans and Indians. But he was weakened by them, and his eyes became irritated to the point where it became hard for him to see.

Douglas often traveled by boat. He survived rapids, floods, and rocks hidden under the surface that destroyed his canoe several times and caused the loss of valuable collections of plants. Once, while walking in the Rockies, he had to cross a racing mountain river fourteen times in one day, wading up to his waist in freezing water! He describes how he was often wet and desperately cold for days and nights on end.

Pack rats ate his seeds and gnawed through his dried plants, and he was plagued by insects. He endured periods of extreme hunger, when he was reduced to eating roots and not only the seeds and berries from his collections but even the dried skins of animal specimens and—on two separate occasions—his packhorse.

His first expedition lasted three years, after which he returned to England. But it was not a happy time for him—he did not fit into the civilized world, and he was soon back at work in America. This time he was no longer alone—he took with him Billy, a little Yorkshire terrier. Billy became his faithful companion during the last years of his life, when he collected in what is now California, and later in the Sandwich Islands.

Douglas and Billy were on their way back to England when their ship stopped in Hawaii, and it was there, when Douglas was only thirty-five years old, that he met an untimely end. He had gone off

David Douglas (1799–1834), one of the greatest plant hunters ever known. He felt out of place during the periods he returned to English society, much preferring the freedom of wild places. I'll bet he hated having to wear these clothes demanded in polite society.
(CREDIT: *CURTIS'S BOTANICAL MAGAZINE*, 1834)

to meet a friend, accompanied by Billy. But he never showed up. One account of the tragedy assumes that he fell into a pit trap. The sounds of a trapped animal alerted two natives, and when they got to the trap, they found a bull, terrified and trying to escape, and under him the gored body of a man—David Douglas.

But there was also the distinct possibility, although never proven, of foul play: Billy, the one witness who saw what happened, could not tell what he knew. He was found guarding his master's possessions and howling as if his heart would break.

The bounty of plants that David Douglas introduced into cultivation is astounding, including his most famous contribution, in 1827—the Douglas fir. He introduced many other recognizable trees, such as the Sitka spruce, sugar pine, ponderosa pine, grand fir, and noble fir, all of which transformed the British landscape and timber industry. Many of our familiar garden shrubs and herbs, such as the flowering currant, salal, lupin, and California Poppy, can also be traced back to Douglas's extraordinary expeditions.

How to Get Them Home?

All the effort, danger, and pain were wasted if plant hunters could not get their specimens back to Europe. And what a task that was. Back in 1482 BC, Queen Hatshepsut of Egypt was sending people to the Land of Punt (probably located in Eastern Ethiopia or Eritrea) to make plant collections for her. They were carried back in reed baskets and jars of earth. Fortunately for the queen (and probably for those who delivered the specimens), the climatic conditions were excellent, and there were many slaves to carry freshwater, fans, sun blinds, and so on to keep the plants well watered, cool, and happy.

But those heroic, brave, and crazy plant hunters of the eighteenth and early nineteenth centuries did not have it so easy. Their precious collections had to be protected from extreme changes in temperature, humidity, and altitude. And they had to endure long journeys—on foot or by horse or by boat—in order to reach a port, and then to survive a long sea journey back to Europe by sailing ship.

Various plant hunters tried different methods. David Douglas, in the 1820s, used rolls of oilcloth for his dried plants, and waxed containers for bulbs. Most of his live plants did not survive. Other collectors tried growing their plants in chests covered by canvas, storing them in barrels, wrapping them in paper, and suspending them in nets from a cabin roof. Some tried putting plants in bladders, their roots sprinkled with damp loam and the neck of the bladder tied around their stems.

A major problem was that most ship captains and their crews thought that these specimens were a confounded nuisance. So while the plant hunters tried to ensure that their precious collections were put in the most protected parts of the deck, the seamen preferred to stow them forward, where they would be least in the way, but where there was also more exposure to salt spray. Or they stuffed them belowdecks, where the plants suffered excess humidity and lack of light and fresh air, were sometimes in sweltering heat and at other times chilled by icy drafts.

Even when the plants *were* in good positions on deck, seamen sloshed water against boxes when swabbing (cleaning). The sailors were supposed to lift the lid of each box for a while each day to let in some air, but often they did not. Moreover, in bad storms the plants were often jettisoned to lighten the weight. Not surprisingly the plant hunters who had suffered so much to obtain their specimens frequently handed out generous bribes to captain, officers, and crew in the hope that the plants would make it home.

In 1819 it was reckoned that up to one thousand plants sent to England from China were lost for every one that survived the voyage and germinated. One collector recommended acclimatizing plants under close guard, prior to the journey, then sending a gardener on board to tend them, and having personnel on hand to speed up their progress through the port of arrival. This was all incredibly costly, yet in spite of this, plant hunters were still sent out to collect and send back as much material as they could.

Finally, in 1834, there was a breakthrough that revolutionized the transport of live plant material around the world—and it came about by accident. Dr. Nathaniel B. Ward was a doctor and amateur naturalist. One day he put a caterpillar to pupate in mold in a glass jar with a lid—and forgot about it. When he remembered, he found that despite the lack of fresh air, two tiny plants were growing in the mold. And, thanks to his passion for natural history, he realized he had stumbled upon the perfect way to transport live plants.

His theory was tested when some English ferns and grasses were placed in two of his sealed glass containers and survived, in perfect condition, a six-month journey to Australia. The same two containers were then planted with Australian plants that were notoriously bad travelers—one species had never survived the voyage to England. But in their airtight containers all the plants flourished despite stormy seas and big fluctuations in temperature. From then on "Wardian cases" of various sizes became the standard method for sending live plant material across the ocean.

Plant Crazes

Some exotic flowers, originally transported from afar, were held in special regard. One example is the dahlia, named for a respected French botanist, Dr. Dahl. Dahlias used to grow in our garden at The Birches. They are beautiful, of course, but it is hard to imagine the frenzy they once roused in the plant fanciers of Europe.

The dahlia originated in Mexico, where it was used not only for food, but also, by the Aztecs, to treat epilepsy. Specimens were sent to a French priest, chief gardener at the Escorial, in the year of the French Revolution. He was not interested in the blooms—he thought that the tuber might be a good alternative to the potato. But it was the blooms that captivated French society. The *Jardin des Plantes* in Paris somehow acquired a few tubers—which they killed by growing them in a hot and humid environment. Other tubers sent to England also rotted.

It was Napoleon's Empress Josephine who managed to propagate them. She was very protective of her plants, and would allow no one else to care for them, doing all the work herself. But eventually she became so successful, and grew so many, that she had to put a gardener in charge. It seems somewhat surprising that, in the face of such proliferation, she refused to part with even one tuber when asked by a lady-in-waiting.

But this lady was determined, and begged her lover, a Polish prince, to steal one. He bribed the gardener to give him not one but one hundred. Of course Josephine came to hear about the theft: the lady-in-waiting and the gardener were fired and the Polish lover exiled. And then, in her fury, she ordered that every one of her dahlias be chopped up and dug into the ground! Never again was anyone to mention the plant in her presence. What an extraordinary reaction—a perfect example of dog in the manger.

Meanwhile a third shipment of dahlias from Mexico was successfully grown in Berlin, and the craze for acquiring dahlias spread through Europe. They were so coveted that in 1836 a bed of them was sold for 70,000 francs—which was an enormous sum at that time. And a single tuber was traded for a diamond.

Tulips, which originated in Turkey, caused another craze when they were first introduced to Europe—which was right in the middle of the Thirty Years' War, the longest and one of the most terrible conflicts in European history, and one that involved all the main powers of the time. Yet even as bloody battles raged, the wealthy citizens of Holland went wild over tulips. Plant hunters were dispatched to scour the Levant (the eastern Mediterranean) region for new varieties, and horticulturists created hybrids. The desire for tulips increased until it became, quite literally, a mania.

Big prices were fetched by bulbs sold to the general public. Speculators met at the house of a wealthy family in Bruges, where they traded in "paper" tulips—bulbs not yet in existence but promised by certificate. More than ten thousand of these nonexistent bulbs were exchanged, creating what we might describe as a Tulip Bubble.

There are many bizarre stories. A single bulb was exchanged for a carriage and a pair of horses, and another for twelve acres of land. One wealthy citizen, having paid a fortune for a particularly rare bulb, then found that a poor shoemaker had the same variety. First he bullied him into selling it for fifteen hundred florins, then he smashed the bulb to pieces in front of him, and finally told him he would have paid ten times as much.

And then there is the tale of a man who, hearing that his long-awaited rare tulip bulb had arrived in record time, together with his order of expensive silks, gave the messenger a lavish tip—and some herrings for his dinner. The messenger, not knowing anything about tulips, saw what he took to be an onion lying there among the silks, picked it up, and ate it along with the herrings. That bulb was worth three thousand guilders—and so, of course, the wretched messenger ended up in jail.

Eventually a law was passed that required tulip bulbs to be paid for with actual money, and gradually the frenzy died away. But not before a number of people had lost entire fortunes.

From the start, Holland managed to get hold of the tulip market, and it is the same today. It is what tourists flock to see in the spring—the great fields of tulips in the Netherlands. Fields and fields of them, in all different colors. They are as much a symbol of the Netherlands as are windmills and clogs.

Modern Plant Hunters

The seventeenth and eighteenth centuries are sometimes referred to as the "Golden Age" for the European countries that were sailing the seven seas, claiming land in the tropics for their colonies. They were certainly not a golden age for the countries that were invaded and whose land, resources, and often people were stolen. But those years did provide the plant hunters of the time a golden opportunity, one that has not since been equaled, to travel on the great sailing ships to far-off places. They were sent out by botanical gardens or nurseries or private collectors—or appointed as botanists to the venture. They were, as we have seen, amazingly brave and amazingly tough, facing hostile natives, pirates, shipwrecks, disease, and more. But they were doing what they wanted to do, and after each expedition most of them willingly went back to face more of the same.

Their kind has no counterpart in the modern world. Botanists are usually part of well-organized expeditions, and the conditions are very different. Of course there are still physical challenges, when they are searching for rare—or new—species in inhospitable, sometimes dangerous, terrain. They may get caught up in political violence and they sometimes get sick. But for the most part their main hardships are bureaucracy and red tape, getting visas to get into a country and permits to collect.

As we shall see in subsequent chapters, some modern plant hunters are no more than poachers in search of quick profit, and in many countries they have brought many plants to the brink of extinction through overharvesting for the commercial markets. We have indeed invaded and pillaged the kingdom of the plants. Fortunately more and more people are fighting to save them and their habitats. And our love affair with plants continues undiminished.

Chapter 6

Botanical Gardens

I was shown this extremely rare tree, Bastardiopsis eggersii, *during my visit to the botanical gardens in Puerto Rico. It has not been seen in the wild in Puerto Rico since 1916. Preserving and trying to propagate endangered species is one of the reasons we need our botanical gardens.*
(CREDIT: © THE JANE GOODALL INSTITUTE / BY SUSANA NAME)

How many times, I wonder, have I found a few hours of peace in a botanical garden? On my lecture tours there are endless interviews, reporters, TV cameras, microphones. And because botanical gardens and arboretums are close to cities yet offer peaceful surroundings, film crews and photographers often select them as the ideal venues to provide the right "atmosphere." But when the interview is over, I always try to stay on a little longer to wander among the gentle plants.

Of course it cannot be the same as time spent in the wilderness—the plants have been removed from their natural habitats, they are captives. But still, when cared for by loving and understanding hands, the captive plants have an aura of well-being. Perhaps they feel somewhat as I do when I am in a city—preferring to be in the country, but still pleased when I am at least among friends.

In a botanical garden in Puerto Rico, a Franciscan priest took me to the "Bamboo Chapel," a small, hidden clearing where the light is dim and green and stands of bamboo meet high overhead. He wanted to create the right atmosphere for a conversation between us for a book he was writing. We spoke of the mystical feelings that sometimes come over me when I am in nature, the sense of oneness with the trees, the plant and animal life around me, and it was getting dark when we finally stopped talking. As we left, we passed a pond and stopped to watch a beautiful white heron, motionless in the fading light, and then saw him catch a fish. He flew low over the water and passed by us so closely that I could hear the beat of his wings.

Another time, I was taken to a famous moss garden in Japan, and I longed to take off my shoes, for there can be few sensual pleasures to rival walking barefoot on a soft expanse of moss. But it was a formal occasion and I had to be content with crouching down and laying my hands on the green living carpet.

There was one visit, to the Africa House of a botanical garden in Munich in Germany, that was especially important for me. I was there for a short interview for some news program. I can close my eyes and almost feel the warm, humid air that was such a blessed contrast to the cold, gray winter day outside, and the feeling that I had arrived in a familiar and loved world—I recognized so many of the plants and trees. I was in communion with my surroundings.

An old gardener was there, tending his plants, loosening the soil around one of the small palms. The film team asked if he would stop digging—just for ten minutes, they said. Looking a bit disgruntled, he stood watching. The interview did not take long, and the gardener went back to his work. I went over to him and, with the help of one of the film team, explained that I wanted to talk to him for a moment. Now looking really fed up, he drove his shovel into the ground and stood with arms crossed. Had he not been inconvenienced enough, he seemed to say.

I told him that I had lived for a long time in an African forest and that this place made me feel at home. I said it was obvious he loved it too, and I wanted to thank him for his work. His expression changed. He wiped his hands on the seat of his trousers, then took my hand in both of his, shaking it up and down. I saw that there were tears in his eyes as he thanked me, and said he was honored to welcome me.

So often when we visit such places, it is the director who shows us around. Very occasionally he or she may call out a gardener for special recognition, but not often. Yet it is the gardeners whose hard work maintains the garden, who have a feeling for the plants that is often, I suspect, the sort of love that I feel for them myself. So I was delighted when I visited the botanical gardens in Puerto Rico, and the director summoned all the gardeners together to introduce themselves and shake hands. I was with Susana Name, who is from Argentina and is my "Spanish voice" in Latin America, and she was able to translate their shy comments.

The Raison d'Être of Botanical Gardens

Botanical gardens are not simply havens of respite from the busy world; they play, and have played for centuries, a tremendously important role in the world of plants. They educate the public, preserve history, and conduct cutting-edge research on ways of growing and propagating plants. These are the places that hold many of the specimens sent back all those years ago by the plant hunters whom I introduced in the last chapter. I hope that by sharing my own experiences I shall encourage more people to go to these wonderful oases of peace, learn about the plants, and explore their world with new eyes and new understanding.

Our modern-day botanical gardens evolved from the ancient "physic gardens," dating back three thousand years. The main purpose of these gardens was to cultivate plants that were believed, rightly or wrongly, to cure a wide range of ailments. They were mostly created in ancient Egypt, Mesopotamia, and the Roman Empire, but they have an especially long and rich history in Europe. Aristotle (384 BCE–322 BCE) is said to have had one in Athens, which he used for teaching purposes. And his pupil Theophrastus, known as the Father of Botany for his work and writing on plants, is thought to have inherited and developed that garden after his teacher's death.

For the most part, the early plant collections in Europe were propagated and tended by monks and their apprentices. And although medicinal plants made up the bulk of these collections, there was often a vegetable patch and orchard as well. Not until the eighth century were gardens designed specifically to celebrate the beauty of God's creation in the form of flowers and other plants.

Over time, as the craze for collecting exotic and rare plants spread, botanical gardens became living museums, trying to acquire and propagate ever more species from ever more distant parts of the world, serving a role in educating the public and providing botanists with places to study and share information. Horticulture became supremely important in the botanical-garden world, and the scientist played an ever more significant role.

Today, in response to a desperate need, a growing number of botanical gardens are engaged in the vital task of protecting plants in the wild and saving species from extinction. I recently learned that twelve thousand of the thirty-three thousand plant species that are listed as globally threatened are known to be in botanical-garden collections. They are being studied and protected, but also displayed, so that visitors can be made more aware of the importance of preserving the beauty and diversity of the plant kingdom.

I cannot think of a better way of illustrating the importance and beauty of botanical gardens than by describing the two I know best, the Chelsea Physic Garden and the Kew Royal Botanic Gardens, established in 1673 and 1759 respectively. Both are in England; both are known around the world.

A Secret Garden in Chelsea

No wonder the Chelsea Physic Garden is sometimes called "the secret garden," for who could guess that such a green and peaceful place was hidden away in the very heart of London? Founded by the Worshipful Society of the Apothecaries of London, this was where their apprentices came to learn about the medicinal secrets of the plant kingdom. But the society was not wealthy, and for a long time the Apothecaries struggled to maintain their garden.

And then, into the picture, comes Sir Hans Sloane, a doctor who was not only interested in the healing powers of plants but was also extremely well connected—and extremely wealthy. He wanted to ensure the success of the physic garden and so bought the property in 1722 and appointed eminently qualified men to take over the running of the place—Isaac Rand as director and Philip Miller as gardener. Miller was a genius at growing the plants, and the enthusiastic Rand began cataloguing their collection and also initiated the exchange of plants and seeds with other botanical establishments. Soon it was the most richly stocked garden in Europe.

I thought of the history of the place as a few of my friends and I looked around on a chilly day not long ago. It was 338 years since the Garden began, 289 years since Sir Hans instilled new energy into it. Dawn Kemp, the general manager, took us into the uncatalogued library collection and pointed out, with real anguish, that these priceless books are housed above the kitchen. She lives in fear of a fire breaking out.

With reverent hands, she pulled out one volume after another—handwritten and bound—from shelves and cupboards. One such was a very large book on ferns published in 1860 by Thomas Moore when he was curator. It is an amazing book, each fern illustrated with the new (at the time) "Nature Printing" technique, which used the actual plant in the process. Moore's fascination with ferns started the British love affair with them, which unfortunately led to a significant plundering of British species by enthusiasts. It was during this time that glass ferneries sprang up—and became an essential part of an upper-class Victorian sitting room.

As we walked around the garden, we kept coming upon educational displays hidden away among the trees, where I found photos and information about some of the colorful people I had come to know during my research for this book. Linnaeus himself, I learned, had visited several times, hoping to persuade Rand and Miller to accept his new classification of plants. They resisted initially, but finally capitulated after they realized how much simpler it would make things.

Just as one example, a well-loved magnolia—originally sent to England by one of our plant hunters, John Bartram—was named by Linnaeus *Magnolia grandiflora.* Before his classifications were accepted, this poor plant was known as: *Magnolia foliis lanceolatisi persistentibus, caul erecto arborea* (Tree with an erect trunk and evergreen leaves). Those wretched apprentice apothecaries, having to learn names like that—how delighted they must have been when things changed!

While wandering through the garden we found one section where the plants and herbs were organized according to their healing properties. Many plant remedies have come to us from ancient folk wisdom, passed down through the ages, and I imagined Sir Hans eagerly trying some of them out on his patients. Research is still going on today—I noticed a yellow flowering plant from South Africa labeled *Hypoxis Hemerocallidlaea Lilliaceae Widley* that had a little plaque beside it stating, "Widely used as a tonic for conditions ranging from bladder infections to tumors. It is now undergoing research as a possible treatment for cancer and HIV."

In the center of the garden is a large and famous mulberry tree, and Dawn told me that one day she had found an old man sitting on a seat under its branches. He told her he was remembering how, as a young boy ninety years ago, he used to gather fruits from that tree and take them to his mother so that she could make mulberry jam.

I looked back at it as I left: we could read the history of the place on the plaques and the old books, but that old tree had seen it all and was part of the history. Linnaeus may well have sat in its shade, perhaps arguing with Rand about the naming of the plants. And maybe it was when he was sitting under this tree, looking up at the leaves against the sky, that Rand suddenly realized the beautiful simplicity and appropriateness of Linnaeus's system. Only the tree knows.

Kew Royal Botanic Gardens

The Royal Botanic Gardens at Kew, now a UNESCO World Heritage Site, is a mecca for plant biologists and plant lovers from all over the world. It was brought to renown by the influential Sir Joseph Banks and, subsequently, by the equally influential Sir Joseph Hooker. Kew's botanists and horticulturists have been involved for hundreds of years in collecting, cultivating, and propagating plants from all over the world. In more recent times Kew's staff have been working to conserve natural habitats and to return some endangered species to the wild.

A couple of years ago I spent a wonderful morning there. It had been raining, but the sun came out and everything was looking its best—if only there had been time to wander about through at least some of the 132 hectares (340 acres) of gardens and take in the energy from some of the ancient trees. But I was there to go behind the scenes into the tropical propagation greenhouses and meet some of the plants I was writing about.

First there was time to catch up, over a quick lunch, with my good friend Carlos Magdalena, Kew's master horticulturist, who was taking me around. From the first time I met him, I was inspired by his passion, his contagious love for his plants. With his shoulder-length dark hair, piercing brown eyes, and ready smile, he is a perfect spokesperson for the plants of the world. He had just returned from a collecting trip to Mauritius, and poured out the news, sometimes hard to understand because he talks so fast in his thick Spanish accent.

Carlos Magdalena, Kew's master horticulturist, is an inspiration to me. I feel immense gratitude toward all the dedicated botanists like Carlos, who travel to remote and far off locations, and sometimes even risk their lives to rescue endangered plants. They possess all the courage and passion of the early plant hunters. (CREDIT: © THE JANE GOODALL INSTITUTE – UK / BY CLAIRE QUARENDON)

Somehow he had got caught up in the frenzy of Mauritius's election day—and just after he arrived, he was told he would have to leave. He had just twenty-four hours to collect some of the specimens he wanted, and he set off to the area where Kew has a project, driving at breakneck speed.

There are so many species in danger of extinction, he said, some with just one or two individuals left in the wild. With so little time, how to choose? He got what he could "all collected in a rush... then flight back to UK. Then sort the hundreds of twigs, saplings, seeds, whatever. Flamed fruits in a sterile jar." He hurriedly spoke about "dustlike orchids' seeds that are unripe, and I have to go to a lab and inoculate in agar-agar..."

I have no idea how you "flame" a fruit, nor how or why you inoculate seeds with agar-agar. It is all part of the incredibly complex world of the master horticulturist.

Next we paid our respects to Kew's Wollemi pine, growing inside its protective cage. These ancient trees from Australia that I mentioned earlier are now being cultivated and sold to botanical gardens and gardeners around the world. I saw another of them when I was visiting Lord Eden, son of Sir Winston Churchill, who lives not far from Bournemouth. And a few years ago I actually planted one at a special ceremony in the beautiful gardens of Adelaide Zoo in Australia. I hear it is growing nicely.

Then Carlos took me to the Palm House, which has been designed to give the impression of a multilayered rain forest. This enormous, architecturally stunning glass-and-iron structure is one of Kew's iconic images and one of the most popular destinations for visitors. It is filled with warm, steamy air and massive exotic palms

I met this towering Eastern Cape Giant Cycad, Encephalartos altensteinii, *in the Palm House at Kew. It is almost certainly the oldest potted plant in existence—the very same individual that was somehow transported all the way from South Africa to London in 1770 by the plant hunter Francis Masson.* (CREDIT: © COPYRIGHT THE BOARD OF TRUSTEES OF THE ROYAL BOTANIC GARDENS, KEW)

from the far corners of the world, many of which, like the bottle palm, are almost extinct in the wild.

My biggest thrill was meeting Kew's venerable cycad, *Encephalartos altensteinii*, or the Eastern Cape giant cycad. I gazed at it in awe, for it was collected in 1770 by Francis Masson and is one of the oldest—possibly *the* oldest—potted plant in the world. I learned that it had been repotted in 2009—a mammoth operation, since the cycad, which has been growing about an inch a year, now weighs slightly over one ton.

Only once, in all its almost 250 years of residence, has it produced a cone—that was one hundred years ago and was such an occasion that the ailing Sir Joseph Banks came to marvel at it. It was to be his last-ever visit to Kew.

The Herbarium

The big botanical gardens all have an herbarium to house collections of plants that have been preserved for scientific study. They are used to study plant taxonomy and geographic distribution, and they provide a historical record of change in vegetation over time. When a plant becomes extinct in a given area—or totally extinct—the only record of its original distribution may be in an herbarium collection. Scientists also use herbarium collections to track changes in plant distribution caused by climate changes and human impacts.

The historic Herbarium at Kew was established in the middle of the 1800s and houses many of the specimens that were collected by the amazing plant hunters of yore. Presiding over these collections is Dr. María de Lourdes Rico Arce—or Lulú, as she likes to be called. She led me past row after row of cupboards filled with drawer after drawer of specimens. Each specimen had been dried and pressed, then stuck on a sheet of archival-quality paper with a label attached describing where the plant had been found, when collected, and by whom. Big fruits or seeds, as well as fragile flowers, roots, inflorescences, and many orchids, are stored in spirits so as to keep their shape for three-dimensional viewing.

As I followed Lulú through the maze of back rooms, we passed plants just brought in from the field, still lying between sheets of newspaper. How well I remember those days in 1960 when my mother and I prepared specimens of plants used by the chimpanzees for food so that they could be identified by Dr. Bernard Verdcourt, the botanist at the herbarium of the Coryndon Museum (now the Nairobi National Museum).

I collected the plant specimens in the forest and took them back to the tent in the evening. There my mother and I would place them carefully between sheets of newspaper flanked by thick absorbent paper, and then we'd press them in specially designed wooden frames so plants could still get air for drying, and finish by pulling straps tight to flatten the unruly leaves.

My mother's job, for the few months she was with me at the start of the study, was to change the papers and try to keep the specimens as dry and mold-free as possible—not easy when the rainy season began. We rigged up a sort of drying rack above a hurricane lamp—but even so, Bernard was horrified by the number of moldy specimens that so often arrived in his herbarium. I wonder if they are still tucked away in a drawer there.

For a moment I was far away, reliving the events of a different time, but Lulú brought me back to the present. There were, she told me, over 7 million specimens stored in the Kew Herbarium. And there are 350,000 "type specimens." A type specimen is very important for botanists, especially taxonomists, because the scientific name of every species is based on that one specimen. They are used to identify material as it is brought in from the field.

If, after an exhaustive search, it seems that a new species has been found, one of the plants from that material will be picked as the type specimen. The plant will be described, named, and published. That name is then fixed for all time.

Most of the type specimens at Kew are original material brought from the field. Just occasionally a very detailed colored drawing or a photograph serves as a type specimen. In the early days it was almost impossible to transport some specimens, and today a plant may be so highly endangered that no material can legally be collected.

Kew's collection forms an irreplaceable international scientific asset, which is surely very valuable to the historian also. Some of the specimens in Kew's collection date back to the eighteenth century, brought or sent from the field by some of those intrepid plant hunters who worked for Sir Joseph Banks and Sir Joseph Hooker. What a magical link to the past—leaves and flowers pressed flat that were collected by David Nelson, then traveled with him on a sailing ship commanded by no less a person than the famous Captain Cook. Others picked by the dour Scotsman David Douglas, who survived hair-raising adventures. One pressed plant had been, perhaps, with Francis Masson when he hid all night from that gang of convicts in Africa. I was miles away again, dreaming of those wild journeys of a bygone era.

Lulú introduced me to some of the modern-day botanists and conservationists who are now working in the Herbarium. The challenges they face are different from those experienced by the plant hunters of days gone by—these contemporary scientists are mostly frustrated by irritating international bureaucracies as they seek permits to send their specimens, or themselves, from one country to another. But they do face physical danger too—there is violent political unrest in so many of the places where they work, as well as the risk of mugging and traffic accidents on treacherous back roads and the increasing violence in many urban areas.

Even so, in the face of the growing number of plants threatened with extinction, more and more herbariums are beginning to work on conservation issues in the field. Together they play a vital role in helping to identify and preserve the rich diversity of the plant life on Planet Earth.

Chapter 7

Seeds

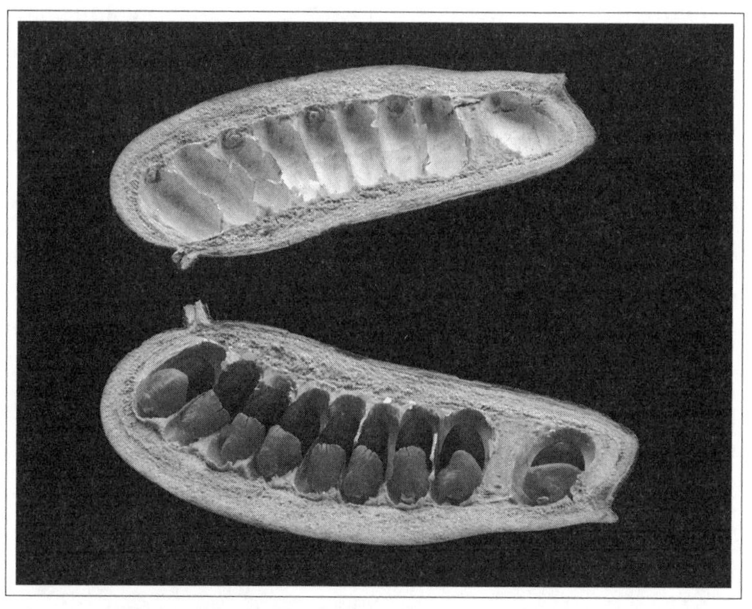

The miraculous seeds of life. Like every plant, each seed is highly unique and intriguing. These orange and black seeds remind me of pharmaceutical capsules, but they are really the beginnings of the Afzelia africana *tree.*
(CREDIT: WOLFGANG STUPPY;)

Seeds have a kind of magic that has fascinated me ever since I was a child. I used to line a glass jam jar with blotting paper, fill it with damp earth or sawdust, and put different kinds of seeds between paper and glass. For me, it was nothing short of a miracle every time I saw those threadlike roots appear and grow downward, and the little shoot bursting through the seed coat and thrusting up toward the light. I loved to look at all the bright-colored pictures of flowers and vegetables on packets of seeds in gardening shops—all the things one could grow if only the soil was right!

Our garden, as I have said, was not a good home for many plants, but I was always hopeful. I sowed the seeds I had chosen in shallow wooden boxes, and watched the little shoots push up from the soil, the husks of the seed coats clinging to the curled-up infant leaves like tiny bonnets. Then I carefully thinned the seedlings out and planted them in a flower bed with great hope and expectation, despite the fact that, year after year, the poor young things were devoured by snails or slugs, or had their roots chewed up by wireworms. Very few ever survived, and eventually I gave up.

I got close to seeds again at Gombe when, in the early days of the chimpanzee study, I would carefully extract them from samples of chimpanzee dung to check on what the elusive apes had been eating. That, of course, is the method chosen by many plants to disperse their seeds—by surrounding them with delicious fruit and thus persuading a variety of animals to transport them, in stomach and gut, throughout their home range.

To provide protection for the precious germ of life within, the seed case is often very tough and hard. But while this helps to protect against chewing teeth, it also makes germination difficult and, as I said earlier, some seeds actually rely on the digestive juices of particular fruit-eating creatures to partly dissolve their protective covering. Only then can the little dormant speck of life inside thrust forth into a world of light. There are other seeds that need fire before they can germinate, and others the abrasive effect of wind and sand.

Indeed, the more I learn about seeds, the more fascinated I become. Recently Wolfgang Stuppy, photographer for Kew, presented me with a marvelous book—*Seeds*. Some of them, when seen through the lens of his powerful camera, have the most bizarre, and sometimes stunningly beautiful appearance. Browsing through the pages of this book is a bit like an adventure in a fantasy world, a whole new experience of design and color.

Rip Van Winkle Seeds

Is it not amazing that a small germ of life can be kept alive—sometimes for hundreds of years—inside a protective case, where it waits, patiently, for the right conditions to germinate? Is it not stretching the imagination when we are told of a seed that germinated after a two-thousand-year sleep? Yet this is what has happened.

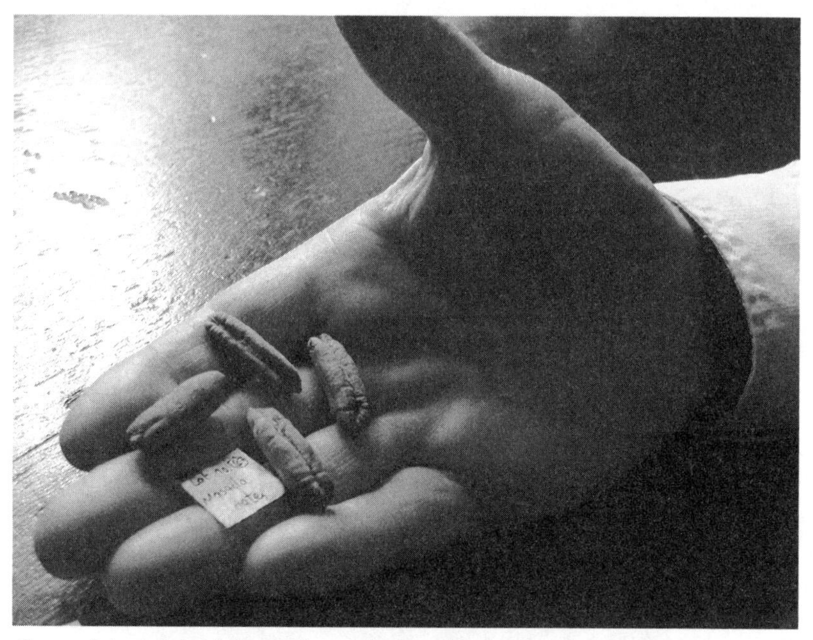

Four of the original date palm seeds found by archaeologists in King Herod's mountain fortress. Carbon dating showed they were two thousand years old—yet one of them germinated! (CREDIT: GUY EISNER)

The story begins with several seeds of the Judean date palm (*Phoenix dactylifera*) found by archaeologists studying the ruins of King Herod's castle fortress Masada on the shores of the Dead Sea. Small fragments of the seed case of two of these date seeds were used for carbon dating. The remaining three were planted—and of these one grew. Its parent was long since dead, along with the palm forests that, at the time, were found throughout the Jordan Valley.

Those palms, forty-foot-tall ancestors of the modern date palm, were believed to have medicinal value, but they were also grown for their delicious –and very large—fruits. As I read the story, I wondered about the people who had eaten the fruit surrounding those seeds.

And that thought set me thinking—all the life and energy, hopes and fears, courage and cruelty of the people who once lived and died in that place are gone. Long since dead and gone forever. Only the crumbling ruins of the castle are left in the desert. Yet within a 2,000-year-old seed, a germ of life was still alive, waiting, waiting, waiting for the right conditions to wake, like Rip Van Winkle, into a strange and different world. And then it put forth roots and shoot and grew into a seedling that was named "Methuselah" after the biblical character, Noah's grandfather, who was said to have lived for 969 years. (Of course this could not be true; someone must have calculated the date wrong, but he was obviously a very old man!) An individual date palm is either male or female, so they had to wait for their plant to mature in order to find out the sex—if it's a female, I was told, it would be called Mrs. Methuselah.

"Methuselah," the male date palm that emerged triumphantly after a long, long sleep. (CREDIT: GUY EISNER)

I was absolutely fascinated by this story of Methuselah and, wanting to learn more, contacted Dr. Sarah Sallon, of Hadassah Medical Organization in Jerusalem, who devised the project, along with Dr. Elaine Solowey, from Kibbutz Ketura, a specialist in growing plants for arid environments, who has been overseeing Methuselah's progress. By good fortunate Sarah was about to visit a friend of hers who lives near Bournemouth, so she was able to pop in and visit. She told me that Methuselah had just flowered—a male! She hopes the archaeologists will let her have more seeds of the same age in the hope that one might be a female. How amazing would that be!

Although Methuselah is the oldest seed to have been woken from a long sleep, there are other very old seeds that have germinated. Such as the single lotus seed (*Nelumbo nucifera*) found in China in an ancient lake bed and carbon-dated at 1,288 years, plus or minus 271 years. Another seed, one from the flowering perennial *Canna compacta*, carbon-dated at about 600 years old, had survived for goodness knows how long in a walnut shell that was used for a ceremonial rattle.

And then there is the delightful story of some seeds collected in China in 1792 that were housed in the British Museum. These seeds, at least 147 years old, started to germinate in 1940 when they were accidentally "watered" by a hose used to extinguish a fire!

Bringing "Dead" Seeds Back to Life?

A miracle of a different sort took place when a couple of seeds of an extinct plant, *Cylindrocline lorencei*, a beautiful flowering shrub, were—quite literally—brought back from the dead. In 1996 only one individual plant remained, growing in the Plaine Champagne area of Mauritius Island. And then this last survivor died also. The only hope for saving the species lay in a few seeds that had been collected by botanist Jean-Yves Lesouëf fourteen years before, and stored in Brest Botanic Gardens in France. Unfortunately, however, all attempts to germinate these seeds failed.

But plant people do not easily give up. Using new techniques, horticulturists found that small clusters of cells in the embryo tissue of just one or two of the seeds were still alive. Eventually, painstakingly, three clones were produced. And finally, in 2003, nine years from the beginning of their efforts, those three clones flowered—and produced seeds!

When I visited Kew, Carlos showed me their plant, donated by the botanical gardens in Brest, derived from one of those original clones. As I looked at it, I felt a sense of awe. What an example of the determination and perseverance of the horticulturists—and thank goodness for the intrepid botanists who have collected seeds around the world and, in so many cases, saved precious life-forms from

Cylindrocline lorencei *at Kew. At one time all that was left of this flowering plant were just a few seeds, and all attempts to get these remaining seeds to germinate failed. This is one of three clones that a team of botanists was able to create from a few live cells of the seemingly "dead" seeds. If this science fiction feat hadn't been successful, this plant would now be officially extinct.* (CREDIT: © COPYRIGHT THE BOARD OF TRUSTEES OF THE ROYAL BOTANIC GARDENS, KEW)

extinction. Plans are now under way to return *Cylindrocline lorencei* to its faraway home on Mauritius.

While I was still gazing at this plant, Carlos smiled and said, "This is as if tomorrow we were to find a frozen mammoth in Siberia, and even though the mammoth is dead, a few cells in the bone marrow were still alive and from it a whole mammoth could be cloned."

Almost one year later, as I was finishing writing this book, I heard how Russian scientists, led by Svetlana Yashina, had been able to regenerate a plant from fruit tissue that had been frozen in the Siberian permafrost for over thirty thousand years! This plant miraculously given new life has been called *Silene stenophylla.* And, most exciting of all, it is fertile, producing white flowers and viable seeds.

It was found in a stash of plants and fruit in the burrow of an Ice Age squirrel 125 feet below the present surface of the permafrost. And in the same ice layer there were the bones of large mammals, such as mammoth, wooly rhinoceros, bison, horse, and deer. The researchers claim that their success with *S. stenophylla* "paves the way for the possible resurrection of Ice Age mammals." Carlos's remark was uncannily prophetic.

Seed Banks: Arks for Plants

The very fact that plants have found such remarkable mechanisms for helping to ensure their future is indeed fortunate in this time of environmental destruction caused by our own species. If we can store seeds in such a way as to enable them to grow at a later date, we may be able to save plant species on the brink of extinction and restore them to nature when we have ensured favorable conditions.

The largest wild-plant seed bank in the world is the Millennium Seed Bank, established at Kew's sister site at Wakehurst Place in West Sussex. In August 2009, I visited this remarkable project. I was taken around by Kew's International Project Coordinator, Dr. Tim Pearce, and we were accompanied by the photographer and seed expert Wolfgang Stuppy, who had given me that glorious book about seeds.

At the time I visited, Tim told me they were storing, for safekeeping, over one billion seeds from thousands of species of plants, including over 95 percent of the United Kingdom's flora. Later, when I checked back with them in 2011, Kew and its partners (one hundred different institutions from more than fifty countries) had collected and conserved seeds from 10 percent of the world's wild flowering plant species. Their goal, providing funds permit, is to conserve 25 percent by 2020.

When we went into the actual storage room—"the Bank"—I had the strangest sensation. There I was in a huge room not unlike the vaults of a bank save that the temperature is minus 20 degrees centigrade, surrounded by millions and millions of sleeping seeds from about thirty thousand species of plants from all over the world. They are kept in small, sealed glass canisters that line the room, labeled with numbers and dates and other important information. Each canister is in its own little locker, into which you can peer through a glass panel.

It was not at all like walking through the Herbarium, for there I was closeted with dead plants; in the seed bank I was sharing the space with thousands of sleeping beauties—awaiting not a kiss from a prince but a thawing and watering. Then would come the unfurling and the great magic as the DNA of each little seed determined the nature of the plant to be.

"It is a strange thought," said Tim, "that this is the most biodiverse place on the whole planet." Indeed, nowhere else can come anywhere close to representing more than thirty thousand different species—and in such a small space.

By the time I left, I had a good idea about the work that goes on in this seed bank, the largest international conservation project for wild plants in the world. The seeds come in almost daily by DHL—sometimes as many as a hundred packages at once. Each sample must be labeled and stamped "Accession into the Collection at Kew." All seeds have been sent voluntarily to the seed bank, mostly by botanical gardens, in a global effort to safeguard the future of the diversity of plant species on Planet Earth. Some need a great deal of cleaning, while others, sent by trained collectors, are more or less ready for the next stage.

Next, onto the "Dry Room," where all water is extracted, and where all sorts of technology is brought into service. There are machines that replicate winnowing, whirling the seeds around, blowing air through them, and shaking them. Sometimes, though, it is necessary to clean delicate seeds by hand to prevent them from being damaged by machinery. After this the seeds are X-rayed, and I was able to see how many of those from a recent acquisition were infested with insect larvae. Tim told me they were especially proud of this X-ray machine, since most seed banks cannot afford such equipment. (Indeed, there are too many hospitals in the developing world that have no X-ray machines—but the one at the seed bank is too small to use on people.)

An important goal of this seed bank is to help improve the quality of collections around the world, and one way of accomplishing this is to share technology. "Today," Tim told me, "there is a gadget that can be used in the field to enable collectors to determine the level of maturity of a seed—when a fruit is ready to be eaten or a seed pod is about to explode." It is obviously important to harvest seeds at the optimum point of maturity. And it is also necessary to collect seeds from different parts of a plant's range to obtain maximum genetic diversity.

"And of course," Tim pointed out, "it is extremely important that the collector notes down as much information as possible and sends it with the seeds: the exact location, other species growing nearby, temperature, humidity, altitude, and so on." I remembered reading how that great plant hunter David Douglas lost the field notebook in which he had kept meticulous records of all the plants he collected in California. It happened when his canoe capsized and was destroyed on rocks—one of the most disastrous of his many accidents, for all that information was lost forever.

Growth by Fire

We now know that some seeds actually need fire in order to germinate—just one more example of the fascinating interrelationships that we find in the natural world. The cones of the lodgepole pine are glued shut by a strong resin, which melts in the heat of a wildfire so that the cone can burst open. Thus the seeds are not dispersed until the conditions are right for the growth of seedlings—when there is diminished litter on the forest floor, giving them space and more light.

Erica verticillata is a beautiful South African plant with stunning magenta conical flowers, that uses fire in a different way. Originally it grew on the Cape Flats, but by 1908 it was listed as extinct. And then, in 1984, a botanist working in the herbarium of the Kirstenbosch National Botanical Garden in Cape Town saw the pressed specimens there, and wondered whether, perhaps, it might still exist. Soon his quest to find the lovely *Erica* became a personal obsession. Eventually he found four different individuals, all in different locations—one was actually growing at Kew and another was right under his nose in the Kirstenbosch Garden!

It had been relatively easy to propagate new plants from cuttings from each of these four survivors, but although they produced seeds, the seeds did not grow. Victoria Wilman, a botanist who helped with the plant's revival, told me that it had taken a while to figure out what was necessary to germinate the seeds. They found that throughout the historic range of *Erica*, periodic fires had occurred naturally every five years or so. And not only did these fires sweep through the thick vegetation, leaving open areas that were then colonized by new plants, but horticulturists found that chemicals in the smoke, coupled with the autumn change in temperature between day and night, stimulated erica seed germination as the winter rains began.

To mimic this situation, material from the plant itself, including old flower heads and green leaves, is ignited and the smoke is collected and allowed to settle. This concentrated smoke extract is then dissolved into the water, which is used for germinating erica seeds. The scientists at Kew told me that they get some of it each year.

The efforts of the South African team have been so successful that Erica has been successfully reintroduced into the wild—the seeds, dispersed by the wind, are viable, and plants are appearing all over the place. And this very beautiful plant is now being grown in gardens.

This is what I love about so many of the horticulturists of the world—the way they are willing to watch and learn from the plants themselves. The innovative experiments they devise, the patience they demonstrate. And they understand the interdependence of life-forms, and realize the need to study the plants in their natural environment. But despite all their scientifically based investigations, some discoveries are made by accident.

As was the case with another endangered South African plant, *Serruria florida*, charmingly named "blushing bride." It was rediscovered in 1900 in the Franschhoek Valley after being listed as extinct, but forty-three years later a bush fire destroyed this only known wild population. Three years later, to botanists' amazement, sixty plants were thriving there. The conclusion that fire was necessary for germination seems, in hindsight, obvious. But at the time such an idea seemed inconceivable, and the area with the precious plants was rigorously protected from fire. The plants decreased in number. Undergrowth was cleared to prevent competition from other plants and give any other seeds a chance to grow. To no avail.

Then an accidental fire again swept through the area—and massive germination took place thereafter. At which point the botanists finally realized, to their amazement, that fire was actually necessary for the propagation of the Blushing Bride—as it is, we now know, for all fynbos species. It is the heating of the soil as the fire sweeps across the ground that breaks seed dormancy.

War, the Tower of London, and a Red Leather Notebook

His understanding about the role of fire was helpful to Dr. Matt Daws when he was put in charge of an exciting project: to try to germinate some old seeds that had an extraordinary history. They had been collected in Cape Town by Jan Teerlank, a Dutch merchant, at the time of the Napoleonic Wars in the early 1800s. Teerlank's vessel had been captured by the British navy while sailing back from Cape Town.

Everything, including a red-leather-covered notebook, was seized. The notebook was handed to the Tower of London and, eventually, ended up in the British National Archives, where, in 2004, it was found by Roelof van Gelden, a visiting scholar from the Netherlands. Inside the little book he found forty tiny packets of seeds, mostly labeled with scientific names, but some that had not been identified. Carbon dating showed they were two hundred years old.

What an incredible find: thirty-two species of plants were represented by those centuries-old seeds, and a few of each were sent to the Millennium Seed Bank. There, Matt Daws first exposed the seeds to smoke. Of twenty-five seeds from one legume, sixteen sprouted. There were eight seeds of another legume, and one of these sprouted. There were just two seeds of acacia type—one had been damaged by insects, but the other sprouted. Two years after germination there were two tiny shrubs, each about four inches high, and a waist-high acacia.

"If seeds can survive that long in such poor conditions, then that's good news for the ones that are stored under ideal conditions in the Millennium Seed Bank," Matt Daws said to me.

A Story of Two Humble Grasses

I want to give an example of a simple European field plant that would have quietly faded into extinction—indeed it was deemed extinct for decades—if not for the existence of seed banks as well as the passion of one botanist.

In the first half of the nineteenth century in two different parts of Europe, two genetically different species of brome were recorded for the first time. The interrupted brome (*Bromus interruptus*) appeared in England, and the more picturesquely named brome of the Ardennes (*Bromus bromoideus*) in Belgium. Each of these grass species had, it seemed, evolved quite independently of the other as a result of sudden major genetic changes. Both were growing in the countryside, where they shared the fields peacefully with their relatives: wheat, barley, and rye. But unlike those cousins, the two new bromes were of no use as human food.

Which is presumably why, some 150 years after their discovery, both of the new bromes had become extinct in the wild. For farming methods changed after World War II, and farmers treated their fields with the new agricultural poisons to make the land more productive (in the short term) and to make the farmers themselves more money, and thus the bromes gradually disappeared with no one noticing. By the time people did notice, the bromes were officially listed as "extinct."

Before the bromes were deemed extinct, back in the early sixties, I was working for my PhD at Cambridge University. I used to take a little tent and camp, on weekends, at the edge of some field in the country, brightened by the red of the poppies that grew there. I remember lying in hidden places in the hay fields and watching the skylarks as they flew higher and ever higher until they were the tiniest of black specks against the deep blue of the summer sky. And still their song could be heard, that glorious spilling of joyous music. I would recite to myself in a quiet voice a few lines from Shelley's "Ode to a Skylark," because poetry was so important to me at that time in my life:

Hail to thee, blithe Spirit!
Bird thou never wert—
That from Heaven or near it
Pourest thy full heart
In profuse strains of unpremeditated art.

The bromes might have been lost to us forever but for the fact that botanists care not only about the showy, exotic plants but are also interested in the smallest and most humble of them.

In 2005, David Aplin, a British botanist who was working in the National Botanic Garden of Belgium, had to give a talk at a conference on plant conservation and wanted to give some examples of Belgian species that had become extinct. He selected the brome of the Ardennes, which had been gone for about seventy years, and began to research its history.

After an exhaustive search he found that even those that had been grown in various botanical gardens had vanished. And then he made a lucky find.

"During my research," he told me, "I discovered a handful of preserved seeds hidden deep in the vaults of our seed bank." He felt a sense of awe. "It was clear that I was probably looking at the last few seeds of this species in existence," he said.

Alpin and the Belgian botanists then contacted their conservation partner, the Millennium Seed Bank, so that the precious seeds could be grown in two separate locations, by two different teams. They were, it seems, only just in time, as less than a quarter of the seeds were still alive. However, these grew successfully and produced viable seeds, some of which are now safely stored in the Millennium Seed Bank, as well as in Belgium.

And what of the British interrupted brome? It, too, has been saved, though its history is less dramatic. Some of the grasses were located growing in pots on the windowsill of a brome-loving botanist. He was able to hand out seeds to other scientists, and the future of *Bromus interruptus* is assured.

The future for both the bromes is now hopeful, and plans for their reintroduction into the countryside are being made under the auspices of the European Native Seed Conservation Network. This is a collaboration recently formed between the Millennium Seed Bank and thirty-one other botanical institutes for the protection of endangered plants. It marks an important step toward the preservation of Europe's botanical biodiversity. And I like to think that my great-grandchildren may lie, as I once did, in fields where skylarks and poppies make a summer afternoon beautiful, and where some of the little bromes once more sway in the breeze.

I happened to notice a quote on a French website as I was searching for information about the brome of the Ardennes, a quote that can apply equally to both of these grasses: "A bearer of hope for the vegetative world."

From my "Nature Notebook." When I was around twelve years old I often picked wildflowers during my walks with my dog, Rusty. I would take them home and paint them—not for a school assignment, just for the love of it. Pictured are the common mallow (purple) and gorse (yellow) flowers. (CREDIT: JANE GOODALL)

Roots have always intrigued me. This mangrove swamp in Abu Dhabi shows the aerial roots rising up above the water, enabling the trees to "breathe." (CREDIT: © XAVIER EICHAKER)

A female Welwitschia in Namibia standing about as high as a man, and estimated to be about 1,500 years old. I have never seen one in its home in the Namib Desert, but I have seen young ones growing in botanical gardens. (CREDIT: THOMAS SCHOCH)

The carnivorous plants have devised many ingenious ways of capturing their prey. The Venus flytrap (*Dionaea muscipula*), fascinated me when I was a child—and it still does today! This plant is growing in the Leiden Botanical Garden. (CREDIT: ROGIER VAN VUGT)

The corpse flower (*Rafflesia arnoldii)* of Sumatra has the largest single bloom in the world. It can measure a yard across, weigh up to fifteen pounds, and carry a distinct smell of rotting flesh—thus, its somewhat sinister name. This one is at the United States Botanic Gardens in Washington, D.C. (CREDIT: U.S. BOTANIC GARDEN)

Children seem especially enchanted by the kingdom of the plants. Two-year-old Isaac grew this narcissus from a bulb at preschool—and he just discovered that it had burst into flower. The photo, capturing his feeling of wonder and amazement, brings back vivid memories of my own childhood experiences of nature's miracles. (CREDIT: HOWARD BERNSTEIN)

"Old Tjikko," a Norway spruce growing on Fulufjället Mountain in Sweden, is the oldest known individual clonal tree. Its trunk may be no more than 600 years old, but its root system was carbon-dated and is estimated to have lived for over 9,550 years. For thousands of years it survived in the harsh climate as a stunted shrub, but warmer weather during the past century has enabled it to grow into a sixteen-foot tree. (CREDIT: KARL BRODOWSKY)

The ancient bristlecone pine forest high in eastern California's White Mountains. I am awe inspired when I look at these tree beings. A researcher cut one of them down, just so he could date it. It was a terrible, wicked thing to do—that tree was over 6,000 years old. How many more years might it have lived? (CREDIT: ROBIN KOBALY)

During a visit to Nepal I took part in a symbolic wedding between two trees. This is the "bride," known as Peepal, decked out in her finery of silk ribbons. The Hindi priest and his five acolytes chanted throughout the service. The "groom" was planted eight yards away by my friend Peter Dalglish. The ceremony is intended to bring good fortune to the house he is building nearby. (CREDIT: MANOJ GAUTAM)

Morning mist gives an air of enchantment to the redwoods and rhododendrons in Redwood National Park in California. (CREDIT: ©THOMAS D. MANGELSEN/ WWW.MANGELSEN.COM)

The original type specimen of the now familiar Douglas fir, collected long ago in North America by the intrepid plant hunter David Douglas and stored in the Herbarium at Kew Botanic Gardens. (CREDIT: © COPYRIGHT THE BOARD OF TRUSTEES OF THE ROYAL BOTANIC GARDENS, KEW)

Kew photographer Wolfgang Stuppy offered me these amazing seed photos for this book. (CREDIT: WOLFGANG STUPPY © COPYRIGHT THE BOARD OF TRUSTEES OF THE ROYAL BOTANIC GARDENS, KEW)

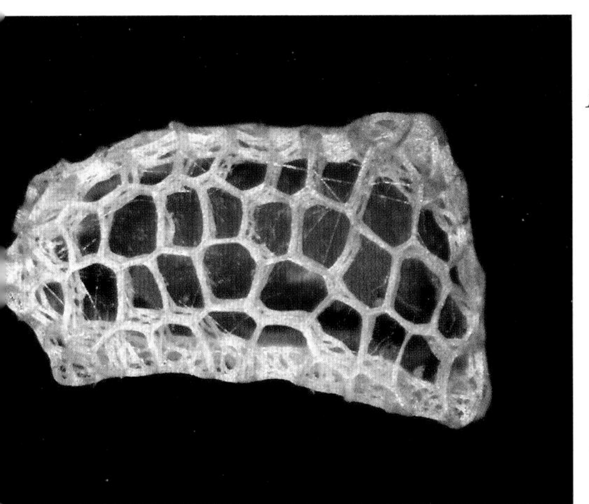

Lamourouxia viscose.

Cochlospermum orinocense.

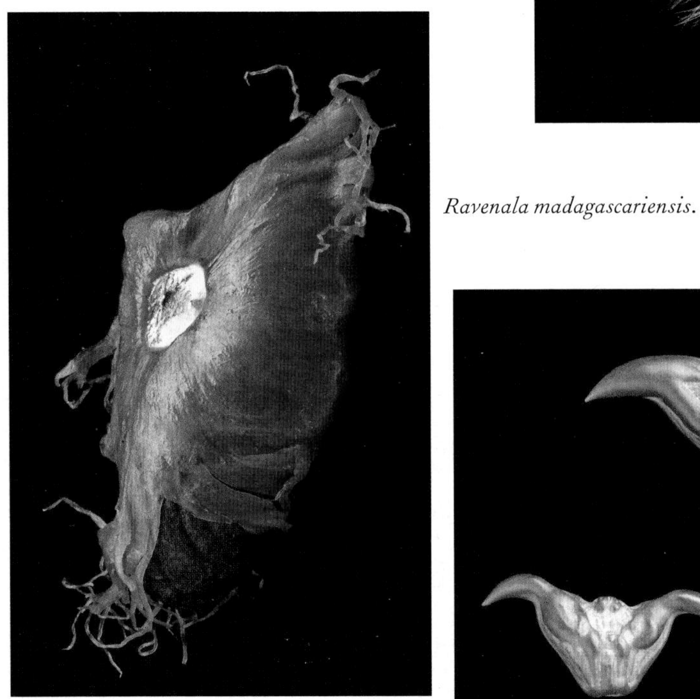

Ravenala madagascariensis.

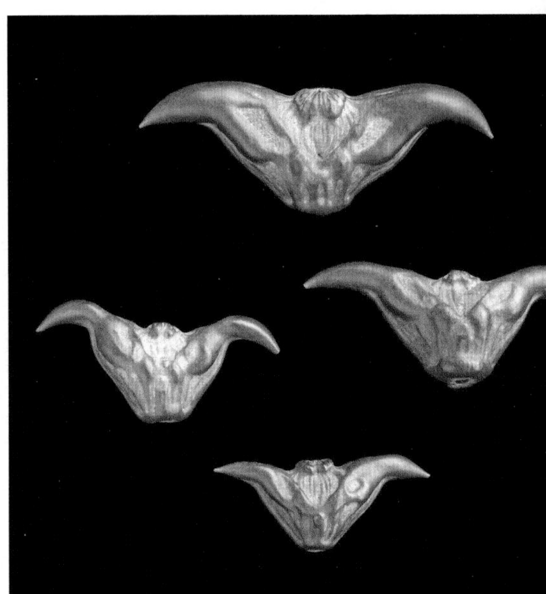

Trapa bicornis.

I was awestruck when I saw this "Seed Cathedral" at the 2010 World Expo in Shanghai, designed in collaboration with Kew Botanic Gardens and the Millennium Seed Bank. Nicknamed "The Dandelion" by the Chinese, it was made of 60,000 transparent fiber-optic rods. At the end of each rod one or more seeds provided by the Kunming Institute of Botany were implanted. (CREDIT: WOLFGANG STUPPY © COPYRIGHT THE BOARD OF TRUSTEES OF THE ROYAL BOTANIC GARDENS, KEW)

A hybrid orchid created and named for me by the Singapore Botanic Gardens, *Spathoglottis Jane Goodall*. What an honor! (CREDIT: BENG CHIAK TAN)

Simon Wellinga successfully cross-pollinated the two "rotten meat orchids" (*Bulbophyllum echinolabium*) in his collection. He grew many orchids and shared them with other breeders. Soon the market was so flooded with them that collectors were no longer motivated to steal the last few growing in the wild. (CREDIT: ROGIER VAN VUGT)

There are only a few groves of this beautiful ground orchid *Eulophia guineensis* growing wild in Gombe National Park. (CREDIT: JANE GOODALL)

The monkey orchid (*Orchis simia*) is found in the high-altitude cloud forests of southeast Ecuador and Peru. As soon as I saw a photo of this amazing flower I knew I had to include it in this book. I can only imagine what it would be like to suddenly come upon all these primate faces in the misty forest. (CREDIT: SCOTT P. MOORE)

Indeed, it is from such stories that I derive the strength to go on fighting for Mother Nature.

Storing Seeds around the Globe

The Millennium Seed Bank is just one among some 1,400 seed banks around the world, although it is the largest. Seed banks often work in collaboration with a botanical garden or a university, have partnerships with other seed banks within the country, and in many cases also with the Millennium Seed Bank. Everywhere the process of collection, cleaning, drying, and storage is more or less the same, though finances may dictate the degree of sophistication possible.

The world's first global seed bank was started in 1920 by a most extraordinary Russian scientist, Nikolai Vavilov. Between 1920 and 1930 he went on one hundred collecting expeditions, searching for both wild and cultivated plants through five continents, including Iran, the United States, South and Central America, the Mediterranean, Ethiopia, and Afghanistan. And he accumulated the seeds of around 200,000 plant species, particularly those of food crops and fruit trees.

Unfortunately, Stalin's Communist regime believed that the science of genetics supported the notion of "inborn class differences" among people, and Vavilov, one of the great scientists of the twentieth century, was proclaimed an "enemy of the people" and was thrown into prison in 1940. The seed bank, which mostly consisted of growing trees and agricultural plants, would have been destroyed but for the heroic efforts of a few loyal botanists who struggled to save it. In 1943, Vavilov died in prison at the age of sixty-three. I just hope he knew his life's work had been saved. The seed bank then survived the Communist era, and was eventually named in Vavilov's honor.

But today a new threat to the Vavilov Institute is posed by developers who want to use the area to build a housing estate. There has been international condemnation of this plan, partly because it would desecrate the efforts of an extraordinary man, but also because of the proven value of this and other seed banks.

In the early 1980s, for example, when a deadly parasite threatened to wipe out almost all of the soybean crops in the United States, the Vavilov Institute was able to supply US farmers with the only variety of soybean that could resist the parasite.

The most extraordinary seed bank collection today is the Svalbard Global Seed Vault, which is dug into the side of a mountain on a remote island halfway between mainland Norway and the North Pole. This "Frozen Garden of Eden" was created in order to secure a duplicate of every country's food-seed collection in a safe, natural deep freeze, so that even if the electricity fails, the thick rock and permafrost will ensure that the seeds remain frozen, since the temperature in the vault would only rise to the level of the surrounding permafrost, about –3.5 degrees C. And even in the worst-case scenario of global warming, the vault rooms will remain naturally frozen for up to two hundred years.

In Celebration of Seeds

Every time I explain to an audience the symbolism that led to naming our youth program "Roots & Shoots," I describe the magic, the life force within a seed that is so powerful that tiny roots, in order to reach the water, can work their way through rocks, and the tiny shoot, in order to reach the sun, can find a way through crevices in a brick wall. And, in the end, the rocks and the walls—symbolizing all the harm we have inflicted on the planet—will be pushed aside and cast down.

This power is illustrated all around us—even in the middle of a city, seeds that have ended up in cracks between the paving stones will push out that tentative shoot, and down below, the roots move slowly, unseen beneath the concrete. Roots & Shoots—the strength of the youth of the world.

Knowing I was going to Shanghai during my 2010 lecture tour in China, and knowing I was writing a book about plants, several people told me to be sure to visit the UK pavilion at the World Expo 2010. They told me that the British designer Thomas Heatherwick and his team had got together with Kew Gardens and the Millennium Seed Bank to plan the structure and that it was "awesome."

By the time I got to Shanghai it was definitely a favorite among the more than seventy pavilions that were built for the expo. The Chinese in particular loved it, and nicknamed it "Pu Gong Ying"—"The Dandelion." It was made of sixty thousand slender, transparent, fiber-optic rods, each one almost twenty-five feet long. And implanted in the tip of each of the rods was one or more seeds, provided by the Kunming Institute of Botany. I still regret that my packed schedule did not allow me to see the interior of this magical place described by Heatherwick as "a tranquil, contemplative space, surrounded by the tens of thousands of points of light." In the daytime the rods acted as optic fibers, drawing daylight in to illuminate the interior. And illuminating the seeds.

But at least I got to see it. And despite all I had read about it and all I had been told, nothing had prepared me for the fantastic sight of "The Seed Cathedral." It was nighttime and from a distance it seemed unreal, ethereal, rising to a height of sixty-five feet above the ground. Light sources inside each of the rods caused the whole structure to shine with an eerie, almost phosphorescent, glow and in the gentle breeze they swayed, a host of giant translucent stems rippling over the exterior of the pavilion.

It was a fitting tribute to the magic power of seeds.

Chapter 8

Orchids

When I look at this orchid I feel a sense of awe. So beautiful, and with my name attached: Spathoglottis Jane Goodall. *I love to see it growing in the Singapore Botanical Gardens among all the other glorious flowers.*
(CREDIT: BENG CHIAK TAN)

With their fantastic designs and colors and sizes, orchids have bewitched us from earliest times. People have lost their lives searching for them in wild and remote parts of the world. Whole industries have grown up around propagating, hybridizing, and selling them. Countless books have been written about them, many illustrated lavishly with superb photographs and paintings. In one of these, *About Orchids*, published at the end of the nineteenth century, one Frederick Boyle wrote, "The plant was expressly designed to comfort the elect of human beings in this age."

Designer flowers, by God, for the elite! But although we can smile—or sneer—at Boyle's supreme arrogance, I have to admit that I always felt there was something artificial and opulent about orchids. Those that I knew when growing up were hothouse orchids. I only saw them in the houses of the wealthy—the kinds of orchids that are, today, an essential part of the decor (sitting rooms and—the indignity of it—bathrooms) in all upmarket hotels.

In the warm tropical air of the National Orchid Garden in the Singapore Botanic Gardens, countless species grow in a more natural setting. I walked around among the trees and rocks where they grow, and in the late-afternoon sun they had an almost mystical beauty. There was one small grove where every orchid had a delicate fragrance. Nearby was an area where hybrid orchids grow, each developed to honor a particular individual. How wonderful to see the orchid named for me—*Spathoglottis Jane Goodall.* Most of the others have been named for members of royal families, presidents, ministers, well-known movie stars, and so on. And now me!

Once I started thinking about these fascinating plants, I decided they needed their own chapter. They comprise the largest family of flowering plants—some 26,000 species, organized in 850 genera, are known, and more than one hundred new species are discovered each year. They make up 8 to 10 percent of all flowering plants. They grow wild in almost every country, colonizing just about every ecological niche—in fact, they are only absent from true desert and frozen ice fields.

I have always thought of orchids as tropical plants and was amazed to discover that about thirteen species are found north of the Arctic Circle—more than in Hawaii, where there are only three! Some orchids are terrestrial, although most grow on rocks or up in trees. A species of orchid is often quite restricted in its range, with many being found in one tree only or in a small group of trees.

The smallest orchid known is *Bulbophyllum minutissimum*, which stands only about a tenth of an inch high; the largest are the vanillas, which are vines that can reach lengths of more than sixty-five feet. In some species of vanilla the leaves have almost vanished, appearing like little scales on the green stem. And the tiny ghost orchid

(*Dendrophylax lindenii*) has no leaves at all and spends most of its life underground, feeding off rotting leaf mulch—all that emerges (very occasionally) is a tiny, inch-long stem, with minute white flowers.

Another little orchid, *Bulbophyllum nocturnum*, discovered by Dutch botanist Ed de Vogel in 2008, is the first true night-blooming species known. Its flowers open at ten p.m. and close at dawn—and they bloom only once.

Orchids are usually pollinated by insects, and for most only one particular species of insect can do the job. Typically one petal is modified to form a landing pad for the desired visitor. About two thirds of orchids offer nectar as a reward to the pollinator. The others are cheats. Their flowers mimic the female of their specific insect pollinator: when the male tries to mate with this fake female, he unknowingly enhances the orchid's but not his own reproductive success! The best known of these cheats is the bee orchid—the flower looks and feels like a female bee and even has the same pheromones. I hope for the bee's sake that he has an enjoyable, though futile, experience.

This extraordinary and fascinating behavior naturally intrigued Charles Darwin, who wrote in a letter to Sir Joseph Hooker of Kew, "I was never more interested in any subject in my life, than in this of orchids." He published a book in 1877 called *The Various Contrivances by Which Orchids Are Fertilized by Insects.*

Once an egg has been fertilized, it produces an incredible number of seeds—as many as four million, I am told. I wonder who had the job of counting them! All in all, we can agree that orchids have a fascinating sex life and are amazingly prolific.

Prince of Orchid Hunters

Many people have developed an almost obsessive fascination for orchids, so it is hardly surprising that a number of the dedicated, crazy plant hunters of the eighteenth and nineteenth centuries set off on expeditions into unmapped, unhealthy, and often dangerous tropical climes in search of new species. The jungles of Central and South America yielded particularly exotic blooms.

The orchid frenzy that seized Europe, though not quite as extreme as the earlier tulip frenzy, nevertheless saw collections and individual plants auctioned for enormous prices. The plant hunters competed with one another, and jealously kept secret new sources of especially exotic species—even going to the extent of providing others with false maps. Many of these men accomplished extraordinary feats of endurance—and a number died. One of them searched the whole length of the Amazon River from source to ocean, and in addition crossed the Andes numerous times, climbing to heights of up to 19,000 feet. Another hunter traveled the same river the other way around, from sea to source.

One man stands out—the Czech, Benedict Roezl, who became known as the "Prince of Orchid Hunters." He had a flair for discovering new and rare species—not only of orchids, incidentally, but of many other beautiful flowers as well—in Latin America and other parts of the world. On one occasion, in 1871, after an unsuccessful trip, he was traveling back by canoe with one native helper. The river was swollen with recent floodwater and was flowing fast. All manner of debris was being swept along, surely posing some danger to their fragile craft. Suddenly Roezl saw that a large uprooted tree that was about to pass them was festooned with all manner of epiphytes, ferns, and mosses. Quickly paddling toward it, they tied their canoe alongside and gathered up the unexpected and amazingly rich bounty of plant life.

Roezl, unlike many of the orchid hunters who perished of disease, wild animals, natives, bandits, or accidents of travel, survived to die peacefully in his own bed back in Prague. This is not to say that he did not have his fair share of adventure—he was, for example, robbed seventeen times. Unlike others of his time, he traveled light, in the manner of many of the famous plant hunters of the previous century. And it was this fact that, on one occasion, almost led to his death, for the bandits who had captured him were angry that he had so little to steal and had their knives out ready to kill him. He was only saved, at the last minute, when one of their number pointed out that it was unlucky to kill a madman, and clearly this man, who traveled with little but stacks of "weeds," must be crazy. They put away their knives and allowed him to carry on with his journey. How interesting that David Douglas had been spared by a group of Native Americans because they, too, had had the same reluctance to harm a crazy person!

Stolen for Beauty

"When a man falls in love with orchids, he'll do anything to possess the one he wants," Norman MacDonald wrote in his 1939 book *The Orchid Hunters: A Jungle Adventure.* "It's like chasing a green-eyed woman or taking cocaine, it's a sort of madness."

This madness, this desperate quest by so many people for more, and yet more new and exotic orchids, unfortunately led to the felling of thousands of forest trees for the epiphytic orchids that grew on them. And because so many of those species are highly endemic, with all individuals of one species being found in a tiny area, the felling of even *one* of their habitat trees may compromise the gene pool of the whole population. In extreme cases every individual orchid has been removed from its habitat. Thus a small island off the coast of Brazil was once blessed with a great abundance of *Leleila elegans.* Botanists wrote in 1847 that never before had they seen such a fantastic biomass of plants. But by 1897, fifty years later, every single orchid had been taken.

Tragically the same greed continues today. Even though in most countries it is illegal to collect orchids without a license that limits the applicant to a strict quota, thousands of plants are collected illegally. Often this is so that new hybrids can be created, propagated, and sold. Dealing with orchids is the most lucrative flower business worldwide, involving some $2 billion per year in legal business, while the illegal markets are likely to be as much again.

Nothing illustrates the madness that seizes orchid people more than the series of events that followed the discovery, in 2002, of

Phragmipedium kovachii. It is a stunningly beautiful orchid from the Amazon rain forest in northeast Peru, with a blue-purple flower that can have a horizontal spread of up to nine and a half inches. This discovery led to a series of international scandals and intrigues that inspired Craig Pittman's recently published book *The Scent of Scandal: Greed, Betrayal, and the World's Most Beautiful Orchid.*

The story began when Michael Kovach, an American orchid collector, stopped at a roadside kiosk in Peru that sold orchids. The vendor, Faustino Medina Bautista, offered him three fantastic orchids. Kovach had never seen anything like them and was sure they were a new species—perhaps his dream would come true and he would get an orchid named for him.

He flew with one of the plants, concealed among other less exotic specimens, to the Marie Selby Botanical Gardens in Sarasota, Florida, famous for its collection of six thousand living orchids. When he walked in with his glorious bloom, there was a gasp of astonishment.

Kovach, of course, should have had an export permit. But this could only have been issued if the orchid was being cultivated in Peru, and it would have needed a name—which can only be given when a detailed description has been published by one of only fifteen recognized orchid taxonomists—none of whom were in Peru. Therefore, legally it is almost impossible to take a new species from its country of origin in the developing world. Yet somehow botanical gardens have continued to describe new species. For the most part, clearly, a blind eye is turned on these illegal transactions.

Unfortunately for the Selby Botanical Gardens, there were others who already knew about Kovach's orchid, since vendor Bautista had been selling them (for less than a dollar apiece) before Kovach turned up there. And a former Selby employee and local orchid taxonomist, Eric Christenson, had obtained a photo from Peruvian scientists, and was working to describe it himself. He planned to name it *P. peruvanum* in honor of its homeland. When Selby's taxonomists heard about this rival effort, they started working around the clock, and managed to get their description published in their own scientific journal just five days ahead of Christenson's.

There was excitement and celebration at Selby. They had described an orchid that was the discovery of the century—"like finding a new species of elephant in the Amazon," said one enthusiast. And Kovach was ecstatic, for this orchid was named for him. But the euphoria was short-lived. Eight days after the published description, possibly tipped off by Christenson, federal agents began investigating the whole situation. Kovach, Selby, and some of its board were found guilty, fined, and put on probation.

In the meantime the orchid quickly became the most sought-after in the world. Prices soared to ten thousand dollars on the black market, and orchid fanatics everywhere were prepared to bend rules and break laws in their obsessive quest to possess it.

And what of the situation in the wild? By 2003 the site where Kovach's three orchids had originated the year before was cleaned out. Another site was found with more than a thousand plants, but a few weeks later, when an enthusiast went to photograph them, he found just two orchids remaining, high on a rocky ledge. By an odd coincidence, when he got back to his hotel, he saw a pickup loaded with seven large rice and coffee sacks, stuffed into which were several hundred of the largest orchids he had ever seen, their leaves some three feet long. They were the last of the plants (except for the two that had escaped) he had just been to hoping to visit in the wild.

No attempt had been made to conceal the stolen orchids, and he was able to track down the name of the thief. He reported him to the Peruvian wildlife authority—but no action was taken. Since then three other sites have been found, two of which have already been plundered.

Five years after discovery, *P. kovachii* orchids were finally being cultivated in Peru: but only three nurseries had been issued permits to collect legally, and they were allowed to take only five orchids each. Yet during those same five years tens of thousands were taken illegally from the wild, few of which will have survived. It is not difficult to see why serious collectors tend to ignore government restrictions.

A Clever Rescue Strategy

One way to protect an endangered wild orchid from the avarice of the collector is to flood the market with captive-bred individuals. This strategy was certainly successful in the case of the "rotting meat" orchid (*Bulbophyllum echinolabium*) which, until recently, was threatened by both overcollection and logging.

I heard the story from Rogier Van Vugt, my friend from Leiden University, in the Netherlands. "This orchid is certainly not pretty," he said, "but it has a charm that is exotic—or, better said, bizarre." It consists of a cluster of swollen green stalks, the younger ones carrying hard, succulent leaves. It may have one or several flower spikes, each of which has just one bloom at a time.

"Each flower," says Rogier, "is an impressive piece of natural art, measuring some thirty centimeters (almost twelve inches) from tip to tip with long, thin brownish green petals and an odd, spiny red lip that is connected to the rest of the flower by a hinge-like system." This is what gives the plant its name—*echinolabium* means "spiny lip."

This orchid, as its name implies, is one of those unusual plants that attract pollinators by smelling like rotting meat. When a fly creeps to the center of the flower, the hinge closes, pressing the insect against sticky pollen grains. In a few moments it is released, after which, with luck, it will visit another stinking flower and deposit pollen on its stigma.

For a while the rotting-meat orchid, which has a very small range, was officially classified as extinct in the wild. However, enthusiast Simon Wellinga, who has many species of orchid growing at his home in the Netherlands, had two *Bulbophyllum echinolabium*. He was propagating them using a method that is now well established—collecting the seeds, sterilizing them, and sowing them on a sterile jellylike substance that contains the nutrients the germinating orchid would get from the mycorrhizal fungi in the wild.

When Simon learned how rare his two plants were, he cross-pollinated them: this resulted in a seedpod containing hundreds of thousands of seeds. He was able to grow some himself, and shared hundreds with other individuals and organizations. He had great success—his seeds germinated into hundreds of young plants, and he shared those too with nurseries and fanciers around Europe. He had also sent seeds to a seed bank in America so that orchid fanciers there soon had the opportunity to grow them as well.

A few years later a very small population of these orchids was rediscovered in the wild. Thanks to Simon and the people who have grown the species on a large scale, the desire to collect from the field is nonexistent, and the newly found wild individuals will at least be safe from poaching.

Orchids as Medicine and Food

It is not only for their beauty that orchids are valued but also for their medicinal properties and as food. The first records of orchid medicinal use date back three thousand years, when the Chinese were using them for a variety of ailments, especially sexual problems. And throughout recorded history, in many parts of the world, a whole variety of orchids were—and still are—believed to have aphrodisiac properties. If you wonder why, just take a look at the tuber of an orchid of the *Orchis* genus. The name of the plant is derived from the Greek word *orchis*, which means "testicles." The toxicologist Paracelsus, referring to one of these tubers, wrote, "Behold the Satyrion root, is it not formed like the male's privy parts? Accordingly, magic discovered it and revealed that it can restore a man's virility and passion." Still today, in various parts of the world, certain orchids are used to treat a whole variety of sexual disorders, from impotence and poor performance to infertility.

In Turkey, where the orchid's aphrodisiac qualities have long been appreciated, they are also used in cultural cuisine. The tubers, especially of the early purple orchid (*O. mascula*) and the military orchid (*O. militaris*), are dried and ground up to create a kind of starchy flour, known as salep, which is used to make a traditional drink—also known as salep. It became popular in England during the seven-

When you look at the tuber of an orchid it is easy to see why its name comes from the Greek word orchis, *meaning "testicles."* (CREDIT: ROGIER VAN VUGT)

teenth and eighteenth centuries, where it was known as "saloop." With the advent of the coffee and tea shops the demand for saloop diminished, but for quite some time it was still offered as an alternative to coffee. Sometimes the British used their own native orchids to make the drink—in this culinary context they were known as "dog stones," which was simply slang for "testicles."

Recently salep has become increasingly popular outside Turkey, and huge numbers of the tubers are exported. As a result, these orchids face extinction, although projects are now under way that employ local people to protect wild orchids, and efforts are being made to cultivate them commercially.

In Africa, too, biologists and conservationists are stepping up efforts to protect some of the continent's rich diversity of orchids, many of which—seven hundred have been listed—have long been valued as medicinal plants and food for humans and livestock. During one of my last visits to Tanzania I heard about one relatively new threat to some of the country's orchids.

The problem originated in neighboring Zambia, where, until the early 2000s, orchid tubers were considered a "famine food." But things began to change: boiled tubers became a fashionable dish in urban areas and led to what has been referred to as an "orchid rush." As a result of this escalating demand, several species of the genera *Disa*, *Haenaria*, and *Satyrium* are now endangered. Another, the leopard orchid, is valued for various medicinal reasons—especially, I am told, as a cure for madness.

The growing shortage of these orchids in Zambia triggered a huge and quite unsustainable illegal trade across the border from Tanzania—in recent years it has been estimated that a staggering four million were smuggled out. In an effort to protect at least some of their orchids, the Tanzanian authorities have made a new and beautiful national park on the Kitulo Plateau—the local people call it Bustani ya Mungu, "God's Garden." This 135-square-mile area is rich in plant diversity—there are fifty species of orchid alone.

And I was happy to hear that efforts are being made not only to protect some of the food-giving orchids in the wild but also to try to grow them commercially—as was the case with the vanilla orchid (*Vanilla planifolia*), which is the source of vanilla flavoring.

The Secrets of Orchid Farming

Vanilla planifolia, like all members of the vanilla genus (more than one hundred have been described), is a vine, and in its homeland of Mexico and Central America it climbs trees in the forest to heights of up to 35 meters (almost 115 feet). Its cream-colored flowers, each blooming for only one day, exude a sweet scent, probably to attract its pollinator, the *Melipona* bee. It is the elongated, fleshy seedpod that provides us with vanilla.

When the pod is ripe, it becomes dark brown or blackish and gives off a powerful scent. It is best to pick the pods just as they start to split open. Traditionally they are then laid out in the sun for a couple of hours each day and wrapped in blankets to "sweat" overnight. After two or three weeks of this treatment, they are dried for a further two to four weeks.

Vanilla was probably first cultivated by the Totonac people of the Vera Cruz region in Mexico—perhaps they found beans cured by long periods in the heat and humidity of the forest. At any rate, they learned to cultivate the vines, and when they were conquered by the Aztecs in 1427, they paid their taxes with vanilla pods. As a result, their rulers became fond of both the taste and aroma, and began using vanilla to flavor their *cacahuatl*, a drink made from water, honey, ground corn, and cacao beans.

In 1519, the Spanish conquistador Hernán Cortés sent vanilla beans, along with cacao beans, from the capital of the Aztec empire back to Europe, where initially vanilla was only used to flavor chocolate. The Aztecs had valued the vanilla not only for its smell and taste but also for its medicinal properties and used it to treat a wide range of problems, from indigestion and headaches to animal bites and poisonings.

Also, while it is not obvious that the Europeans valued the vanilla beans as medicine, they were delighted to have a new and exotic aphrodisiac. And many people do find the taste and smell of vanilla erotic and invigorating—which is why it is added to so many perfumes and used in aromatherapy.

Well into the seventeenth century, no one knew how to cultivate vanilla orchids outside their natural habitat. Plantations were started in many countries with a suitable climate, but the orchids never bore fruit. Not until 1836 did Charles Morren, Belgian horticulturist and professor, realize that the vanilla flower needed the *Melipona* bee! He developed a method for hand pollination, but it was time-consuming and costly.

It was twelve-year-old Edmond Albius, whose mother had worked on a vanilla plantation on Réunion (a small island off Madagascar), who revolutionized vanilla farming. He developed and perfected a method of hand-pollination that was superior to all previous ones and that is still in use today.

Orchids in Peril

The biggest threat to most orchid species is the destruction of their habitat. Thousands of species live in rain forest trees and are often driven close to extinction, or even over the brink, as a result of the felling of tropical forests for timber or farmland. Without doubt many endemic species—which may live on one tree only—become extinct before they are discovered and described.

It is not only in the tropics that orchids are threatened. It is the same all over the globe, wherever we humans have moved in with our growing numbers, our hoes and spades, bulldozers and chainsaws, roads and developments. In addition to which, since most orchids rely on insects for fertilization, our use of pesticides has wreaked havoc. And now there is climate change.

Fortunately there are very many orchid enthusiasts working to save them, protecting them in their natural habitat, and seeking to propagate them in captivity. I met one of them during a recent visit to Australia and was delighted by his enthusiasm. Paul Scannell, from the Albury Botanic Gardens in New South Wales, is particularly passionate about one species of very beautiful and very endangered orchid, the crimson spider orchid (*Caladenia concolor*). In his area of the box woodlands there are just eighteen individual plants: they would not be there but for Paul.

"It's a fragile environment," he told me, "badly degraded as a result of land clearing, trail bikes, and four-wheel drives, deliberately lit fires, firewood and bush rock collecting, cattle breaking through fences, predation by native animals—and years of drought."

It is the involvement of the local people, including the Aboriginal Wiradjuri community, that is saving this orchid. As soon as Paul alerted them to what was going on, they began raising money and building fences around the habitat. The scientists, meanwhile, were working out a recovery plan. "But if we had waited for that," Paul told me, "the orchid would probably be extinct by now."

Paul organizes surveys during which volunteers check on known plants and search for new ones. They note where new fences must be constructed and old ones repaired to keep the orchids and their habitat safe from livestock and vehicles. It is hard work, and it is ongoing, for at any moment some new threat may confront the team.

But orchid people will never give up. I had a letter from Paul a few months ago. "Our beautiful crimson spider orchids, with their intricate and complicated lives," he wrote, "have survived everything nature has thrown at them over the ages. The eighteen plants in our local population have continued to defy the odds and remain static in their numbers."

Hopefully a way to increase those numbers will soon be found: many orchids can now be propagated in botanical gardens, by horticulturists. All around the world they are doing well in captivity, and already, where the habitat is suitable, some have been reintroduced back into the wild. And there are plans to reintroduce many more.

Saved by a Stapler

My Dutch botanist friend Rogier told me a quite marvelous story about a friend of his, Tom Velardi, who is saving orchids in his own, very special way. When Tom tired of his hectic life in the United States, he set off for Japan with nothing but one suitcase and some books and became an English teacher in the city of Fukuoka. Tom, a nature lover, delights in the native flora of Japan and loves to photograph the plants while hiking in the mountains.

There are a few species of very small epiphytic orchids in the forests there, but they are rarely seen, as they often grow high up in the trees. In the stormy season, however, many branches break off and end up on the forest floor. And that is when Tom sometimes finds tiny orchids growing on them. Knowing that these plants need fresh air and light to grow and are sure to die if he leaves them on a fallen branch, Tom collects the plants and nurtures them at home. Then, when the storms are over, he returns the orchids to the trees, each one to the correct host, since they are very selective and particular.

How does Tom accomplish this?

"I simply use a stapler, and staple them to the trees! They are very small staples and don't penetrate beyond the bark of the tree, but it seems to hold the plant well, until it can grow new roots. And the staple rusts away in time. Not a very elegant solution, but it seems to work fine. And they seem to enjoy their new home."

Tom is just one of the people who love orchids. Neither collector nor scientist, but just one of the growing number of people who respect the natural world and are prepared to do their bit to help when there is a problem. And, as we all know, there are very many problems today.

It wasn't until I began to gather material for this chapter that I realized the full extent of the influence that orchids have exerted through history. Down through the ages discoveries of the most beautiful species have roused passions that have led to cheating, crime, and the most flagrant disregard of national and international law. It is the stuff of great drama and intrigue—and indeed many writers have explored the orchid sagas.

But this terrible history of greed and exploitation is only part of the story. A new breed of orchid lovers is now coming to the fore—those who are equally passionate, but for a different reason. Those that are prepared to fight to protect beautiful endangered orchids in their natural habitat, and to persevere in efforts to restore others to their rightful homes in the wild.

Chapter 9

Gardens and Gardening

Four generations of gardeners: my son Grub, me, my mother Vanne, and my grandmother Danny in the Birches' garden. (CREDIT: JANE GOODALL)

In many ways, as I have explained, The Birches garden was less than ideal. It was dark, shaded by trees. The soil was sandy and in some places made acid by pine needles and rhododendrons. Yet for me as a child it was a magical and perfect garden—a place where I waited for the first spikes of leaves breaking through the earth in spring and wondered whether they would become a crocus or a hyacinth, a place where I could watch the swelling of the buds on the trees and the unfurling of tiny leaves.

The garden was not just a place for growing things and learning about nature. It was also a place for nurturing the soul. Gardeners have always known that working with the soil and growing and harvesting plants can lift the spirits and make you feel better. I can see Danny now, kneeling on her little mat, trowel in hand, aches and pains temporarily forgotten. And Uncle Eric, home for the weekend during World War II, digging the flowerbeds, battling with dandelions, and feeding the hydrangeas with rusty nails and old bits of iron to improve their color. It helped him to forget the horrors of the wounded who filled Whipps Cross Hospital after every enemy bombing raid on London. He didn't talk about it, but I knew there were people who had lost limbs, lost their eyes, lost family members. When I was eleven years old and found out about the Holocaust, I turned to the garden and Beech in my confusion, seeking the reassurance of that living, green space as I tried to come to terms with my growing awareness of evil.

The wonderful thing is that we still have The Birches and its garden. Of course there have been changes, but much is the same. It was my aunt Olly who introduced the idea of growing flowers in tubs. Today Judy has greatly increased their number, and some are used for apple, plum, and cherry trees. In the spring there are still the primroses and violets of childhood. And we still have the same three peony plants and the hydrangeas and some of Olly's roses, though they are very old now, and dying. The pine trees and rhododendrons, and Beech and Nooky, along with most of the other childhood trees are fine.

A new addition to the garden, growing in the middle of the lawn by the birdbath that was installed by Uncle Eric and the stone frog "Jeremy Fisher," who has been sitting there for more than eighty years, is a young Japanese maple, planted for my mother after she died because she always loved their color. Some of her ashes were sprinkled among its roots when it was planted, and we added some of Olly's when she died a year later. That tree has thrived. Something else new is a pond introduced by Judy, which grows water lilies and other water plants. She and her daughter, Pip, are planning to make a new rockery in memory of Danny.

How lucky we are to have this place so rich with the memories of childhoods long gone, and now creating new memories for the two little boys—Judy's grandsons—who in their turn play and dream in this magic garden.

Gardens of the Ancient World

Our human love of flowers and gardens goes way, way back in time. I remember reading, as a child, about the Hanging Gardens of Babylon that were said to have been suspended from heaven on golden chains. According to one of the earliest accounts, these gardens were built on the bank of the Euphrates by King Nebuchadnezzar II, who ruled between 605 and 562 BC. He had them built for his wife, who was homesick for the trees and flowers of her native Persia. Water from the river was continuously driven up pipes laid beside stone steps that rose in tiers, as in a theater. The highest garden was seventy-five by one hundred feet square, and huge trees grew up there. The gardens were an architectural miracle.

Other historians believe that the gardens were built by King Sennacherib of Assyria (reigning 705–681 BC) in quite a different place, close to his palace on the Tigris. And there are those who think that the Hanging Gardens were merely poetic fantasy, that they never existed at all. If they did, then what happened to them? There is speculation that an earthquake destroyed them at the end of the second century BC. At any rate, I like to believe that they were real, one of the Seven Wonders of the Ancient World.

Whatever we think about those particular gardens, we certainly can be sure that gardens and gardening have been part of human culture for thousands of years. Elaborate gardens were created in China, and then Persia (where the oldest archaeological proof of a garden layout has been discovered). In the Western Hemisphere, gardens—as opposed to fields for the cultivation of food crops—seem first to have proliferated in Italy around the temples and later within walled enclosures close to the houses of the wealthy. The ash that rained down during the eruption of Vesuvius in AD 79 has preserved not only temple gardens but also hundreds of these domestic gardens. I well remember learning about the horrifying event when I was at school, wondering what they went through, all those hundreds of doomed citizens—perhaps it was similar to the experience of those who lived in Nagasaki and Hiroshima when the atomic bombs were dropped. The difference, of course, was that one was an "act of God," while the other was the result of humanity's inhumanity.

Different styles of gardens have developed in different countries, and styles change over time. The wealthy, with their large estates, have developed whole landscapes with streams and woodlands in addition to the more formal flowerbeds, ponds, and fountains. The traditional English cottage garden displays a wealth of colorful flowers—hollyhocks and delphiniums and roses, cheerfully rubbing shoulders in tiny spaces. Formal Japanese gardens place rocks and water and plants to create an atmosphere of serenity, a place for meditation. I have been fortunate, for my travels around the world have enabled me to visit many extremely beautiful gardens of many types.

One of these visits, on a cool but sunny May day in 2010, was to the Val de Marne Rose Garden. Situated about four miles south of Paris, it was created in 1894—the first public garden in the world to be dedicated entirely to roses. It is a magnificent place, with over thirteen thousand bushes representing some 3,200 varieties. Collected from around the world, they grow in the hundreds in the different flowerbeds, while others climb walls and arches, trellises and pergolas. The riot of colors, ranging from pure white to dark crimson, almost purple, set against the green of the spring leaves and grass borders, was truly a banquet for the eyes. And the fragrances... nothing heavy and cloying here, nothing like the overwhelming scent of frangipani and tiger lilies. No, a series of delicate scents, each one a delight.

I was greeted by Christian Hanak, known as a rose author—or "poet," as he calls himself—and Guillaume Didier, a rose breeder. The two had worked together, for the eight years that it takes, to produce a glorious new variety of rose, and I was invited to "baptize" it. A singular honor, for not only do I have a love of roses, but this particular rose was named for me—the Jane Goodall rose.

It is a climbing rose (*Generosa*) with delicate pink blooms, glossy dark-green leaves, and a strong stem—with very strong thorns. The young plant I met that day had six blooms, but when fully mature, Christian told me, it will flower abundantly and climb up to ten feet high, reaching toward the sky. I love what he says about it, this poet: "the ultimate romantic flower... it has the natural grace of simple beauty... a rose that knows not to reveal its heart until the end of flowering, when it can no longer hide its secret." And a couple of the blooms had revealed their secrets—exquisite orange-pink colors right in their center. Best of all, this rose has the most exquisite fragrance, delicate yet strong, without being overpowering.

A small group of people had been invited for the ceremony. Speeches were made, the Jane Goodall rose was planted in the garden, and we scattered handfuls of rose petals over her. And then I kissed a leaf, as I always do to mark ceremonial plantings. Corks popped, and soft-pink rose-flavored champagne was passed around. I poured a little for the rose, and the baptism was complete.

We all left with light hearts and raised spirits. That is what time in a garden, among our favorite flowers, can do for us.

Gardening to Heal Body and Soul

It was soon after this that I learned how another rose tree had been planted to help a traumatized victim of war. There is, in London, a wonderful organization called Freedom from Torture. They treat survivors, and therapists have found that even the most severely traumatized victims can benefit from spending time in nature. A skilled and sensitive horticulturist has designed a peaceful and sheltered garden where therapists can spend time, one-on-one, with their patients. Slowly, gradually, the power of soil, flowers, and trees begins to work its healing magic.

Precious, a young woman from a war-torn part of Africa, was

one of the most severely traumatized patients. She had brought with her a dark burden of terrible memories—memories that could have destroyed her. Not only had she been gang-raped by soldiers, but worse still, forced to watch as they slashed off the head of her six-month-old baby. She had somehow managed to escape and was helped, by friends, to get to England. When she reached Freedom from Torture, she was on the brink of mental disintegration.

Each day she spent time in the garden alone with her therapist and nature. Gradually she was able to tell her story. And one day she planted a rosebush—in memory of her son. That was the start of her long, hard journey back into the world through the dark memories of her terrible ordeal.

There is now scientific research that proves that gardening can benefit people suffering from stress and depression. Firstly, there is a physical benefit, for it tones the body, and this affects mental health. Secondly, the work of gardening involves the right brain; people focus on the immediate task before them, and in that way the worries that circle around in their thoughts, which are produced by the left brain, are alleviated.

When questioned, the patients who were part of the study said the best reward was not the success of their plantings but the reduction of stress that came from the gardening itself. It seems that the soothing colors, the textures, and the smell of plants and soil has an uplifting effect on one's mind and spirits.

Just half an hour of gardening can help to raise morale and help us to face the problems thrown at us by life. And although an actual garden is best, even tending a few potted plants can have a remarkably beneficial effect.

Gardening for Prisoners

Probably because of the calming effect on the psyche, an increasing number of prisons are launching gardening programs: on-site food gardens improve the nutritional intake of inmates, and this, in addition to the calming effects described above, can reduce violence and improve the participants' mental health. Some programs teach horticultural skills that can be used upon inmates' release (slashing recidivism rates). And some may even produce surplus food that can be sent to food banks or other community centers or services.

In October 2011, I had an opportunity to visit such a program when Drew Reynolds, one of the teachers at the Oak Creek Youth Correctional Facility in Albany, Oregon, asked if I could possibly squeeze in a visit with the girls during my packed schedule. That is how I heard about a garden that seven of the teenage girls had created. It all started when they learned that the state's "Oregon Youth in Action" program was offering cash awards to worthy school projects that supported healthy living.

They had already been inspired by Michelle Obama's mission to improve nutrition and fight obesity. And they knew that she had an organic kitchen garden at the White House. With the help of Drew, the girls applied for the award, proposing that they start an organic vegetable garden so they could learn about plants and gardening and incorporate better food into the correctional facility's kitchen. The award required the girls to testify about their plans in front of the state legislature and speak about the value of their project. Because they were confined to the facility, they had to testify by phone. They were very nervous, but together they wrote a speech and read it over the phone.

After they heard that they had won the award, the First Lady of Oregon drove out to the facility to hand deliver a $2,000 check and a certificate. The girls were given a small piece of ground tucked behind one of the facility's buildings, and they used the money to pay for compost so that they could create a nourishing soil bed for plants and seeds. The novice gardeners had a lot to learn—many of them had never done any hands-on work with plants or gardening. Some were only just beginning to learn where food came from or how it was grown. One girl asked if you could grow candy corn there!

The girls chose what they would plant, and they tended and harvested the vegetables. Some of them worked in the kitchen, learning how to prepare and cook what they had grown. They told me proudly that they had been able to produce 219 pounds of food that summer out of their small "test garden" and that almost all of it was used in the kitchen for meals at the facility. I later learned from Drew that because their garden was so successful, the facility has now committed to giving them additional space as well as providing them with a 30-by-48-foot greenhouse.

The original group of girls who won the award received a lot of positive attention and felt incredibly proud. Because girls come and go, others have taken over the gardening, and it has become a very popular activity. If they could, Drew says, many of them would spend all their days gardening during the warmer months.

If only every child could know the joy of a garden, there would, I am sure, be less violence on the streets. Remember how that intrepid plant hunter, David Douglas, abandoned his unruly behavior when he began to work, as a child, in a garden? It has been found that areas in a city that are enhanced with green places and window boxes see a drop in crime rates. Enlightened inner-city schools realize this and make an effort to give the children at least some experience with planting things, watching flowers bloom, growing something they can eat—even if it is only in pots in the schoolroom. But that is a lot better than nothing.

Perhaps the best endorsement of the effect of a garden on the well-being of the gardener comes from that most inspirational of people, Nelson Mandela. He survived twenty-one years in Robben Island Prison in South Africa, and this is something he wrote in his autobiography:

"A garden is one of the few things in prison that one could control. Being a custodian of this patch of earth offered a small taste of freedom."

Renewal on the Reservation

Nowhere is the power of gardens and gardening more apparent than in Pine Ridge, an Oglala Lakota (Sioux) Native American reservation located in South Dakota. When I first went to the "Rez," it was a place that offered almost no hope to the people living there, displaced from their traditional hunting grounds by the white man. Unemployment was over 80 percent—and everywhere I went, I met families struggling in all arenas of survival. There was lots of trash; mangy dogs whelped under trailers; many of the adults were either alcoholics or on drugs; and suicides (especially among the youth) were all too common, much above the national average for the United States.

Patricia Hammond is a Lakota living near the reservation, where she works every single day. Jason Schoch was originally from a small rural North Dakota town and a farming family who, when I met him, was keen to do something for the Native Americans and the small towns of the Dakotas. Soon after that, he and Patricia met, they fell in love, and he moved to join her in Pine Ridge.

We all recognized the potential benefit of establishing a Roots & Shoots program on the reservation as a way to engage and empower youth. We hoped it would help not only to reconnect the Native children to the animal and plant world around them but also foster respect for their own cultural traditions. Patricia and Jason started by working with some of the children to prepare the soil and plant a vegetable garden, working with as many of the young people as they could persuade to join them.

"We chose a garden," Jason told me, "because it was relatively simple and could lead to immediate change right in their backyards." They both told me that knowledge of plants has always been important in the indigenous community. Patricia said, "So we both knew we needed to connect these vegetables growing in the garden with the native plants and the natural world and their own culture, as well as their physical health. But we knew the garden was key—just talking about these things would not have helped."

At first it was an uphill battle. The garden was trashed time and again. But something magic happened: a few of the older boys, including gang members, seeing how upset their younger brothers and sisters were when their hard work was destroyed, began to protect their garden.

The tribal elders, having been let down so many times by the white man and his broken promises, were initially mistrustful of this new program that came from outside the Lakota culture. For months they watched and waited. And then, finally, they gave the Roots & Shoots program their support. That was the breakthrough that Patricia and Jason had so desperately needed. From then on, the garden became a gathering place where the grandparents joined in, teaching the children about the importance of bees as pollinators, and worms for aerating the soil. The garden was a stepping-stone toward teaching them about the natural native plants that had

Lakota Native American Patricia Hammond helped start a Roots & Shoots gardening program on the Pine Ridge Reservation in South Dakota. One of the goals of the program is to teach children about indigenous plant food and medicine. Through gardening, native wisdom is once again being passed down through the generations. (CREDIT: JASON T. SCHOCH)

always played such an important role in their culture. It was the start of repairing the growing disconnect between youth and the natural world that has always been at the heart of Lakota culture. And it also began to re-bridge the disconnect between youth and the elders.

The Roots & Shoots group started hiking out to the prairie to learn about indigenous wild food and medicinal plants. They collected seeds and started a native-plant garden. With a garden nearby, one of the elders, who said it was too hard for him to travel out to the prairie, could then finally begin to pass on his knowledge to the young people.

Since the first garden was planted in 2006, sixteen more have been created, and all have a section for native plants. Indigenous knowledge, once again, is being passed down from the wise elder medicine men and women, who still remember their old culture, to the next generation. There is a new feeling of hope now—at least among some people in Pine Ridge Reservation.

Guerrilla Gardeners

Now that we understand how gardens and plants can raise our spirits, we should be really grateful to the people who are defying the law to become "guerrilla gardeners." A few months ago I was on a bus heading toward Victoria Station. As we drove through a particularly dreary neighborhood of faded office blocks, I suddenly noticed one roundabout that was bright with assorted flowers. It was in stark contrast to the other roundabouts, and I was curious.

That was my introduction to guerrilla gardening in London. A growing number of middle-class, well-dressed, well-spoken, "respectable" people, frustrated by the dreary appearance of the neighborhoods where they live or work, are growing flowers on any unused land they can find—along the edges of the roads, on patches of earth around the base of trees—and on roundabouts. It is, apparently, illegal to do this, so even though the police usually ignore them, these visionary gardeners do their work at night.

As a matter of principle, surely if people want to create beauty in shabby places, they should not be prevented? This is certainly the view of Richard Reynolds, the unofficial leader of what is known as the "Growing Movement" in London. He began brightening roundabouts in the drab concrete area of the intersection of Elephant and Castle in central London in 2004 and immediately captured the media's attention. He has even written a book for those interested in joining him—*A Handbook on Guerrilla Gardening: Fighting Filth with Fork and Flowers.* "Going out there and taking responsibility for a shared space, along with other people can warm the soul," he says.

Another act of rebellion that I love is the tossing of a "seed bomb" or "green grenade"—which is simply a clay ball mixed with flower seeds that germinate easily. These bombs are thrown up onto embankments, behind railings, and other hard-to-reach places where guerrilla gardeners can't plant the seeds by hand. When the rain comes, the clay dissolves, the seeds take root, and soon patches of bright flowers bring smiles to closed city faces. At least, that is the idea.

Certainly it works for me. When I am walking through some alien town, I love it when I pass an urban garden and am suddenly gifted with an unexpected scent of lilies of the valley, or the fragrance of roses, or the smell of new-mown grass. Indeed, I always try to detour so as to go through a park where the light is softened as it filters through the leaves—and instantly my heart is lightened and the world seems a better place. Most people, when I ask them, say they feel the same.

New Gardens for a Changing World

Gardening is changing. Until recently, modern landscaping and gardening was oriented more toward maintaining lawns and decorating beds with flowers and shrubs. In order to keep the grass green and exotic decorative plants alive, gardeners relied on liberal doses of water as well as chemical fertilizers, pesticides, and "weed killers," such as Roundup Ready.

At one time a young man was paid, one day a week, to help Olly with the garden at The Birches. We did not realize that he was using herbicide on the lawn to get rid of moss and other small weeds, as well as a particularly vicious pesticide to deal with the snails and slugs. When we found out, we were horrified. About six months after we dispensed with his services, we heard, for the first time in several years, the *bang, bang, bang* of a song thrush smashing open snails against a rock. Gradually other birds reappeared, and now the whole area is protected for conservation and the use of chemicals strongly discouraged.

So many people are concerned about the terrible environmental degradation of our planet, and so often they feel helpless and hopeless in the face of all that is wrong. The most important thing, as I am constantly saying, is to think about small ways in which we can make a difference—every day. And people lucky enough to have gardens can truly make a difference by maintaining the land in an environmentally friendly way.

Right now the biggest new gardening trend in the United States is the elimination of fertilizer-dependent and water-draining grass lawns. Instead, gardeners are discovering the joys of creating more environmentally friendly habitats with native trees and plants—those that have been living in the area for hundreds of years and are adapted to the climate.

My botanist friend Robin Kobaly is an advisor to people who want to grow drought-tolerant gardens with native plants in the Southwest. She says that people are especially enthusiastic about native plants when they live in arid areas, but even in other parts of the country, where there's more rainfall, gardeners are getting sick of the amount of water it takes to keep grass lawns green. At the moment, gardening with drought-tolerant native plants is just a popular eco-conscious trend. But soon, five to six years from now, Robin believes, "it will be imperative for everyone to change how they landscape and garden as the overriding reality of the lack of water becomes apparent."

This new gardening movement not only reduces water waste but also provides an attractive habitat for the local wildlife. Last month Gombe videographer Bill Wallauer wrote to tell me about how he and his wife, Kristin, were transforming their "typical ridiculous American lawn" into a native plant habitat for bees and other insects and birds and a whole host of small creatures.

Bill put in a stream, a pond, and a wetland for water-loving plant species. He created two areas of high-wildlife-value shrub species, planted numerous coneflower and aster species, and is propagating native grass.

"My favorite spot is our beautiful native-woodland-wildflowers area, which has species like wild ginger, wild leak, and trillium," he recently wrote to me. So far he has recorded thirty-seven bird species in their "tiny little backyard."

I have to say that while it may seem small to him after the wilderness of Gombe, it is clearly rather large compared to the postage-stamp-size gardens that most people have—if they have a garden at all. But even the smallest of gardens can make a difference for the wildlife that is struggling to survive. Almost everyone I meet wants to save wild animals and insects, but they often don't realize how important it is to preserve the anchors of the wildlife community—the native plants.

In urban areas where the gardens and yards are often small, some communities are joining together to create wildlife havens. There is, for example, the "Pollinator Pathway" in Seattle—where a group of neighbors have transformed the scruffy strips of grass in front of their homes, between the sidewalk and the street, into a mile-long bee-pollinator corridor, planted with native plants that attract and nourish bees.

Other neighborhoods and individual properties are havens for migrating birds. Robin tells her gardening clients, "Think of your garden as a gas station for migrating birds, a place where they can fill up their tanks—they can't migrate if they don't have fuel."

It is exciting to think that our gardens can be part of a growing effort to restore health to our planet. To this end, enormous efforts are also being made by young people all around the world through the JGI Roots & Shoots program.

Children—The New Garden Warriors

I mentioned Roots & Shoots earlier when I explained how I started the Alligator Club as a child. But let me pause here to explain what Roots & Shoots actually is, and why gardens and gardening play such a large part in many of its programs. R&S is a global movement that encourages young people to become involved in projects that have a positive impact on the world around them. Its most important message is that every individual matters and has a role to play, that each of us makes a difference every day, and that the cumulative result of thousands of millions of even small efforts results in major change.

It started in 1991 with twelve secondary-school students in Dar es Salaam, Tanzania. Now, at the start of 2012, there are programs in some 130 countries with around fifteen thousand active groups involving young people from preschool through university—and beyond, for more and more adults are forming groups.

Hundreds and thousands of these groups can solve many of the problems their elders have created for them. I have seen how it changes the lives of young people, gives them a sense of purpose, rekindles hope.

R&S members are determined to make a difference, prepared to roll up their sleeves and take action, to walk the talk. For the most part, it is the young people themselves who, after discussing local problems, decide what to do to try to solve them. They are asked to choose three projects about which individual group members feel passionate—one to help people, one to help animals, and one to help the environment. The three projects they end up choosing vary depending on the nature of the problems and the age of the members, their culture, whether they are from inner-city or rural environments, and which country they come from. By taking action, seeing the difference they can make, knowing that there are other young people just like them all around the world, the R&S members become empowered, filled with enthusiasm and hope.

A great many of the R&S groups choose to care for their school gardens and learn about plants. In Tanzania, schoolyards that were once made up of dry, trampled dirt are now made beautiful with many trees. They not only provide shade but also hold the soil in place. I especially loved visiting the Tanzanian group that was helping to clear a space in the wilderness by the school to build a library—and one eight-year-old took me to where they had created a similar-sized habitat "for the insects that lost their homes." Cactus Roots & Shoots Club at Mjimpya Secondary School in Kilimanjaro has a project called Green Mjimpya. To make their school beautiful, they have created various flower gardens grown from seeds they have collected from native plants in the adjacent forest reserve.

In the United States and Europe, provided the schools give permission, a lot of R&S groups are building wildlife habitats, planting native species, putting up bird nesting boxes and designing woodpiles for insects. Many Roots & Shoots groups around the world are also creating butterfly gardens. In Taiwan the "Green Thumb" project now persuades as many schools as possible to plant indigenous species of flowering plants, in an effort to restore something of the magic of a country once known as Formosa, "the land of the butterflies."

The Garden of Eden—Lost?

So far I have not mentioned the Garden of Eden—yet that story is part of my earliest childhood memories, and is certainly one of the best-known and most famous gardens of all for Jews and Christians alike. I used to love to think of Adam and Eve at the dawn of time, before the loss of innocence, and imagine what their garden was like. A place of rich biodiversity, when we humans were part of it all.

Today it seems that this garden represents, symbolically, not just the loss of innocence but the loss of the connection between Man and Mother Nature. As a species we have tried to separate ourselves from the other animals. In our arrogance we have tried to dominate the natural world. Fortunately the Garden of Eden has not yet been utterly destroyed.

Let us, symbolically, work together to restore harmony to that garden. Let us strive to replant everything that, over the ages, we have destroyed as a result of greed and ignorance, poverty and apathy. But we had better not plant another apple tree there!

PART THREE

Uses and Abuses of Plants

Chapter 10

Plants That Can Heal

Part of our TACARE mission in Gombe is to learn about and protect the knowledge of the traditional healers. Recently I visited Mzee Yusuph Rubondo in his tiny house, and he told me that before he became a healer he had learned about witchcraft. He said this was probably why he has become an expert in curing patients who have been "bewitched." (CREDIT: © THE JANE GOODALL INSTITUTE – TANZANIA / BY DR. SHADRACK M. KAMENYA)

Many of the medicines my sister and I were given as children were based directly on ancient folk wisdom passed down, often orally, by those who were knowledgeable about the healing properties of different plants. They had wonderful names, our medicines—witch hazel, slippery elm, syrup of figs, friar's balsam, dill water. Unfortunately, the taste of these plant extracts was usually not as delightful as their names implied—but my grandmother, Danny, was implacable, and as she stood over us, spoon in hand, we had no choice but to "open wide" and swallow the revolting stuff.

One of Danny's favorites was Squill and Tilleul—which I always thought of as "Squills and Tooloo." It was a disgusting cough medicine made, I have now discovered, from the resin of tolu (*Myroxylon balsamum*), a tree native to Colombia that acts as an expectorant, and from the bulb of squill, a Eurasian and African plant of the genus *Scilla.* No wonder I hated the stuff—squill is also used to make rat poison!

Gradually these old remedies went out of fashion, but now some of them are once again back on the shelves as herbal and holistic medicine in the United States and across Europe. And there are new cures coming into fashion now that have been "discovered" in plants from remote jungles—discovered by Western medicine, that is, though they have been used for hundreds of years by the indigenous healers, who have a deep knowledge of and communication with plants.

Healers of the Waha Tribe

Part of the Jane Goodall Institute's TACARE ("Take Care") program in Tanzania is devoted to learning about the local traditional medicines, mostly by talking with the indigenous healers, or traditional medicine practitioners, as they are often called.

I was fascinated by this aspect from the start, as was Emmanuel Mtiti, director of TACARE, and Aristides Kashula, our forester. Kashula was the first of our team who began traveling to different villages to talk to the medicine men and women. And although it was not easy, he gradually won their confidence and eventually they began to share their knowledge.

This was important—more and more of the medicinal plants were becoming highly endangered due to habitat destruction, and knowledge of their uses was also endangered as the old traditional healers died and youth, for the most part, was scornful of the old ways. So we wanted to try to protect, cultivate, and learn about that wisdom before it was too late. We have now been able to work with a total of eighty-six medicine men and women, all of whom agreed that almost every plant has some kind of healing power. The medicine may be contained in leaf, flower, seeds, pith, root, or bark. It would take a long time to make a complete "herbal" of local medicinal plants—indeed, it would be almost impossible, for different healers use plants in different ways, to cure different diseases.

In February 2012, I went with Shadrack Kamenya, a member of our Gombe research team, to meet with two of these healers in their homes. These days only a few of the very oldest women still wear the traditional clothing of the past—the two men I met with were dressed in normal Western-style shirts and trousers. And although their parents had spoken only the local Kiha language, these men spoke Kiswahili, the national language of Tanzania, as well.

First we visited with Mzee (the respectful form of address for an elder) Mikidadi Almasi Mfumya of Bubango Village. We sat on low stools just inside the door to the tiny living room (only about six feet by five feet) of the house (itself only a little more than thirteen feet square) where he lives with his family. He told us he was now sixty-five years old and that many of the plants he knew as a young man had disappeared along with the destruction of the forests around his village.

He had a large collection of jars and pots and gourds for mixing and storing his remedies. Many of them, he explained proudly, had been handed down from his grandmother. He picked up one or two of the wooden bowls to show us, handling them with reverence and respect. It was from his grandmother, he said, that his own mother had learned the skills that she had passed on to him.

What he is best known for, Mzee Mikidadi told us, is treating snakebites. He uses ground-up leaves that he buys from the Wabembe, the indigenous people of eastern Congo, many of whom have settled in the Kigoma region. I asked him if he had cured a lot of people and he assured me that they almost always recovered if they got to him soon enough. And he was sure his mother was still helping. "Her spirit talks to me," he said, "and so I know when patients are coming and can have all the medicine ready when they arrive."

Mzee Mikidadi took us around his little plot at the back of the house where he is now growing his own medicines. Trees and plants thrived in a riot of green leaves, gnarled trunks, and tangling vines. He showed us one young ntuligwa tree (*Flacourtia indica*), growing on a termite mound. He had had to get it from some distance away, since all such trees have vanished from his area. Traditional wisdom maintains that the medicine is always most effective if the leaves from which it is made are picked from trees that are growing on a termite mound.

I was fascinated to hear that Mzee Mikidadi always talks to a plant, asking it for permission, before using it for medicine. "I always leave a gift," he told us, "an offering for the spirit of the plant. And then I return to take what I need." I have been told exactly the same by a First Nation healer, who speaks to his plants and leaves them gifts of tobacco.

We said good-bye to Mikidadi and drove to Chankele Village to talk with Mzee Yusuph Rubondo, a well-respected elder who thinks—but has no way of knowing for certain—that he is eighty-five years old. When he started practicing as a young man, there were, he said, many chimpanzees in the thick forest all around his village. And all the medicinal plants were there. He told us he had acquired his knowledge from his mother and father, both of whom were healers: his mother had learned from her father, but his father had learned from a man who was not closely related at all.

We followed him into his house (also very small—the whole structure no bigger than twenty-by-twenty-two feet), and I sat with him on a rush mat laid out on the earth floor at one end of the living room. It was somehow mysterious in there, dimly lit by the light that came in through the one very small window. Arranged neatly on the ground beside him was a fascinating collection of little jars and bottles, most of them carefully wrapped in plastic bags. This was his "drugstore" of powders, dry leaves, seeds, and so on that he uses to treat a whole host of different medical conditions, ranging from toothache to coughs, from rheumatism to fevers.

He had started off, he said, learning about witchcraft—and perhaps that was what had helped him to become an expert in curing patients who had been bewitched. I asked him if he saw many such people, and what their symptoms were.

There were many, he said. Some arrive lethargic and dull. Others are shouting and screaming, occasionally trying to take off their clothes, and then he needs help to restrain them and hold them down, before he can treat them.

The medicine he uses comes from a plant that he dries and grinds into a powder. He called it *kikali,* but it may be that he was simply using the Kiswahili word to indicate that it was strong medicine. He took the lid from a container made from a small round polished gourd, chestnut brown in the dim light, and showed me a pale gray-brown powder. Then, taking a pinch, he demonstrated how he treated a patient by rubbing it into his own arm. After that, with a mischievous twinkle in his eyes, he did the same to me!

I could have sat listening for a long time as he talked of the changes he had seen in his long life. Some, he said, are good changes—he likes his cell phone. But other changes have been disastrous, such as the growth of the population, the changing weather patterns, and the gradual destruction of the forests that supply most of the medicines he needs. Many of the plants that were once common in his backyard must now be searched for, farther and farther away.

Two of our own Gombe staff are skilled in the use of medicinal plants, and Shadrack, who has talked with them at length, tells me how some of the plants have helped people with diseases such as herpes zoster infections, typhoid, amoebic dysentery, peptic and duodenal ulcers, malaria, diabetes, high blood pressure—and HIV-AIDS.

I asked Shadrack if there was proof that anyone had actually been cured of HIV-AIDS. He said he had met several people who had been diagnosed with the condition, who had arrived from various regions of Tanzania looking thin and very sick. And then, following their treatment, which lasted a few weeks, they had gone off looking well and healthy. But there was no proof, he said, that they had actually become HIV negative. Still, if there is a medicinal plant that alleviates the symptoms and gives people better health and longer life expectancy, this would be wonderful.

Animal Physicians

How did traditional healers first learn about the healing properties of plants? Through trial and error? Some kind of instinct? Or perhaps, from watching animals?

About a century ago a Tanzanian medicine man, Babu Kalunde, discovered that the roots of a plant known as *mulengelele* to the local Watongwe people, was powerful medicine, and as a result probably saved the lives of many people in his village when there was an epidemic of a dysentery-like illness. Babu had watched a young porcupine that had symptoms similar to the sick people digging up a *mulengelele* and eating its roots. He was amazed, as he knew the plant was extremely poisonous. But now the situation was desperate, so Babu took a small dose himself. There were no ill effects, so he persuaded the sick people to try the plant—and it helped. To this day the Watongwe use *mulengelele* as medicine. Babu's grandson, now a respected elder and healer himself, uses it to treat gonorrhea and syphilis.

Probably everyone who has owned a dog has watched him or her eating grass. I have known many dogs over the years—two of them zealously selected blade after blade, chewing them up with great gusto. Occasionally this would cause them to vomit.

There has been much speculation as to why dogs eat grass. Some believe that they just like the taste—as I love eating spinach leaves. Others think dogs do it instinctively when they feel unwell to stimulate a vomiting response, which may help them to get rid of whatever made them feel sick. There is a school of thought that believes the grass may help to clear the intestines of parasites. Or that the dog needs more fiber in the diet: one poodle, who had regularly eaten grass for eight years, stopped once she was fed a high-fiber diet.

That animals have an instinct to cure themselves seems pretty conclusive. A recent study showed that female monarch butterflies infected with a deadly parasite lay their eggs on a particular species of milkweed that reduces the risk of the caterpillars becoming infected. They thus provide their young with medicine. Other tests show that sick domestic animals, when given a choice of foods, mineral supplements, and so on, will chose one known to be useful in treating their symptoms, perhaps detecting the medicinal properties through smell.

It should not be surprising that chimpanzees are also able to treat some of their own illnesses. In the 1960s, during the early years of my study at Gombe, we used to check the chimpanzees' dung to get some idea of the frequency with which they ate different foods. We found many seeds that had been swallowed along with the fruit—the plant was using the chimps to distribute its progeny. And every so often we found long, narrow leaves with stiff hairs underneath that had been swallowed whole. I pressed them (after a thorough washing!), along with the other food plants, and sent them to Bernard Verdcourt to identify at the herbarium in Nairobi. They were, he said, leaves of *Aspilia pluriseta*. Richard Wrangham, before he became an eminent professor at Harvard, had studied chimpanzee feeding behavior at Gombe and he noticed that the chimpanzees used their tongues and lips to roll *Aspilia* leaves into a sort of cylinder with the plant hairs on the outside. Instead of chewing them, they would then swallow them whole. When he heard that the local villagers used this plant as medicine as well, we were all excited.

Since then Dr. Mike Huffman has made detailed studies of the use of *Aspilia* by chimpanzees, lowland gorillas, and bonobos. At first it was suspected that the leaves contained some kind of chemical, but in fact it is the physical characteristics of the leaves that is significant—as they pass through the stomach and intestines, the stiff hairs flush out the nematodes and tapeworms that tend to multiply during the rainy season.

Many animals medicate themselves with plants. This chimpanzee is chewing Aspilia pluriseta *to help flush out nematodes and tapeworms from the gut that flourish during the rainy season.* (CREDIT: MICHAEL A. HUFFMAN)

Some hundred miles south of Gombe is the Mahale Mountains National Park, site of an intensive chimpanzee study carried out by the Japanese since 1966. There the chimpanzees make use of the extraordinarily bitter pith of *Vernonia amygdalina*. This plant, found in most African countries, is used by people as a treatment for, among other things, malaria, internal parasites, and lack of appetite. It is also used by chimpanzees infested in the rainy season with the nodule worm *Oesophagostomum stephanostomum*. Mike told me of two cases when chimpanzees who were clearly sick—they had lost weight, were lethargic, and were known to have a nematode infestation—had spent time chewing *Vernonia* pith. Between twenty and twenty-four hours afterward, both showed definite signs of recovery.

Subsequent research in the lab has shown that *Vernonia* pith is indeed effective against certain microorganisms that infect both chimpanzees and humans. The scientists also isolated two chemical compounds from the pith that actually suppressed egg-laying activity in a common parasitic worm. How chimpanzees know they should take these medicinal plants is still a mystery. Mike suspects the chimps—and many other animals—are actually using even more plant species as medicines.

And not only as medicines: in Calcutta, Dr. Dushim Sengupta and other naturalists observed that a pair of house sparrows lined their nests with neem leaves at hatching time. It seems they somehow know that the leaves act as a pesticide. To make sure that it had not been an accidental choice, the nest lining was removed—again the birds selected neem leaves as a replacement.

The Neem Tree—"Nature's Drugstore"

The neem (*Azadirachta indica*) is an evergreen that can reach heights of forty to fifty feet. It originated in India, where it is common in backyards—and it continues to grow in suitable wild habitats as well. For more than 4,500 years Indians have known that all parts of the neem tree have medicinal value—extracts from leaves, bark, flowers, seeds, and roots have been and are being used to treat an incredible number of different medical conditions. The Indians' appreciation of its virtues is reflected in its many names: "heal all," "nature's drugstore," "village pharma," "panacea for all disease"—and in one area, "the sacred tree."

It has been especially valued for its properties as a pesticide, and various preparations are used to protect crops in the fields. Oil from its seed protects stored crops for around twenty months. Neem "cakes" dug into the earth promote good growth, repelling insect pests and plant diseases, storing nitrogen, and encouraging the proliferation of earthworms to aerate the soil.

In 1939, during a terrible plague of locusts in Sudan, someone noticed that whereas the voracious insects consumed just about everything that grew, leaving leafless trees and bare fields, the neem trees were still green once they had moved on. The locusts would land on the foliage—but then fly off. They were repelled.

For the first time Western scientists began to investigate the value of the neem tree—although it would be another thirty years or so before Dr. Larry Johnson would write, "Western medicine, pharmaceutical and agricultural companies are becoming increasingly interested. Soon it may be perceived as one of the most valuable trees on the planet."

The neem tree was brought to Africa by the Indians and now grows in many parts of the continent. The word we use for it in Tanzania is *arabaini*, which in Kiswahili means "forty" and refers to the fact that it has at least forty different uses, including the treatment of malaria.

"Try one," my son Grub urges me, handing me a small green leaf from the neem tree in our garden in Dar es Salaam. I know how it tastes, but I bruise the little leaf with my teeth anyway. At once my face contorts—it is incredibly bitter. I reject the rest, and watch with amazement as Grub, who has already chewed up five of these leaves, swallows a couple more. He has a headache and thinks it could be heralding a bout of malaria—he has been forgetting to chew his daily couple of leaves and is now making up for it.

I have a Tanzanian friend, Christopher Liundi, who grew up in Dar es Salaam. His mother had forced him to drink an infusion of neem leaves once a week. "It was so bitter I could hardly get it down without vomiting," he told me. But it was worth it—Chris has *never* had malaria, a miracle for someone living in an area so teeming with malarial mosquitoes.

My mother and I both got very sick with malaria when we first got to Gombe. Side by side we lay in our shared ex-army tent, too weak to go into town to seek treatment. We eventually recovered, though I think my mother, whose temperature rose to 105 degrees Fahrenheit for five days running, nearly died.

The Roots of Quinine

Indeed, malaria is a common and often deadly disease throughout the tropics, especially for small children and people newly arrived in a malaria area. But it was not the neem but the cinchona tree (*Cinchona* spp.) that would provide a cure. Without that discovery, the history of colonial settlements in Asia, Africa, and the Americas might have been very different.

There are some twenty-three species of cinchona, all found in the eastern Andes—in Ecuador, Peru, and Bolivia. It is the bark of this tree that is so important—it contains a bitter substance from which, eventually, quinine was extracted. I knew about quinine from an early age, as I had an aunt and uncle living in India, and then my father was stationed in the Far East during World War II. They all told me about the quinine tablets they had to take each day to protect against malaria. It was because of the small amount of quinine found in tonic water that "gin and tonic" became the drink of choice for expats in the tropics. And I cannot resist adding here that when there was a bad outbreak of avian malaria in Calcutta, Dr. Sengupta's little sparrows actually exchanged the neem leaf lining of their nests for those of the paradise flower tree (*Caesalpinia pulcherrima*), which is rich in quinine. They also ate the leaves.

In the sixteenth century, Spanish settlers in South America discovered that local indigenous people had, for hundreds of years, been using powdered cinchona bark as a cure for fevers, and it seems that Jesuit priests first introduced the wonder bark to Spain. By 1650 regular shipments were being sent from Peru to Spain, from whence it was traded to other European countries. Word spread and the demand grew. By the early 1800s cinchona bark was seen as essential for the health of all those administering the European colonies in tropical areas around the world.

As all this bark came from trees growing in the wild, it soon became impossible to meet the constantly increasing need for the bark, and prices soared. Finally, in 1820, two scientists were able to extract, from the bark, an alkaloid chemical that had antimalarial properties; they named it "quinine." But even though quinine soon became commercially available, demand for the complete, natural cinchona bark continued, and in the mid-1850s, Peru stopped permits for the export of cinchona seeds and seedlings, hoping to retain control over the very lucrative trade.

The British promptly sent that intrepid explorer of the Amazon Richard Spruce to find another supply that they could grow in their overseas colonies. He was able to get some seeds and plants of a cinchona, *C. succirubra*, from Ecuador. They grew readily, and cinchona soon became the most widely planted species in British colonial India, Sri Lanka, Jamaica. and East Africa.

At about the time Spruce was searching for seeds in Ecuador, one Charles Ledger bought seeds of a species of *Cinchona* from an aboriginal trader in Bolivia. He tried to sell them to the British, but as Spruce's collection had just arrived, no one was interested. Spruce therefore sold his seeds to the Dutch, and this led to their extremely successful *Cinchona* plantations in Java.

It is hard to overemphasize the major role that quinine, our gift from the *Cinchona* tree, has played in world history. Only when colonialists had access to this drug did West Africa cease to be known as "The White Man's Grave." It was when supplies from plantations in Java were cut off during World War II that the United States established its own plantations in Costa Rica. But before these trees could mature and provide a new source of quinine, hundreds of thousands of US troops died in Africa and the South Pacific due to lack of the drug. Indeed, it is said that there were more deaths from malaria than from all the bullets and bombs combined.

Quinine is still used in treating some forms of malaria that have become resistant to the latest drugs, though usually as a last resort because it can have some unpleasant side effects. I know about these from personal experience. I was in Dar es Salaam, suffering from one of my frequent bouts of the disease, and was persuaded to seek help from the physician attached to the American embassy at the time. He took a blood test and, staring at the multitude of parasites wiggling about under his microscope, concluded that my death was imminent. Afterward he told me that the only other person he had seen with as high a count had indeed died. Panicking, he gave me a double dose of quinine. It cured the malaria, but I was almost stone deaf and had blurred vision for several days.

Miracle Drug of Folk Medicine

Another plant whose incredible power to heal was "discovered" by Western medicine is the rosy periwinkle, a common little plant in southeast Madagascar. In 1655 a traveler took some of the pretty plants to Paris for ornamental purposes, and by the eighteenth century it had proliferated in many gardens and botanical gardens throughout much of Europe. Soon it had escaped to colonize suitable areas in the country as well as vacant lots. Gradually it adapted to the different climates in which in now lives, becoming a garden annual in temperate zones and a perennial shrublet in the tropics. We have rosy periwinkles in our garden in Dar es Salaam.

But this plant is a lot more than an attractive garden flower. In its native Madagascar, traditional healers always used it as a remedy for a number of diseases. And as it traveled farther and farther around the world, more and more people began talking about its healing properties. It became the miracle drug of folk medicine, prescribed by herbalists in southern Africa, India, Australia, and the Philippines—for constipation, toothache, malaria, abortions, and diabetes. It was this last claim that attracted the attention of Western medicine, and although it was never substantiated, the various tests that were carried out revealed that it could arrest blood cancers.

One of the interested people was Dr. Robert Noble, of Toronto, and in 1958 he suggested that it just might be a cure for childhood leukemia. Other scientists were able to isolate the active principle, vincristine sulphate, from dried periwinkles—but it took twelve tons of dried periwinkles for one ounce of vincristine sulphate, and there were bad side effects, including loss of hair. Clearly more work had to be done, but the team persevered, and today it is the main weapon against childhood leukemia. Many have recovered completely because of the medication derived from the little rosy periwinkle.

Biopiracy—The Theft of Indigenous Knowledge

Today, because of the continuing growth of the human population and increasing destruction of the environment, the endemic plants of Madagascar are disappearing. It was only because of its attractive appearance that the rosy periwinkle survived. How many other plants with properties that could heal our human and animal diseases are becoming extinct every year in different parts of the world? Is there anything that can be done?

It is more than likely that the medical profession and the pharmaceutical companies ended up making money through exploiting the rosy periwinkle—though of course, it costs a great deal to develop drugs of this sort, and many plants, after rigorous testing, fail to yield anything useful. But if some percentage of the profit were paid to the traditional healers in Madagascar—or in other countries for other products—would this not encourage them to protect their medicinal plants? There is a major controversy raging over this question.

When I was thirteen years old, my uncle Eric, who was a surgeon, told us about a new anesthetic that originated in the rain forests of South America. There it was used to poison the arrows and darts of various native tribes. At his hospital they were calling it "jungle juice," or curare. It had been derived, as I now know, from two different plants found in Central and South America, a small tree (*Strychnos toxifera*) and a liana (*Chondrodendron tomentosum*). Interestingly, the extracts from these plants, though highly lethal when injected or rubbed onto a wound, are harmless when taken orally—which explains why poisoned prey can be eaten with no ill effects.

In 1935, when I was only one year old, someone had come up with the idea that curare might be useful in Western medicine. How right they were, and by 1947 it had been synthesized and was making its debut as a "wonder drug" that would relax muscles during surgery. That was when my uncle began to use it and that was when I first began to think about the indigenous people who had discovered the power of the vine that could kill.

No Westerner knows more about the relationship of plants and the shamans of the Amazon rain forest than Dr. Mark Plotkin. Ever since he went there as a young man as part of a group surveying crocodiles, and was introduced to the indigenous Indian tribes by Dr. Richard Schulte, he was hooked. Mark has now spent a quarter of a century learning about the many medicinal plants that are used in the forests, as well as searching for new plants that can heal.

*Mark Plotkin (*right*) has spent a quarter of a century learning about and documenting the indigenous wisdom of the Amazon. Here he attends a recent unprecedented gathering of shamans from seven tribes. They realize that it is desperately important to share their knowledge, to pass it on, to preserve it before it is too late.* (CREDIT: MARK PLOTKIN)

It was Mark who first drew my attention to the fact that some Western drug companies were sometimes making huge profits from medicines made from plants growing in the rain forests of the Amazon, plants that had been used by the shamanic healers for hundreds of years. He was trying to develop new rules to ensure that the indigenous people of the forest got a fair share of these profits.

One of the most powerful voices speaking out against this theft of indigenous wisdom by Western corporations is the philosopher and environmental activist Dr. Vandana Shiva. Calling it "biopiracy," she describes it as a new sort of colonialism. "In the old way they took over the land—now they are taking over life."

She describes the successful efforts of American companies to patent a chemical found in the neem tree for use as a pesticide. It began in 1971 when Robert Larson brought neem seeds to the United States and was able to extract the active pesticide ingredient (an isolated molecule named azadirachtin). He got a patent, and fourteen years later sold it to W. R. Grace & Co.

Since then, about a dozen patents for neem-tree products have been granted to US companies and two to Japanese companies. W. R. Grace, owning four of these companies, set up a base of operations in India and tried to buy the technology of Indian scientists who were working to develop their own products from the neem tree—not surprisingly, there was strong opposition.

Meanwhile W. R. Grace continued to develop new neem-derived products. In 1992 the US National Research Council published a report on the neem tree designed "to open up the Western world's corporate eyes to the seemingly endless variety of products the tree might offer." After which an article in *Science* magazine stated that "squeezing bucks out of neem ought to be relatively easy."

Vandana Shiva was incensed. In one of her many articles she writes, "W. R. Grace's aggressive interest in Indian neem production has provoked a chorus of objections from Indian scientists, farmers and political activists, who assert that multinational companies have no right to expropriate the fruit of centuries of indigenous experimentation and several decades of Indian scientific research." Of course, all this has led to a heated and ongoing transcontinental debate about the ethics of intellectual property and patent rights.

It is important to protect the rights of the indigenous communities, important that they have access to their traditional healing plants, and important that they be able to maintain their cultural traditions and practice their healing skills. And in order to protect the environment and nurture the plants they need, it will be important that we help them, that they get some share of the millions of dollars made by the pharmaceutical companies, governments, and private investors.

Only in this way can we hope to protect the diversity of plant life upon which, ultimately, we all depend.

We Are Losing Our Medicinal Plants

As a result of habitat destruction many of our known medicinal plants are, as we have seen, becoming endangered. Many are also threatened by overharvesting. Recently scientists found that the bark of the American yew provides a source of taxotere, which is used to treat breast, ovarian, and cervical cancer. This tree has been widely used by Native American tribes for its medicinal value, as well as for purification and smudging ceremonies. My Native American friend Chitcus used to collect small amounts of the yew bark each year, but now, he told me, the trees where he used to go are almost all destroyed.

"There is no need to kill the tree to collect the bark," said Chitcus. "You should leave one to two feet of trunk and then it will regenerate. But now the collectors, in order to harvest every last bit of bark for taxotere, cut it level to the ground." And, thus, kill it.

In India and Sri Lanka, where Ayurvedic medicine originated (and in which, incidentally, the neem tree plays an important role), most of the herbs are still harvested from the wild. When this medicine became more popular in the West, exports grew rapidly, and suddenly, in 2010, it was found that 93 percent of the traditional herbs were endangered. Partly this was due to habitat loss, but mostly because of greedy, reckless harvesting by those who sought immediate profit. Collectors were tearing the whole plant out of the ground, whether or not all parts were needed, thus reducing the chance for the harvested area to recover.

Some of the most common over-the-counter herbal remedies in the United States, such as wild ginseng (*Panax quinquefolius*), goldenseal (*Hydrastis canadensis*), and Echinacea, also known as purple coneflower (*Echinacea angustifolia*), are also listed as endangered, mainly because of the increase of unsustainable harvesting methods.

The Future of Ancient Wisdom

What a tragedy that, just as we are beginning to appreciate the wisdom and knowledge of traditional healers and shamans, so many of the plants are vanishing—or gone. Fortunately, people are waking up. Old Mzee Rubondo, the traditional healer in Tanzania, realized he had to do something about his vanishing medicinal plants on the day he had to travel 160 miles to find one that he desperately needed—a plant that had once grown close to home. That was an expensive journey that he could ill afford—the loss of the forest was a personal loss that was also hindering his work and affecting the health of his community.

That was when he decided to take part in our TACARE programs. He knew about them—he told us that our conservation initiatives were really making a difference, and that in all the places where he had searched for particular plants, people had talked about our work and were more willing to help him. Mzee Rubondo, and many of the other traditional healers, are now taking an active role in collecting and protecting medicinal plants, and helping to restore forest habitat.

Mzee Rubondo was particularly appreciative of the Jane Goodall Institute's (JGI) environmental education program, as he, along with other healers in the area, believe that if people know which plants are used to treat different diseases, they will be more likely to help in protecting them. They all encourage Roots & Shoots club members to learn the names and uses of the plants that grow in the area. They are desperate to pass their wisdom down to the next generation.

During my last visit to Kigoma I visited the Roots & Shoots group of Sokoine Primary School. They showed me the regenera-

In Tanzania the Roots & Shoots members of Sokoine Primary School are learning how to identify and draw their local indigenous medicinal plants.
(CREDIT: SMITA DHARSI)

tion that has taken place in the fifteen-acre forested area they have been protecting since 2004. Club members, with the help of local volunteer Isaack Ezekia, have been identifying all the rare plants growing there, especially the medicinal plants. Isaack told me they are so enthusiastic that when he offered to hold a workshop during their holidays, they all wanted to take part. He taught them more about the uses of the plants, their scientific names, and how to draw them. Isaack did not realize that the father of one of the pupils, Fedrick Fowahedi, was a well-known traditional healer, and was apprehensive when the child said he was taking specimens of the plants home to ask his father if what he had learned was true. To Isaack's immense relief he was told he had got it all right.

*Tanzanian Roots & Shoots volunteer Isaack Ezekia (*center*) is teaching the local primary school children about their medicinal plants. R&S member Fedrick Fowahedi (*left*), the eleven-year-old son of a respected traditional healer, is one of those responsible for caring for the school's forest garden. He has been watching over this endangered tree that he had found and transplanted in the garden, and was eager to explain how its leaves and bark are used to cure a variety of illnesses.* (CREDIT: NICOLAS IBARGUEN)

Now the members are eager to write a science book for children that will include names and usage of all traditional medicinal plants found in the forest.

In the Amazon, too, says Mark Plotkin, there is a race to preserve the ancient cultures of the indigenous people before it is too late. The shamans, traditionally leaders as well as medicine men, were finding it increasingly difficult to pass on their knowledge. As in so many parts of the world, the younger generations tended to scorn the old traditions.

The Amazon Conservation Trust was set up in part to try to help the shamans and the women healers with the vital task of passing on their wisdom. An imaginative program pairs a shaman with a young apprentice whom he can teach about medicinal plants. They make a medicinal plant garden, and the apprentice, if he can write, keeps a written record of the shaman's knowledge—for which he gets a small stipend. The program is working. There was a recent unprecedented gathering of shamans from seven tribes who met together to share knowledge, discuss problems, and celebrate successes.

I suspect that some of those shamans share the sentiments of old Mzee Rubondo in Tanzania. When I asked what he thought about the future of his work, he replied, "We cannot afford to lose our plants, because agreeing to lose them is like agreeing to die. But if we replant lost species and conserve the forests, then our plants will survive—and so will we."

Hope for the Wild Medicinal Plants

Twenty years ago, when it was already clear that the growing demand for medicinal plants from the wild was creating huge ecological and social problems, international guidelines were drawn up to regulate harvesting of these wild herbs. It was a good beginning, but it did not go far enough in addressing the typically conflicting needs of the local people's commercial markets on the one hand and the protection of the environment on the other.

Then in 2008 the FairWild Foundation was established to develop new standards for harvesting wild plants (for medicinal or any other commercial purpose)—standards designed to create a more sustainable and fair system for managing the collecting, as well as the trading, of wild plants and their products.

Most recently, in 2012, the FairWild Foundation co-organized a highly significant event, the first of its kind. It was called "Wild Thing...I Think I Love You: Wild Plants and the Herbal Industry." More than eighty delegates attended, representing collection operations, traders, makers of final products, NGOs, government agencies, and intergovernmental organizations. It was clear that the participants all understood that in order to ensure future supplies, there was an urgent need to ensure that environmentally and socially ethical standards be used in the collection and trading of wild plants.

Gradually the message is spreading, and practices are changing. The Sri Lankan government is not only developing community-farming projects that will grow Ayurvedic herbal plants, the sale of which will directly benefit local economies, but also making it a priority to preserve the Mihinthale Sanctuary, where there is a high level of medicinal plant diversity.

The government of India has defined "sustainable harvest protocols" for endangered wild medicinal plants, designed to prevent people from ripping out entire crops or decimating a habitat. It has also created conservation areas in India where there is the greatest diversity of medicinal plants, and hired locals to monitor and protect these areas. And the Japanese government recently sent a big delegation to India to learn about all this.

An important question that is receiving a good deal of attention concerns the feasibility or desirability of taking endangered plants from the wild and domesticating them. The problem is that almost all traditional healers maintain that medicine harvested from a wild, free plant is more effective. I think of Mikidadi's little plot, where his plants grow in the same glorious confusion of biodiversity as in a forest, and where his ntuligwa tree is faithfully planted on a termite nest. We are finally beginning to understand how different life-forms in a given habitat are interdependent. If medicinal plants are grown as a monoculture, can they always provide the same benefits as their wild counterparts?

China in particular has problems with overharvesting medicinal plants in the wild. Herbal medicine has been part of the Chinese culture for at least two thousand years, and it has become increasingly popular both in China itself and throughout much of the Western world. Many people from the United States and Europe working in Tanzania, find the Chinese herbal drug qinghaosu a more effective treatment for many kinds of malaria than the typical Western drugs. And it is much less toxic.

This popularity of Chinese medicines means, of course, that many of China's medicinal plants have become endangered in the wild. But there is hope—recently a consortium of organizations, including World Wildlife Fund, TRAFFIC, and the International Union for Conservation of Nature, worked closely with villagers to introduce new ways to harvest medicinal plants sustainably while also making a good profit.

During my last visit to China, I was invited, along with a small group, to visit Jane Tsao's organic farm near Chengdu. After showing us around the fields and greenhouses, Jane took us to a lovely, unspoiled woodland area along the banks of a river where she is setting up a small nature reserve. As we walked in the shade of the tall trees, following narrow paths through ferns and shrubs of the woodland floor, I noticed a small, dilapidated wooden hut half-hidden among the trees.

During my recent visit to an organic farm near Chengdu, I was fascinated to find, pinned to the wall of a disused forester's hut, this faded print of Li Shizhen (145–208 AD). Author of a giant encyclopaedia on the uses of plants in medicine, he is widely revered throughout China today as a sort of patron saint of Chinese herbal medicine. (CREDIT: JANE GOODALL)

"It was once a forester's hut," Jane told us. "Now we are going to restore it and make a tiny education center." It will provide information about the various local plants and trees that have medicinal properties. And it will also showcase some of the herbalists of the past who were wise in knowledge of nature.

The portraits of those bygone healers, unprotected and faded, were pinned to the walls. I stood looking at them, my mind wandering to the very different China in which they had lived. And it seemed to me that despite their stern demeanor, they were offering a blessing on those who were trying to protect the natural world that they had loved.

Chapter 11

Plants That Can Harm

*When scraped, the seedpod of the opium poppy (*Papaver somniferum*) oozes the white goo used to make opium. The seedpod, innocent in itself, has been called the "storage vessel for the dreams of the damned."*
(CREDIT: TEUN SPAANS; CUT AND PHOTO MADE FOR EDUCATIONAL PURPOSES)

As I was thinking about this book, I began to ask people, "Which five plants do you think have had the biggest impacts on human history?" Most came up with the primary plants used in agriculture. But a surprising number said cannabis and quite a few mentioned tobacco. Of course they were right—those plants, along with the opium poppy, coca, and others, including plants used to make alcoholic beverages, have indeed impacted tens of millions of human lives around the world. And so I decided that I wanted to talk about the plants behind the addictions that can lead to so much antisocial and self-destructive behavior.

Most of these plants have rich and noble histories, having been used as healing medicines or as part of traditional sacred rituals. The medicines derived from these plants, when used responsibly, can have very positive human benefits. Unfortunately they have been and are most terribly *mis*used. So that, in the minds of many, the plants themselves are associated with drug and alcohol abuse. Yet in and of themselves the plants are all innocent.

It was not until the nineteenth century that addictive substances such as heroin, cocaine, and mescaline were extracted from these plants, and for a while they were completely unregulated. They were perceived as medicinal, prescribed by physicians, and could be bought anywhere. During the American Civil War, for example, morphine was freely administered to wounded soldiers, who were provided with a supply and syringes. And then, increasingly, such substances were used for "recreational" purposes, and the ugly scenario of drug addiction arrived. But it grew slowly and quietly: not until the early 1900s, when there were thousands of addicts worldwide, did countries gradually realize what had happened and introduce laws to try to deal with the problem.

The "War on Drugs," which began with Present Nixon in 1971, continues to be fought relentlessly as the US government persecutes and fights illegal drug use and sales within its borders. And of course the United States also offers military aid to collaborating countries, trying to reduce illegal drug trafficking into the United States. In Mexico today armed conflict between rival drug cartels—as well as between the cartels and the Mexican government—has escalated. Mexican drug cartels now dominate wholesale illicit drug markets for cannabis and heroin in the United States.

I have never in my life experimented with any drugs. The thought of becoming addicted—to drugs or anything else—has always horrified me. But as an adolescent I read a good deal of poetry, and I was intrigued by those Romantic poets, such as Samuel Taylor Coleridge and Percy Bysshe Shelley, who became hopelessly addicted to opium. I used to fantasize about the dimly lit opium dens where intellectual young men lay around smoking pipes and translating their extraordinary experiences into writing. I wondered whether my imagination, stimulated by opium, would produce wonderful and original poetry. It was purely academic curiosity—there was no way I could have got ahold of opium even had I wanted to. Nor were these young men smoking opium, of course—they were taking laudanum (an herbal tincture that contained about 10 percent opium), as I later discovered.

Marijuana, of course, is much easier to get, but I was never tempted to even *try* a "joint." Nor, to my knowledge, have I eaten a laced cookie. But hundreds of people I know have used "weed" at one time in their lives. And I know of so many families that have been torn apart by drug addiction.

Marijuana, Weed, Pot—*Cannabis sativa, C. indica, and C. ruderalis*

Cannabis originated in Central and South Asia, possibly first in the mountainous region northwest of the Himalayas. It has a very ancient history of ritual and recreational use. Charred cannabis seeds were found in a ritual brazier at a burial site in what is now Romania that dates back to the third millennium BC. For thousands of years it has been used in religious ceremonies in India and Nepal. And in 480 BC, Herodotus, that renowned Greek historian, describes how it was inhaled as a vapor in religious rituals and also for personal pleasure, "inducing a state of bliss."

Medical use of marijuana, some say, dates to 2,737 BC in China. A basket of leaf fragments and seeds was recently uncovered beside a shaman who was estimated to have been buried somewhere between 25,000 and 28,000 years ago. And it is certain that it was widely used by traditional healers in India and other Eastern countries during British colonial times, especially for nausea and vomiting, the control of muscle spasms, and as a sedative and relaxant. A British physician who was working in India took note of this and other medical usages, and decided to collect some samples and send them back to the United Kingdom for study. As a result of this "discovery," cannabis became widely prescribed by physicians and sold in pharmacies throughout the English-speaking world, including America, during the late eighteenth and early nineteenth centuries.

Cannabis arrived in France by a different route. Two French scholars, who accompanied the French army during the Napoleonic conquest of Egypt, took note of its psychoactive effects. They collected, in 1878, samples to send back to France, where many studies were made of the effect of smoking the drug on users, particularly a group of writers and poets who maintained that it was "a route to aestheticism and self-realization." That was one hundred years before similar observations were documented in America.

Although the use of cannabis as a recreational drug spread far and wide, its use by physicians dropped. Newer drugs that had longer shelf lives and more consistent quality gradually began to displace cannabis. In the early twentieth century, as countries started cracking down on the use of recreational drugs in general, the growing, possession, and use of cannabis was criminalized in many parts of the world. And this included its use for medicinal purposes.

Today there is a great deal of controversy over cannabis in the United States and the United Kingdom, and mounting pressure on governments to legalize its use. Two scientific studies, commissioned by the US and UK governments, both concluded that cannabis was not addictive and did not lead to the use of other drugs. And that there was definite evidence that cannabis was useful in treating a number of different medical problems, especially for patients with incurable diseases, postoperative pain, and muscular dystrophy. The studies asserted that the benefits would definitely outweigh any risks that might be involved. The controversy is ongoing—meanwhile several US states have legalized its medical use.

As a result of the frequent raids on illegal marijuana crops growing in the United States, growers began to cultivate the plant indoors, where there was less likelihood of detection by the authorities. The renowned botanist Michael Pollan vividly spells out the consequences of indoor cultivation in his book *The Botany of Desire: A Plant's Eye View of the World.* Suddenly marijuana growing was put into the hands of botanist types who were willing to monitor the plants obsessively while using advanced technology and state-of the-art grow rooms to ensure the most optimal growing conditions and highest potency levels. And so, he concludes, "It stands out as one of the richer ironies of the drug war that the creation of a powerful new taboo against marijuana led directly to the creation of a powerful new plant."

In the United Kingdom there was a recent exposé of the methods of illegal marijuana growers. They rent apartments in the less respectable areas of town, revamp the interiors so that, in essence, they become indoor greenhouses, and then before they can be discovered, they move on, leaving no address and no way for the landlord to recover the cost of expensive reconstruction.

Before we leave the subject of cannabis, I want to emphasize the difference between hemp and recreational marijuana. The species grown for hemp, *C. sativa sativa*, contains only 0.3 percent of tetrahydrocannabinol (THC)—which is the psychoactive ingredient that makes marijuana appealing to users, whereas the species *C. sativa indica*, grown for marijuana, has as much as 2 to 20 percent THC. Moreover, *C. sativa sativa* has low fiber content, whereas hemp is very rich in fiber content.

At one time hemp was grown widely in America and in other parts of the world, and for many different purposes. However, because of its association with cannabis, it became illegal to grow it in the United States—although recently certain states and individuals are working to change the law. This is because the often-maligned and even demonized hemp is, in fact, one of the most helpful of plants to humans, and can be used for many different products, such as rope, clothing, bricks, and oil extracts. It's also one of the best of the "mop crops"—a kind of plant that actually absorbs toxins from the environment and can be used to clean up polluted areas.

The Opium Poppy—*Papaver somniferum*

Beautiful and dangerous, but with many healing gifts for us, the opium poppy originated in India. It is harvested when the seedpod has reached full size but is still green. When the pod is scraped, a white latex oozes out. This is removed and dried, and it is this final goo-like product that is known as opium. That is why the seedpod has been called a "storage vessel for the dreams of the damned." Opium has up to 12 percent morphine, and it is from the morphine that heroin—with twice the potency of opium—has been produced. Codeine is another derivative of morphine.

The opium poppy has been cultivated—for medicinal, ritual, and food purposes—from Neolithic times. Fragments of the plant, carbon-dated at 4,200 BC, have been found in burial sites in Mesopotamia, where it was known as the "joy plant." In ancient Egypt it was used by priests, magicians, and warriors. From there it was traded to countries around the Mediterranean Sea and to Europe. In ancient Greece it was used as an anesthetic during surgery—and, in very small doses, in powdered and diluted form, to quiet a crying child. In addition, it was mixed with hemlock to induce painless death.

Opium was also used for medical purposes in Europe until the years of the Inquisition, in the twelfth century, when everything that came from "the Orient" was suspect, and the use of opium was discontinued for two hundred years. As it was the only anesthetic known at the time, this must have resulted in much suffering. When it was finally reintroduced into Europe in 1527, for medicinal purposes, it was widely and enthusiastically prescribed for all manner of conditions including sleeplessness, diarrhea, and pain relief, especially during surgery.

By the eighteenth century, laudanum—an alcoholic herbal preparation containing 10 percent powdered opium (the equivalent of 1 percent morphine, and imported cheaply from the Orient)—was prescribed by physicians, at least in England, for almost every condition under the sun. It was mixed with just about everything—mercury, hashish, cayenne pepper, ether, chloroform, belladonna—and whiskey, wine, and brandy. Because it was prescribed so frequently, and for such a plethora of ailments, many people became addicted.

It achieved notoriety because of the Romantic writers and musicians who used it, among them Lord Byron, Thomas de Quincey, Shelley, Keats, Lewis Carroll, Edgar Allan Poe, Charles Dickens, and Brahms—the list is very long. Samuel Taylor Coleridge's famous autobiographical book *Confessions of an English Opium Eater* was widely read. In it Coleridge explains how the drug, which had been prescribed for excruciating intestinal pains, became addictive and gradually destroyed him. I found it very harrowing to read.

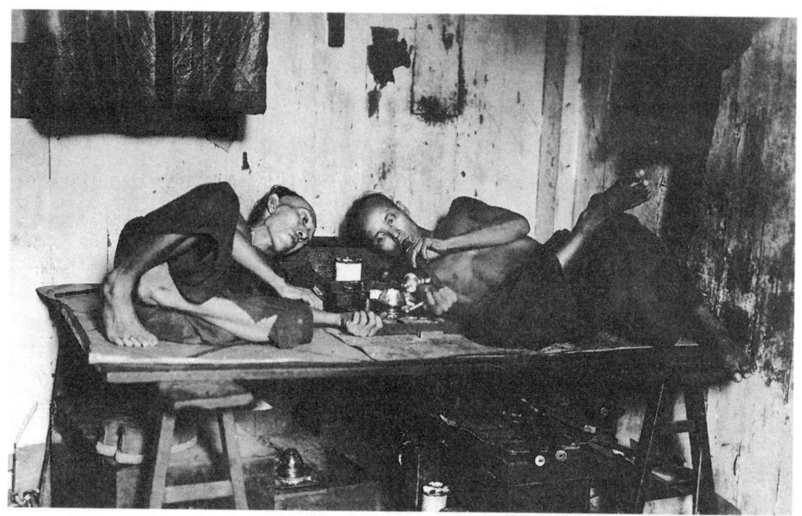

An opium den in Manila's Chinatown somewhere between 1900 and 1920. The clothing and hairstyles of the smokers identify them as ethnic Chinese. Under their "bed" is a cache of equipment, including four opium pipes and two opium lamps. The horrors of opium addiction were not fully understood until the early twentieth century—and by then there were thousands of hopelessly addicted, lost souls throughout many parts of the world.
(CREDIT: COURTESY OF THE STEVEN MARTIN COLLECTION/ASIAN AMERICAN COMPARATIVE COLLECTION, UNIVERSITY OF IDAHO)

In fact, the use of processed opium as a drug, in one form or another, predates written history. It was introduced to China, most likely by an Arab trader, probably in AD 400, but not used as a recreational drug until the fifteenth century. At first almost no one could afford it, but by the sixteenth century, British traders had begun to import cheaper opium from India. Soon it was being smoked in pipes, mixed with tobacco—the term *pipe dream* was first coined to refer to the fantasies that arose from smoking these pipes. Gradually more and more people became addicted, and during the late 1700s, the emperor of China tried to prohibit its import and use.

The British, however, were not prepared to give up such a profitable business, and found ways to smuggle the drug into the country. Eventually the emperor ordered all opium in the country to be destroyed. The British continued to bring in the drug, and relations between China and Britain became increasingly hostile. This led to the First Opium War, in 1839–42.

The conflict ended with the Chinese signing a treaty that was not at all to their benefit, and they found ways to ignore its terms. Eventually this led to the Second Opium War, 1856–60. The treaty that ended this second conflict plunged the Chinese into what one of their historians has described as "a century of humiliation." By the 1890s, nine hundred tons of opium per year were being imported into China and countless hundreds of her citizens were addicted.

It never occurred to me, when I was learning about those wars at school, how utterly shocking and horrifying it all was. The British government was not only condoning the pushing and smuggling of drugs, it was actively engaged in the trade—a sort of monstrous nineteenth-century drug cartel operating proudly under the British flag. But, of course, the horrors of addiction were not realized—not until the early twentieth century was the true effect of addiction understood, and laws put in place, in many countries, to regulate its use.

Now, as we all know, the main area of conflict is Afghanistan, but it's a very different kind of conflict from *those* opium wars. The cultivation of opium poppies in the region provides income for hundreds of farmers. In 2000, the growing of opium poppies was banned by the Taliban. But after their withdrawal, cultivation gradually increased, despite the efforts of America and the United Kingdom to encourage the growing of alternative crops.

It is grown in other countries too—legally and illegally. A friend of mine, Michael Watts, told me that recently he was with a group of people walking in the foothills of Mount Sinai on the Sinai Peninsula. They passed a field of beautiful flowers and some members of the group started walking in that direction, wanting to photograph them. Their guide became extremely agitated. "He caught my eye," said Michael. "He wanted to stop everyone but didn't know what to say. So I said, 'Tell them!' " The guide then pointed out the men with guns guarding the field. It was a crop of opium poppies!

Coca—*Erythroxylum coca*

Coca is a small evergreen bush native to western South America. It was domesticated in pre-Columbian times and has been cultivated for its leaves for some two to three thousand years. The leaves are picked for the first time when the plant is three years old, and from then on it is harvested, mostly by women, three times a year.

From pre-Inca times until the present, coca has played an important part in the religious ceremonies of the Andean people of Peru, Bolivia, Ecuador, and Colombia, as well as northern Argentina and Chile. The Incas thought that Coca was of divine origin, and for many years only nobles and certain other favored classes were allowed to use it. After the decline of the Incas, it was more widely used by all classes of people, but it was still highly respected so that, before planting their fields, farmers would invite a shaman to hold a ceremony, chewing coca leaves and sometime playing music.

Christin Jones, who helped us track down and secure permissions for the photos in this book, was participating in an archaeology dig at a site called Tiwanaku in Bolivia. She told me, "Before we could break ground, a shaman had to come to perform a ceremony. He used coca leaves to predict the success of our dig." Christin said she "sat around chewing coca leaves" along with the rest of the local community while the Aymara women spun yarn to wrap around a llama fetus, which was then burned as a sacrifice to Pachamama, Mother Earth.

Many people in Peru carry coca leaves with them, keeping them in little bags, often exquisitely woven. The leaves should be dried for at least three days before chewing. Leaves are sometimes chewed with a little bicarbonate of soda, which increases their stimulating effect, or drunk in an infusion of coca-leaf tea.

Initially the Spanish invaders forbade the use of coca, but then, realizing it would enable them to get more work out of their slaves, it was routinely issued to them. I find it fascinating that distances were measured in "cocalas"—the distance a load can be carried under the stimulation of one chew of coca leaves. Coca can also be used as an anesthetic, and for relieving the pain of headaches, wounds, and so on. Sharing leaves symbolizes solidarity among friends and partners—the Andean people sit around drinking coca tea just as we sit down for afternoon tea in England. Well, some of us still do.

In the mid-nineteenth century, soon after cocaine had been isolated from coca leaves in 1859, a variety of "coca-wines" were produced in Europe and became very popular. They were sold as tonics and were appreciated by, among others, the actress Sarah Bernhardt, Queen Victoria, Thomas Edison, and Pope Leo XIII. The original Coca-Cola was among the early tonics. About this time the Dutch successfully developed coca plantations in Java, and the Japanese in Formosa (Taiwan), but efforts by other European countries to grow this plant in their colonies were not very successful.

With the isolation of cocaine from coca leaves, the story of the guiltless coca plant, once held sacred by the people of the land from which it originated, turned rather grim. The ensuing problems with drug addiction and drug smuggling caused coca to be viciously attacked (along with opium poppies and cannabis) in the War on Drugs. From 2000 on, fields of coca plants were sprayed repeatedly with toxic herbicides from planes. By 2004 the large-scale coca-growing fields had been more or less destroyed, but the overall cultivation of coca had not decreased. Instead farmers simply moved to harder-to-find places and planted again. They had no cash-crop alternative, and they became increasingly desperate as their own food crops were eliminated along with the coca by the deadly rain of toxic chemicals. Which, of course, has had deadly consequences for the environment as a whole.

Meanwhile the violence between government and FARC (the Revolutionary Armed Forces of Colombia, or the "People's Army") increased, as did the power of the drug traffickers and cartels. In 2008 the United Nations monitoring body, which is clearly influenced by United States policies, requested the governments of Bolivia and Peru to abolish all use of coca (including chewing leaves), and to make it a criminal offense to be in possession of coca leaves. This directive was not well received. In fact, one legislator in Peru stood up and defiantly chewed a handful of leaves during a session of Congress—dozens of politicians followed suit. I would love to have been a fly on the wall!

How ironic that these plants, used for healing during hundreds of years, should lead to so much violence, desperation, poverty, and death. And that a plant that in itself is incapable of harming people, should be existing under a death sentence.

It is good news for the Andeans that the presidents of Peru, Bolivia, and Venezuela are defending the traditional use of coca, and are fighting orders from the International Union for Conservation of Nature (IUCN) to ban its cultivation and to destroy all wild plants. And it is good news also for *Erythroxylum coca* itself.

The Peyote Cactus

In 1956, during the year I spent working in London just before I went to Africa, I met an artist—a real Chelsea artist who often wore a smock. Charles was always very neat, with artistically long hair in a pageboy bob. He confided to me that he was taking part in an "experiment" to learn about the effects of mescaline—a substance I now know is extracted from a cactus. He never told me for whom he worked. In his studio, and under supervision, he would take a dose of a specified strength, and the effect on his painting was subsequently analyzed.

"I was looking at a square box," he told me, "and suddenly it was completely flat, like a table mat." Colors became extraordinarily vivid and intense, and he saw recurring patterns of stripes, spheres, and dots of many brilliant shades. It reminded me of a book I read by Aldous Huxley, who described what he experienced under the influence of mescaline as "animated stained glass illuminated from light coming through eyelids."

Mescaline is a naturally occurring psychedelic alkaloid found in small amounts in some plants of the bean family, but mainly in several species of cactus—the San Pedro (*Echinopsis pachanoi*), the Peruvian Torch (*E. peruviana*), and especially the peyote (*Lophophora williamsii*), which has been used by Mexico's Native Americans in religious ceremonies for more than three thousand years.

When I was in Mexico, I was told how mescaline was extracted from the peyote cactus. First the cactus is cut down to ground level. The taproot then grows a new "head"—which is cut off and dried. I was shown one of the disk-shaped buttons. This head may be chewed, or soaked to make a drink. As it is very bitter, it is often ground into a powder and put into capsules so that you can get the effect without tasting it.

Peyote has been used medicinally in many different contexts by several Native American cultures. The Tarahumara of northwest Mexico held long-distance races from village to village, sometimes running fifty miles. They would chew peyote and rub it on their legs for the purpose of strengthening them and also protecting them from evil forces. The long-distance runners of northwest Mexico's Tepehuán people did the same. The Kiowa people, who were indigenous to the Great Plains, used peyote to treat flu, scarlet fever, tuberculosis, and venereal diseases. And it has also been used to alleviate pain from toothache and in childbirth, and for treating skin disease, rheumatism, diabetes, and blindness.

As is so often the case, indigenous wisdom is based on sound biochemical fact. Thus peyocactin, a substance extracted from mescaline buttons, has strong antibacterial properties. Tests have shown that it is effective against eighteen different strains of penicillin-resistant *Staphylococcus aureus*, several other bacteria, and a fungus. The US Dispensatory includes peyocactin in preparations to treat, among other things, hysteria and asthma.

Tobacco—*Nicotiana*

Even though I have never smoked, I have some very personal connections to tobacco. My first husband died of his addiction—he got emphysema, which is a very unpleasant way to go. In the end he *had* to smoke—it made him cough and cough, the only way to rid his lungs of the nasty deposit of phlegm. Furthermore, the tobacco farming that began in Tanzania in 1984 has destroyed vast areas of forest that include a good deal of chimpanzee habitat, and the same is true in other areas around the world.

The tobacco plant itself is, of course, as blameless as all the other plants in this chapter. Yet even though I know this, I somehow cannot help disliking it—the commercially grown version, that is. And it doesn't help that this plant is in the nightshade family since I instantly think of deadly nightshade. Poor, innocent tobacco plant—I'm sorry!

Let me hasten to add that my illogical feeling of disapproval definitely does not extend to the wild tobacco plants. Among the indigenous peoples of the Americas tobacco has, for hundreds of years, been used in sacred ceremonies—as it still is—for it is believed to have many healing properties. In South and Central America the Indians smoked tobacco in pipes of many shapes and sizes, often elaborately decorated. It was sometimes chewed or used as snuff to "clear the head." Tobacco was also used as a remedy for such varied conditions as asthma, bites and stings, urinary and bowel complaints, fevers, convulsions, nervous ailments, sore eyes, and skin diseases. Some tribes cultivate tobacco as an insecticide to protect themselves against parasites.

In North America the use of tobacco was similar. By most, if not all, of the indigenous peoples, tobacco was held sacred and, in one way or another, played a role in most major life events, from birth to burial—as it does to this day. Some tribes planted it separately from other crops and there were special rituals for sowing and harvesting. It is thought to be a gift from the Creator, and that the smoke takes thoughts and prayers to heaven.

As is the case in South and Central America, the most important ceremony for most North American tribes is the smoking of the peace pipe, sharing the smoke between the individual making the smoke and those receiving it. The smoking of a peace pipe would symbolically seal a treaty or pact to end war with another tribe.

Sometimes tobacco is given as an offering to Mother Earth, placed on the ground or beside sacred rocks or trees. And as we saw in the last chapter, a traditional healer may leave tobacco as an offering to the spirit of a plant before returning to take it, or part of it, for medicine.

A twist of tobacco is almost always a component of the medicine bag, a small leather pouch containing various sacred items. I have been gifted a few by Native American friends. I have been told that tobacco is the one object common to all medicine bags—but I cannot know for sure, because it is not permitted that one should look inside.

It seems that the very first person to bring tobacco to Europe, in 1493, was Ramón Pane, who accompanied Columbus on his second voyage. But the plant was named for Jean Nicot, a French ambassador to Portugal, who sent tobacco leaves back to the French court as medicine—and subsequently popularized it as snuff. In England, Sir Walter Raleigh advocated the smoking of this "weed" in pipes in the British court. When he first began smoking, it is said that a manservant, entering the room and seeing his master wreathed in smoke, rushed for a pail of water with which he doused the unfortunate smoker! Soon, though, pipe smoking became fashionable at court—even Queen Elizabeth I was persuaded to try it.

Gradually, throughout the seventeenth century, the habit of

smoking pipes spread though all of Europe. The demand increased, and this led to the proliferation of huge plantations in the southern United States.

The Arrival of "Cancer Sticks"

The commercial production of cigarettes, appropriately nicknamed "cancer sticks," began in South America. In 1853 one Luis Susini designed a machine that could produce 3,600 "cigarets" per hour, and set up the very first factory in Cuba. By 1921 cigarettes were in mass production, with machines that could turn out 8,000 per minute. Thus the stage was set for the growth of a multibillion-dollar industry that would compromise the health of hundreds of thousands of people around the world. And, incidentally, that of the countless dogs used in unnecessary tests designed to prove that inhaled cigarette smoke can be harmful—as was abundantly clear from clinical observations of people.

Some recent statistics for America are quite shocking. One in five of 445,000 deaths during one year was attributable to smoking. This was a higher number than the total number of deaths caused by HIV, drugs, alcohol, car accidents, suicides, and murders combined. During the same year 90 percent of all lung cancer deaths in men, and 80 percent in women, were caused by smoking, as were 90 percent of the deaths from lung diseases such as emphysema and bronchitis. In addition, smokers have an increased risk of coronary and lung disease, as well as stroke and lung cancer. And, rather horribly, even the health of those who breathe in the smoke of others may be compromised.

One of the most vivid descriptions of the harmful nature of tobacco was written by Britain's King James I in 1604:

> In my opinion there cannot be a more base, and yet hurtful, corruption in a Country, than is the vile use (or other abuse) of taking Tobacco in this Kingdome. A custome loathsome to the eye, hateful to the Nose,

> Harmfull to the braine, dangerous to the lungs, and in the blacke stinkey fume thereof resembling the horrible stygian smoke of the pit that is bottomless.

How ironic that Jamestown, the birthplace of the New World tobacco plantations, was named for him.

Alcohol

Alcoholic beverages can be made out of many plants, though, in the Western world we are most familiar with those made from hops, grains, and grapes. In Asia rice is often used, and in Africa it is millet, bananas, and the sap of palm trees. I have tried almost all of them.

My mother, Vanne, maintained that a little drink in the evening was medicinal: after a hard day's work it served to change the mood, enable one to relax, and clear the mind of daytime worries. She could not drink wine—it simply did not agree with her. Her "poison" was whiskey—meaning Scottish whiskey, or Scotch, as Americans call it—and she liked to have, each evening, a little "tot." That is a "shot" in America, a "wee dram" in Scotland.

So it became a tradition: wherever I was in the world, at around seven p.m., I would try to get ahold of some kind of a drink (water would do, in a pinch!) and raise my glass to Vanne and the family. Thus, over the miles, we toasted one another and each felt better. My sister and I kept up this family tradition even after Vanne's death. We were fantasizing one evening, Judy and I, and imagining Vanne up on some beautiful white fluffy cloud, where angels played harps and everywhere beautiful flowers bloomed.

"And I bet," said Judy, "that if there is any whiskey up there, Mum will have got ahold of a glass." Other family members have joined Vanne on the cloud, and friends and their loved ones, and of course my dog Rusty and my chimpanzee friend David Greybeard. And so, with a growing number of people around the world, I raise my glass each evening in a toast to "The Cloud Contingent." Silly, perhaps, but somehow immensely comforting.

As for the therapeutic value of the little drink in the evening, several scientific studies have shown that people who drink lightly live longer than those who do not drink at all. The problem is that sometimes when people are under stress, one drink doesn't do the trick. Better have another. Maybe the worries are still there, so why not a third? This is the path to alcoholism. And, alas, addiction to alcohol is only too common.

The Grapevine

At one time there were two large glass conservatories attached to the back of The Birches, leading onto the garden. One of them was a place to sit where all the sun's rays were captured through walls and roof so that it was warm in winter. The other served as a sort of greenhouse—festooned with Uncle Eric's grapevine. Alas, the grapes never developed into juicy, delicious fruits, but remained small, undeveloped, and far too sour to eat.

When bombs fell close by during World War II, the glass was cracked, and sadly both conservatories had to be dismantled. But Judy has planted a new grapevine, in memory of Uncle Eric. It is an outdoor plant and obtains its nourishment not from the poor Birches soil but from a richer and more suitable soil imported and placed in a tub. It is three years old now, and last year, Judy says, the fruits were large and sweet.

We know that wine was made in ancient Egypt—there are hieroglyphics that record the cultivation of the grape there. And the ancient Greeks, Phoenicians, and Romans all grew vines and drank wine. From there the cultivation of the grape spread throughout Europe. Grapes can be black, purple, crimson, dark blue, yellow, green, orange, or pink. They have been cultivated for wine making all over the world where the conditions are right—they need warm, sunny days for the ripening, and sharp frosts in winter.

Until quite recently the wine snobs believed that the only wine worth drinking came from French vineyards. Gradually, though, the vineyards of other countries have built up their own reputations. The first sustainable vineyard in California was planted at a mission under the direction of the Jesuit Father Junípero Serra. Subsequently he established seven others at different missions, and became known as "the Father of California Wine"—originally known as "mission wine."

There are many species of grapes of the *Vitis* genus across North America, most of which, until recently, were not considered suitable for wine. But today many of these grapes are grown for wine throughout the United States.

Tanzania has been making efforts to cultivate grapes for good wine in the Dodoma region for many years. Benedictine monks were producing Bihawana wine in the 1970s. Derek and I used to buy it sometimes—it was more like port, but very good. But the Dodoma wines grown in the same region (both red and white) were hit-or-miss affairs. Sometimes one was lucky, but some bottles actually gave people hallucinations—and terrible hangovers. Perhaps the menu at a safari lodge, sometime in the seventies, sums it up best: "This Dodoma wine has all the subtlety of a charging rhino." I am still puzzling about the meaning. And no—I did not try it! More recently Cetewico, another brand from the same region, has come onto the market and is apparently very good. I shall have to buy some and try for myself.

Hops

My father didn't really like wine, and he hated spirits—his drink was "bitters," the English term for pale ale. He taught me to appreciate the British way of pouring the beer that resulted in a big "head" of foam. In 1956 I worked as a waitress at the Hawthorns Hotel in Bournemouth in order to save money for my fare to Africa. The doorman always used to offer me the opportunity to suck up this foam from the top of his lunchtime pint. I didn't actually like it much, but never had the heart to tell him.

The British like their beer room temperature. My second husband, Derek, hated the American culture of cold beer and used to ask his host to warm it in the microwave!

Beer is made from malt, but a key ingredient is hops, the female flower clusters of *Humulus lupulus.* This plant, native to temperate areas of the Northern Hemisphere, is a vigorous climbing herbaceous perennial that retreats into a rhizome (underground stem) during autumn. When cultivated, it is trained to climb up and along ropes in a "hop garden." Whenever I went to stay with a friend in Kent during my summer holidays, I used to pass field after field of hops, rows and rows of plants trained to grow along rope lattices in precise green lines.

Hops were first cultivated in the eighth and ninth centuries AD in Bohemian gardens in Bavaria and other parts of Europe. The first documented use of the plant as a "bittering" agent in the making of beer is in the eleventh century—before the use of the hop, breweries used other plants, such as dandelions, burdock root, marigold, and heather to counteract the sweetness of the malt.

Homemade Beverages

I used to stay with a friend in Kigoma who bought grapes grown around Dodoma in Tanzania, and fermented them in huge barrels in the guest room. I would hear strange noises of bubbling—rather like Macbeth's witches—"bubble, bubble, toil and trouble." I don't remember, though, ever tasting the wine that resulted! Dodoma grapes are tiny, with a skin that is dark purple and very thick and very sour—so I always bite a hole in it first and squish the fruit out into my mouth. The flesh itself is sweet and delicious, but it has very, very many seeds.

Of course, all kinds of other plants are used in East Africa to make alcoholic drinks, or "pombe"—it depends on the area and what grows there. In some places pombe is made from millet seeds. In the villages around Gombe in the Kigoma region of Tanzania, one kind of small, very sweet banana is the preferred ingredient—the fruits are fermented in great pits. And when I first arrived in Kenya back in 1957, the staff on my friend's farm would make a potent brew from wheat, which was placed to ferment in bottles in the heat of the hay in the barn. Unfortunately, the brew sometimes overheated and exploded. If anyone heard it, the guys were in trouble, for making pombe was strictly illegal in those days. And I used to worry that the horses might swallow slivers of glass.

In many parts of Central and West Africa the local drink of choice is palm wine. JGI is working with a number of villages in Congo-Brazzaville, where we have a sanctuary for the care of orphan chimpanzees. As in all the African countries where we seek to conserve chimpanzees and their forests, it is important to improve the standard of living of villagers in the area and encourage them to start environmentally sustainable projects.

And sometimes—as when we opened a small schoolroom in the village of Mpili—we join the villagers for a celebration. On that occasion everyone gathered together in a large clearing, the elders and "VIPs" (I was honored to be there with project manager Victor de la Torres Sans sitting on benches under a thatched awning). Someone had a guitar, there were several drummers, and young men filled jugs from two huge tubs of freshly brewed palm wine and went around filling our glasses and cups with liberal amounts of the very potent beverage.

There we were, drinks in hand, awaiting some words from the chief. He made a short speech thanking us for our contribution. I made a short speech thanking them for all their help. And then, very solemnly and before drinking, we poured a few drops of our palm wine onto the ground—for the ancestors. After that the party began. I had been warned that I would not like the local brew, but I found it quite delicious.

When the Sacred Gets Co-opted

Plants have played a major role in healing and in sacred ceremonies. But alas, the greed and commercialism of the modern world has changed everything. To become rich and powerful, the drug barons will go to any lengths to obtain and push their products, which today are often chemical compounds extracted from the original plants. The corporate greed machine uses any method to advertise and sell its goods, urging teenagers onto the wrong path with corrupting advertising and cheap, often harmful, alcoholic beverages. For years the cigarette was a sex symbol, the pipe a sign of tough manliness.

How tragic that people are killed in the drug wars by bullets as well as by overdose. That there are those who, like my first husband, Hugo, die coughing up their lungs. And how terribly unfortunate that the plants themselves are so often considered the "enemy"—to be eradicated whenever possible. Poor, innocent plants. And when they are uprooted and sprayed the entire environment is damaged.

We must just hope that somehow the triple evils of drug addiction, alcohol addiction, and nicotine addiction can be tackled at their source and that the plants can be left in peace.

Chapter 12

Plantations

The cotton gin was invented in 1793. It enabled the seed to be separated out from the fiber quickly so that cotton became a more profitable crop. This increased the need for slaves—and 80,000 were imported from Africa between 1790 and 1808, when further importation was banned. The slave, forced to turn the handle round and round and round, appears to be grimacing; he probably would be beaten if he stopped. (CREDIT: WILLIAM L. SHEPPARD, PUBLISHED IN *HARPER'S WEEKLY*, DECEMBER 1869)

Just as the use of plants for drugs has led to so much human suffering, so, too, has the cultivation of plants. With the dawn of agriculture the days of the hunter-gatherers were, to all intents and purposes, over and the gradual changing and destroying of the natural world began. And during the hundreds of years from the first simple farms to the introduction of mechanized farming, we had one of the darkest chapters in human history—the slave trade.

The early plantations were the forerunners of today's industrial farming. They exploited people, and destroyed lush habitats to create unsustainable monocultures. All for the sake of financial gain for the colonial plantation owners and the European countries from which they came. Slavery had a lasting impact on the population dynamics of the countries where the slaves were sent, as the ratio of African slaves to free men hugely increased. And this, of course, has led to many of todays' socioeconomic problems. The brutality lasted for years—and in fact, as we shall see, in some parts of the world slavery in agriculture continues to this day.

Of course the plants were innocent—in many cases they were victims themselves. I remember the first plantation I saw—a sugarcane plantation in Uganda. Miles and miles of what was once tropical forest bulldozed, the trees destroyed, the land forced to host a monoculture of plantation crops. And the plants, marshaled into rows, endless row after row, like prisoners lined up for roll call. Forced to grow on soil poisoned with chemicals, then sprayed with more chemicals, and blamed by environmentalists for greedily sucking up more than their fair share of water. I imagined them humiliated, dejected, ashamed of the harm they were compelled to inflict on the land.

Although slaves were not, of course, forced to work on that sugarcane plantation, I found myself remembering *Uncle Tom's Cabin*, that powerful antislavery novel written by Harriet Beecher Stowe in 1852, which, it has been said, helped lay the groundwork for the Civil War. It was a very popular book in England at the time it was published, and my mother used to read it to us on winter nights around the fire. I cried and cried, and it left me with a horror of slavery. It also, in a way, prepared me for the gruesome descriptions of life in the German concentration camps during World War II. Oddly, *Uncle Tom's Cabin* was apparently a favorite book of Adolf Hitler—perhaps the horrific cruelty described gave him ideas when it came to the treatment of Jews.

Crimes against Plants and Humanity

During the eighteenth and nineteenth centuries the European powers were hungrily grabbing and laying claim to land around the world. In part this was to plunder the natural resources—minerals, timber, and so forth. But it was also to establish plantations that would allow them to grow economically valuable plants, from different parts of the world, free from any restrictions on exports and costly tariffs. The development of these plantations thus went hand in hand with the expansion of the colonies—particularly those of Britain, France, Holland, Spain, and Portugal—in tropical and subtropical countries including those in the Caribbean and the Americas.

However, in order to be economically successful, the colonial invaders needed plentiful supplies of cheap labor—and it was this that led to the transatlantic slave trade.

The first African slaves were traded by the Portuguese in the sixteenth century, and during the following four hundred years or so an estimated twelve million people were abducted from their homes, mainly from West and Central Africa, and shipped to the European colonies. Most were forced to work on the plantations. And those plantations not only led to massive human suffering but were (and still are) extremely damaging to the environment. Large areas of land are cleared, trees felled, fertilizers (chemical today) added to the soil, and monocultures established. Very often plantation crops are greedy for water, and this has often meant severe depletion of natural supplies. All of this results in loss of biodiversity.

Among the plants typically grown on plantations, certain of them were especially lucrative for the planter, such as sugarcane, tobacco, cotton, rice—and for a while, indigo. Other plantation crops include coffee, tea, and cacao, as well as figs, sisal, dates, vanilla, and olives. And there are plantations of trees, too, grown for timber and wood pulp—the fast-growing conifers, notably pine and spruce, and the eucalyptus, which is especially thirsty for water. And, of course, plantations of oil palms are proliferating today, at the expense of hundreds of square miles of tropical old-growth forests, to produce palm oil, not only for inclusion in many food products but also for biofuel.

The demand for palm oil is rising in the United States and Europe because it is touted as a "clean" and "green" alternative to petroleum. Indonesia is the world's top producer of palm oil, and prices jumped by almost 70 percent in 2010. But palm oil plantations devastate the forest and create a monoculture on the land. This situation is a cause for ever-growing international concern, particularly because it is pushing the orangutans to extinction. The only remaining forest habitats of the red apes are the lowland forests of Borneo and Sumatra—the same rain forests that are being bulldozed to make way for palm oil plantations. Over the years, Birute Galdikas has fought off loggers, poachers, and miners, but nothing has posed as great a threat as palm oil.

"When you get up in the air," she wrote, "you start gasping in horror; there's nothing but palm oil in an area that used to be plush

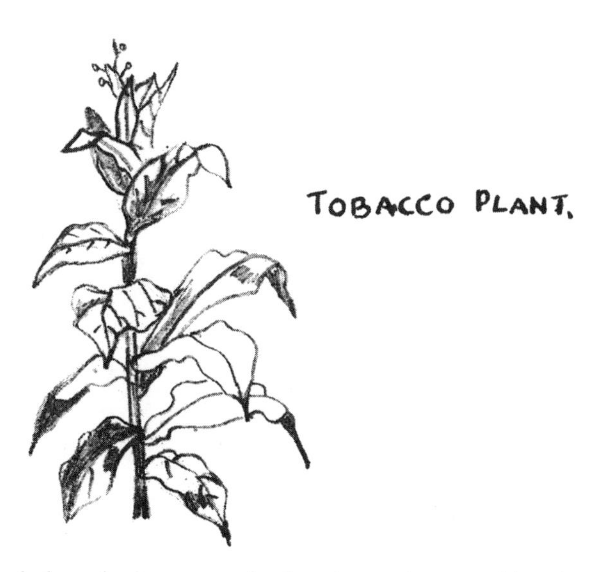

I learned about food crops at school and spent hours making drawings of them. This small drawing of tobacco and the other one later in this chapter of cotton come from a school notebook saved by my mother.
(CREDIT: JANE GOODALL)

rain forest. Elsewhere, there's burned-out land, which now extends even within the borders of the park."

The plantation crops I have chosen to write about are tobacco, rice, and cotton. Together they illustrate how their cultivation has provided huge economic benefits to plantation owners while causing massive human suffering and environmental degradation.

Tobacco—*Nicotiana*

I have already discussed the long history of tobacco use among indigenous people, who grew it for its medicinal properties and also used it in their ceremonies. In 1549 the Portuguese colonialists found tobacco in Brazil, where it was being cultivated by the indigenous people. Realizing its value, they enslaved the native tribes, seized their land, and forced them to work on their own fields.

The first North American tobacco plantation was established in Jamestown, Virginia, in 1618. When the colonists arrived from Britain, approximately thirty thousand Algonquian Indians lived in the region, most of whom were led by Powhatan, father of the famous Pocahontas, who became the wife of the Englishman John Rolfe—and it was Rolfe who was responsible for starting the tobacco plantations.

Rolfe had learned to smoke tobacco (or "drink" tobacco, as some called it) before he left England—it was a fad that had started after the Spanish brought back *Nicotiana tabacum* from the Caribbean. The Indians in Virginia used tobacco too, only it was a different native species, *Nicotiana rustica*. Rolfe despised this local tobacco and convinced a shipmaster to bring him *N. tabacum* seeds from Trinidad and Venezuela. Pocahontas was a smart and resourceful young woman—and it seems she may have helped Rolfe learn the native methods for growing and curing tobacco. Six years later Rolfe returned to England with his wife—and with the first samples of the New World tobacco. It was an immediate hit, and the tobacco plantations prospered and proliferated from then on.

Jamestown was turned around as a result of the successful method for producing tobacco. In fact, the people of Jamestown went crazy over this new crop. Tobacco was planted everywhere, not only in the fields but in the streets, the marketplace—even the cemetery! Also most people stopped growing other crops, and in the end it was necessary to make a ruling that everyone who grew tobacco must also plant two acres of corn, or else there might have been some very hungry people!

There was another major problem. Tobacco production rapidly exhausts the soil of nutrients, so the colonists had to keep creating new plantations, sprawling out farther and farther, claiming riverbanks and systematically taking over Indian land.

Then, too, initially there was a real shortage of workers, since the land was originally occupied for the exploitation of natural resources rather than for settlement. Before the African slave trade was established, plantation owners took whatever labor they could get, including criminals.

Those early settlers also lured young men from England with promises of riches. Full of enthusiasm, their fares paid, these hapless youths were indentured on arrival and forced to work in the fields. Often they ran away, but in either case they did not live long. And so the tobacco plants flourished and the planters grew rich, even as those working the fields suffered and died. Soon tobacco was a far more profitable crop than sugarcane, and was sometimes used as currency: In 1619 a man could import a wife from England for 120 pounds of tobacco!

Tobacco and Slavery

In 1620 (or by some accounts 1619) twenty African slaves were sold in Jamestown by a trading vessel that had stolen them from a slave boat. They were the first, but some fifteen years later African slaves were being regularly imported to Jamestown, direct from Britain and the Caribbean. Even so, in 1648 there were still only three hundred or so working there at any one time—because of a 30 percent mortality rate. Then, during the 1660s, the crash in sugar prices came, and African slaves were sold off by their owners in the Caribbean to the plantation owners in Virginia, who were still greedy for more and more cheap labor to fuel the ever-expanding tobacco industry.

By 1790 a slave ship departed from British ports for Africa every other day—gathering captives from West African slavers and transporting them across the Atlantic. Very many were destined to toil in the tobacco plantations. How ironic that among the items taken out to West Africa from Britain to trade with dealers in exchange for slaves were rolls of tobacco soaked in molasses—tobacco that had been cultivated, harvested, and cured by African slaves in the Americas.

Before the importation of Africans was well under way, many Native Americans were captured to work in the tobacco fields. Sometimes the planters actually bought them from the tribes, many of which at that time kept prisoners of war as servants. As time went on, the tribes began trading more and more of these captives, along with furs, for guns, knives, and other white-man goods. The British sometimes encouraged friendly Indians to send out raiding parties against other tribes so that they could buy the prisoners of war to work on the production of tobacco, and ever more tobacco.

While most people are aware of the horrors of the African slave trade, many do not realize that tens of thousands of Native Americans were also enslaved during the frenzy of tobacco growing, and the death rate among them was high from new diseases and inhumane treatment. In fact by the middle of the eighteenth century many of the tribes of the southeastern United States had been virtually destroyed. Eventually some of the remaining tribes formed a confederation to resist capture.

Current Abuses and Hazards

At one time tobacco was called "green gold." But all that changed after the Civil War, when tobacco could no longer profit from the labor of slaves. The crop continues to be cultivated in the United States, but the world's major producers are now in China, Pakistan, Brazil, India, and Malawi. And human-rights groups are now concerned with a new form of slavery—child laborers. While some children may work on their family tobacco farms, many are forced to work alone on plantations, laboring for long hours, low pay, and enduring abuse from their supervisors.

The environmental legacy is dire as well. Tobacco plantations have caused major deforestation in developing countries. In Tanzania I have seen firsthand the adverse effects on the environment of tobacco farms. Firstly, large areas of forest are clear-cut for the plantation, and a huge amount of wood is needed for curing the leaves. In Brazil alone the industry uses sixty million trees per year.

Secondly, because tobacco is sensitive and prone to many diseases, massive amounts of pesticides and herbicides are used to keep it on life support. These chemicals, of course, cause terrible harm to the surrounding water, plants, and animals. These poisons also pose health hazards to the laborers who apply them. Children, in particular, are harmed by the herbicides used.

Thirdly, the tobacco plant draws nutrients from the soil at a higher rate than any other major crop, and thus the cultivated land becomes increasingly dependent on fertilizers. Which, along with the pesticides and herbicides, causes terrible contamination of water.

Once again we return to the blameless tobacco plant, which was once respectfully cultivated by indigenous people for use as sacred weed for ceremonies and spiritual contemplation. How sad that it was eventually forced into such a horrible industry. For when it became part of the profit-driven colonial empire, tobacco was forever corrupted on the worldwide stage. There is nothing positive to say about the tobacco industry.

Rice—*Oryza sativa and O. glaberrima*

Rice did not figure largely in our diet when we were children except in the form of rice puddings—which I hated, not because I disliked rice but because I did not like milk! Thus, I would only eat it when it was overcooked (by most standards) with no trace of liquid milk to be seen. It was the potato that formed our staple food back then. After all, we did not grow rice in England, and during the war years, I doubt we imported very much. But rice is definitely the most important cereal staple for a very large proportion of the global population, especially in the Far East, India, South Asia, the Middle East, Latin America, and parts of Africa. It provides about one fifth of the calories consumed by humans worldwide. Asian farmers are responsible for about 90 percent of the total global rice production.

Rice is a member of the grass family. The stems of the Asian rice plant (*O. sativa*) have long, slender leaves growing from each node, and small wind-pollinated flowers develop on branch-like spikes that arch or droop over. The resulting seeds are harvested for rice. It was first domesticated in about 10,000 BC in the Yangtze River Valley in China: before that there is archaeological evidence that the people were collecting and eating grains from wild rice plants. The cultivation of rice then spread to other parts of China and Southeast Asia, and to India and Nepal. It was introduced as a food to Europe during medieval times.

Even today rice is still harvested by hand in many countries—dried, then milled with a rice husker to remove the outer husk or chaff. At this stage it is brown rice. Further processing results in white rice, which lacks some nutrients but keeps longer. It is a crop that is very labor intensive and needs high rainfall—the traditional method for growing rice is to flood low-lying areas in order to create paddy fields into which the seedlings are planted.

African rice (*O. glaberrima*) originated in the Niger Delta in West Africa and was eaten there for some 3,500 years. But although rice farming spread to Senegal, it did not travel outside of West Africa and when, somewhere between the sixth and eleventh centuries, Asian rice was introduced, perhaps by Arab traders, the cultivation of African rice decreased.

Rice Plantations—The Worst for Slaves

It was the conditions for slaves working on the rice plantations of the eighteenth century that were the most horrific of all. When the first of these were being established in America, most of the slaves were Native American. But they were ill suited to the brutal life, so the death rate was high. In the early 1700s plantation owners started buying slaves from Africa. They discovered that those from the rice-growing areas of West Africa had an understanding of the process far greater than their own. Growers—particularly those in South Carolina—who were prepared to pay a much higher price for these slaves profited, as the productivity of their plantations greatly increased.

In all, they converted some 150,000 acres of virgin land into tidal rice plantations. First they had to clear the land, using oxen to help them move tree stumps and pull loads of soil away. (Probably ghastly work for the animals too.) Next they had to excavate the ditches that would bring tidal waters into the fields—and construct sluice gates that would allow access only to the freshwater from the surface while keeping out the salty water from below that would kill the seedlings.

Then they had to build levees up to six feet high around the field. The field was drained for sowing and then flooded for growing the rice plants. Eventually the plants were left totally submerged for two months. For weeks on end, from dawn to dusk, both men and women labored in the fields, up to their ankles or midcalf in mud and water, swarmed by mosquitoes in the stifling heat and humidity. As if this was not enough, there was the danger of snakes and alligators.

And finally came the harvest, cutting the plants with iron sickles, stacking them on a mule or ox wagon, and after they had dried out, threshing them with flails to separate out the grains, a long and arduous process. If they failed to make their quota, they were whipped on their naked backs, women and children as well as men.

It is not surprising that mortality rates were high. In 1778, eighty people were abducted into slavery from North Africa to establish rice plantations—half died within the first year. Many were so desperate they tried to run away, even though they knew the punishment they would face when caught—as they usually were. I read of one especially brutal overseer who gave each one a hundred lashes

The cruelty of the white plantation owners to their African slaves was horrendous. The conditions were so bad, especially on the rice plantations, that slaves frequently tried to run away, even knowing the savage beating they would receive if caught. They were beaten for many other reasons, including failure to meet their quotas. (CREDIT: HENRY LOUIS STEPHENS)

when they were caught. Still his slaves attempted to escape. He eventually solved this problem by chaining them to each other around the neck, chaining to each one his spade, and forcing them to dig ditches, month in and month out. He boasted that he kept them in this way for two years.

After the Civil War and the emancipation of the slaves, rice growing declined, but it was not given up entirely in America. Some one hundred varieties are grown across the country today. (The so-called "wild rice" is the seeds of *Zizania aquatica*, which is also of the grass family, but not closely related to rice at all.)

Paddy Fields Wreaking Havoc

There are serious environmental concerns about the ongoing large-scale farming of rice. The flooding of the paddy fields means that the organic matter, buried under water and deprived of exposure to the air, starts to ferment. In the wet season the microbes in the soil convert carbon into methane gas, which is a greenhouse gas that is twenty times more potent than CO_2. Another major concern is that as a result of climate change, sea levels are rising, so the paddy fields will remain submerged for longer—and produce ever more methane.

The production of rice is severely taxing to the environment wherever it is grown commercially. For example, rice cultivation was introduced to Australia, where it grew well but only as a result of extensive irrigation—and this can be a major problem in areas without heavy rainfall. During the recent cycle of drought an unnatural demand was placed on the waters of the Murray-Darling Basin river system.

When I was visiting Australia in 2008, water from the river basin had actually stopped flowing into the sea, so that, at high tide, seawater entered the river delta, making the water in the delta more saline than that of the ocean and greatly compromising the ecology of the region. During those same years, of course, rice growers suffered huge losses. The very heavy rains that ended the drought restored the level of the river and washed the saline water back into the sea. But the same thing is likely to happen again.

In some countries, such as the Philippines and Thailand, governments seeking self-reliance in rice production have sought to squeeze out two harvests a year—with unfortunate consequences. Canals were built to irrigate the paddy fields in the dry season—and this meant other crops suffered. Moreover, this ignored the wisdom of growing rice in the rainy season only, so that the soil has a chance to recover from the months it is forced to remain underwater. Also, rotating rice with other crops is far more sensible, as it impedes the survival of rice pests and limits the output of methane.

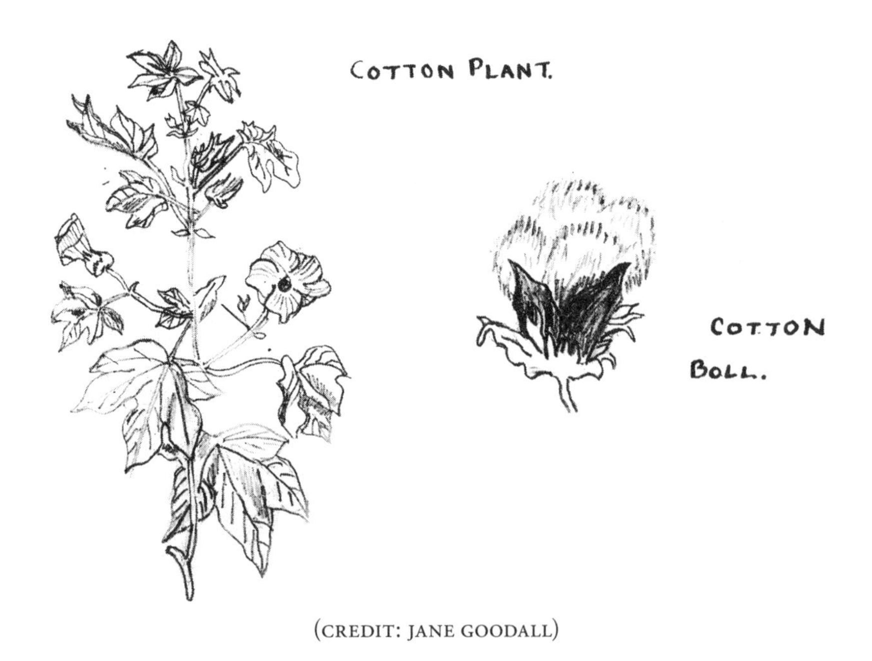

(CREDIT: JANE GOODALL)

Cotton—*Gossypium spp.*

The material of choice for wearing in hot climates has always been cotton, for it allows your skin to "breathe." Although synthetic materials now provide some competition, there is still a huge demand for cotton—it is a wonderful material. Unfortunately, as we shall see, commercial production of cotton has resulted in horrendous human suffering and horrendous damage to the environment.

Cotton is produced from a shrub-like plant, with an attractive flower. The seeds develop and are protected in what is called a boll—one cotton bush may have as many as one hundred bolls. Inside is a mass of soft, white, fluffy fibers that assist in the dispersal of seeds, enabling them to float through the air in the wind.

These fluffy fibers led to a very strange myth that seems to have originated in central Asia. It was described by John Mandeville's 1371 book, *The Travels of Sir John Mandeville*: "There grew in India a wonderful tree which bore tiny lambs on the endes of its branches. These branches are so pliable that they bend down to allow the lambs to feed when they are hungry." There are stories of this preposterous plant in other sources as well, and while there is some variation, all agree that when the lambs (which are made of flesh and blood) can reach no more grass, they die—at which point they can be eaten!

Wild cotton plants grow in subtropical regions in Australia, Africa, Asia, and the Americas and four species (*Gossypium hirsutum,*

Cottonseeds are protected, in the seedpod or boll, by a mass of soft, white, fluffy fibers. These fibers led to the bizarre myth of a wonderful tree in India that grew tiny lambs of flesh and blood on the ends of its branches. This drawing comes from John Mandeville's 1371 book, The Travels of Sir John Mandeville.

G. barbadense, G. arboreum, and *G. herbaceum*) have probably been domesticated since antiquity. The uses of cotton fibers were discovered separately in the Old and New Worlds: fragments of cotton fabric, both dated at around 5,000 BC, have been found in Pakistan and Mexico. It was not until late medieval times that the cotton fibers were imported to England for the mills. Presumably, it was the similarity of cotton fibers to sheep's wool that lent credence to the bizarre story of the lamb tree.

Because cotton fabric has always been valued, many of the early settlers in America established cotton plantations, and as it was a very labor-intensive crop, they purchased African slaves in huge numbers. Britain initially imported raw material from India, but this supply eventually proved insufficient for her rapidly expanding manufacturing industry, and so she turned to American and Caribbean plantations to keep up with demand. The French were also importing cotton from New World plantations.

Then, during the American Civil War, there were embargoes on cotton exports from America, so the British and French turned to Egyptian cotton. But as soon as it became practical, they returned to buying the cheaper cotton from America. As a result, in 1876, the Egyptian government declared bankruptcy—and this was a main factor enabling the British to annex Egypt into their colonial empire in 1882.

In post–Civil War America the production and sale of cotton in the South continued to finance much of the development of the North, and right up to the middle of the nineteenth century it was still the main cash crop. In 1850 there were an estimated 1.8 to 2.5 million slaves in America, and 75 percent were involved in the production of cotton.

Current Dangers in the Cotton Fields

We shudder when we think of those days. How shocking to realize that the production of cotton is still causing untold human suffering. For one thing in many of the cotton-producing countries

(India, Egypt, Pakistan, Turkmenistan, Tajikistan, and Uzbekistan) enforced child labor is what is keeping down the cost of production. Human-rights groups are particularly targeting Uzbekistan. For example, its schools are closed during the cotton harvest, and children as young as seven are forced to work in the fields. Each child must fulfill his or her quota or risk detentions and sometimes lower grades. If they run away, they may be expelled. These children—tens of thousands each year—must work long hours, often with inadequate food and in horrible conditions. Fortunately, as information about this situation leaks out, many international clothing companies are actually boycotting Uzbek cotton.

Another shocking fact about the cotton industry is that workers, including children, are often forced to work in the fields during or after crop spraying. Vast amounts of pesticides are used each year on cotton crops, many of which are banned or restricted in the West. A report by the Environmental Justice Foundation in collaboration with the Pesticide Action Network in the United Kingdom, titled "The Deadly Chemicals in Cotton," states that of the estimated two billion dollars worth of pesticides sprayed each year globally, nearly half are labeled "hazardous" by the World Health Organization. Two of them, Aldicarb and Endosulfan, are particularly deadly. Endosulfan can cause paralysis, coma, and seizures, and it is the number-one cause of deaths by poison in West Africa (where children are actually trafficked for the cotton industry). Yet Endosulfan is the most widely used pesticide in the world. No wonder cotton is also said to be the "dirtiest crop."

It is also one of the thirstiest crops—requiring six pints of water for each boll that matures. The water used for irrigating the cotton fields of Central Asia contributed hugely to draining the Aral Sea, said to be one of the most staggering disasters of the twentieth century.

Cotton, in terms of dollars earned by the exporting countries, is the most valuable nonfood agricultural product. But if a *correct* balance sheet were produced, one that added in the costs incurred by the cotton pickers, their families, and the environment, the product would not seem to be so "valuable" after all. How ironic that a little plant that produces such soft and aesthetically pleasing material, in itself as innocent as the mythical lamb it was once thought to nurture, should lead to so much suffering and devastation. So much so that I feel guilty when I think of all the cotton garments I have worn over the years.

But it is, of course, possible to grow organic cotton, and the demand for it, at present, outstrips availability. It is not always easy to find organic-cotton garments, and they are usually more expensive. But as with everything organic, it is worth the effort, just to know that we are supporting sustainable production. It is healthier for the cotton pickers, who are no longer exposed to all those chemicals, and, provided the garments are fair trade, the terrible exploitation of children will stop. Finally, it is much better for us, since nonorganic cotton is loaded with chemical residues that we absorb through our skin.

A Terrible Legacy

The exploitation of the poor or weak by the strong and powerful has always been a part of human history. The great plantations of the seventeenth through nineteenth centuries were profitable because of the use of cheap slave labor along with total disregard for environmental concern. Increasingly machinery took over from human sweat and muscle—which left thousands of ex-slaves uprooted from their own countries, stranded in alien cultures. Machinery also increasingly took over from draft animals.

We still have a long way to go before injustice is stamped out. In both rich and poor nations, developed and developing, there are still many ruthless business practices. Too often the natural world is exploited as, in the interests of increased profit, exhausted and chemically poisoned soil is forced to produce two crops per year instead of one, and more wilderness areas are destroyed for agriculture. Even plant nature is being bent to serve this greed, as their genetic inheritance is contaminated with the introduction of artificially modified genes. Moreover, in many developing countries slave labor is not a thing of the past, and crops are grown as a result of the sweat of people, including children, who have little option but to accept this servitude because of poverty, cultural norms, and lack of education. In the developed world too, illegal immigrant workers are often treated as slaves and work for a pittance in terrible conditions, unable to complain.

And, of course, the destruction of the environment, the cruelty inflicted on the natural world, plant and animal alike, and the terrible legacy we are leaving for the generations to come is ongoing.

Chapter 13

Food Crops

Wheat was the first farmed food crop, cultivated approximately eleven thousand years ago in Egypt. This etching, from the tomb of Ramesses III (who ruled from 1186 BC to 1155 BC), shows the step-by-step process of making bread from wheat at the royal bakery. (CREDIT: OXFORD ENCYCLOPEDIA OF ANCIENT EGYPT, EDITED BY DONALD B. REDFORD (2001) P. 197. BY PERMISSION OF OXFORD UNIVERSITY PRESS, INC.)

The gradual changes in farming techniques that have taken place over the ages enabled the digging stick to be replaced with hoe and scythe, then hoe and scythe with the ox or horse-drawn plow, and these with mechanized tractor, combine harvester, and so on, each new innovation enabling a farmer to work a larger area with fewer people.

The original organic fertilizers such as rotting vegetation and animal dung, especially guano, became increasingly supplemented by and then substituted with a variety of chemically synthesized fertilizers that, while beneficial to the farmer in many ways, began to take a terrible toll on the quality of the soil and to affect human health.

Various methods for irrigation of crops were devised over the ages. There were the irrigation ditches and hand-pumped artesian wells. Then boreholes were drilled so that water could be pumped up from deep down under the ground, from the aquifers. Then came center pivots, with their long arms distributing water in a wide circle around them. When you fly over the American prairies in the summer, you look down on hundreds of green circles on brown grass. Groundwater levels sank and aquifers were shrinking. And as more and more land could be used for agriculture, with corresponding growth of human populations in the urban areas, water from rivers was diverted for irrigation and more and more dams were constructed. There have been devastating environmental impacts.

The crops that, today, provide staple foods for millions of people around the world, and play a major role in sustaining our growing populations, are maize (which Americans call corn), rice, wheat, and potatoes. Maize comes first in terms of quantity produced globally—the UN figures for 2007 show that 784 million tons were produced globally. This compared with 651 million tons of rice, 602 million tons of wheat, and 320 tons of potatoes. A high proportion of the maize produced, however, is converted into biofuel.

Wheat—*Triticum spp.*

I am starting with wheat because it was among the founder crops at the dawn of agriculture—archaeological evidence shows that it was grown on the first-known farms carbon-dated to 9,000 BC. And because we use the grains to make bread, and bread has always been an intrinsic part of my own diet.

My grandmother Danny used to bake bread, and that heady aroma is a treasured memory from early days at The Birches. I can see her now, mixing the dough in a large ceramic bowl, wheat flour and water and yeast. Kneading it with her knuckles, letting us help by pulling it into ropes, then kneading it again, and finally covering it with a cloth and leaving it in the hot cupboard overnight to rise, through the action of the yeast. The next morning it would be baked in the oven. I would always try to steal the crust while the loaf was still warm and eat it with butter and homemade jam—even though Danny disapproved, as it was not good for the loaf. My sister makes bread today, but in a machine, and though the smell is wonderful, it does not seem quite as powerful. However, there are still artisanal bakeries in Europe where I can stand outside on the street, all my olfactory senses enraptured by the aroma in the air, and recapture the sensation of absolute bliss I knew as a child when Danny baked bread.

When I first visited Brazzaville and Pointe-Noire in the Republic of the Congo, both fairly small towns in a developing country, I discovered, to my surprise, that there were countless little cafés that emitted the same mouthwatering smell of baking bread. But of course it should not have surprised me, for Congo-Brazzaville is an ex-French colony. And in all their colonies the French introduced the art of producing delectable croissants, brioches, and crispy-crunchy French bread.

Wheat is a kind of grass. There are four species of wild wheat, and it is thought that their grains were collected for consumption long before the plant was first domesticated in the Fertile Crescent region in southeast Turkey. About a thousand years later, in 8,000 BC, the cultivation of wheat began to spread throughout the ancient world, first to Greece, Cyprus, and India, then to Egypt and Spain. By 3,000 BC it was being cultivated in England and Scandinavia, and a thousand years later it had reached China.

Not only was wheat among the first crops to be cultivated on a large scale, but surplus grain could be stored for long periods of time. This meant that numbers of people, many of whom were not involved in food production or procurement, could live permanently in one place. It thus played an important role in the development of the first settlements.

Today wheat is grown on more land than any other commercial crop—about 600 million acres around the world, and it thrives in amazingly diverse habitats, from near the Arctic to the Equator, from sea level to the plains of Tibet, four thousand miles above sea level. Its grains are ground into flour that is transformed into bread and a thousand and one other culinary products. It is a leading source of vegetable protein, containing more than many other cereals. Wholegrain wheat is also rich in vitamins and minerals. Only the unfortunate people who must have a gluten-free diet are deprived of the beneficence of wheat. And even they, most experts agree, can drink Scotch whiskey, made from fermented wheat grains, provided the beverage has been properly distilled.

After World War II the British government decided to develop wheat growing in Tanganyika (now Tanzania), initially to help feed war-ravaged Britain, and subsequently other parts of Europe. Ex-servicemen were offered the opportunity to get degrees in agriculture, and given the chance of managing wheat farms in one of three areas (most of Tanzania is too arid for successful wheat farming—as was one of the three areas selected).

My late husband, Derek Bryceson, was one of those men. He had served as a pilot and was shot down early in the war, losing partial use of both legs. Nevertheless, having obtained his degree at Cambridge University, he was able to persuade the authorities that he would be able to handle one of the farms on the slopes of Mount Kilimanjaro. He was very successful, only leaving his farm in order to support Julius Nyerere in his campaign for the presidency of the newly independent country. When I met Derek, he had become a member of Nyerere's first government—at the time he was the only freely elected white MP in black Africa. He was also the director of Tanzania National Parks.

Derek did not talk much about his farming years, but he frequently told me how he had loved to look out across his wheat fields, the young green of the new growth, the golden stems rippling in the wind before harvest. And this against the backdrop of Mount Kilimanjaro, tallest mountain in Africa, crowned by a snow-covered peak.

Potato—*Solanum tuberosum*

Toward the end of March 2012, I was in the United States being driven from the airport to the University of Wisconsin. The country there is flat, and we passed through farmland. I asked our driver what crops were produced. Corn, sugar beet, and potatoes, he told me. My mind drifted back in time to the days in England when I used to help with the potato picking on the farm owned by Miss Bush, who also ran a small riding stable. It was backbreaking work, potato picking by hand. I and two or three others, each with a large sack, followed after the plow—or whatever machine it was that moved through the rows, digging up the earth. We put the exposed potatoes into our sacks, working quickly to try to keep up—but it was certainly worth it, as it earned me free rides.

During the first year that I helped with the potato picking, a beautiful Shire horse named Paddy pulled the plow, but by the following year he had been retired and replaced by a tractor. I was very proud when I was allowed to drive that, but not nearly as happy as I was when I had been allowed to walk along leading Paddy by his bridle.

After a day's work, we had to sort the potatoes into three different categories—those suitable for market, those that were slightly damaged or too small (those went for making chips and potato crisps), and the badly damaged ones (which were fed to the pigs).

The potato is the starchy tuber of a plant distantly related to deadly nightshade. It originated in the South American Andes, where it still grows wild. It was first domesticated seven to ten thousand years ago and has been an essential crop in the Andes since the Pre-Columbian era. It was "discovered" by the Spanish conquerors of the Inca empire in the second half of the sixteenth century. Spanish boats carried the delicacy to Spain, from where it reached England and was gradually transported around Europe—and eventually farther and farther around the world—by British sailors.

Initially the European farmers were suspicious of the strange new food, but it soon became a well-loved staple across Europe, especially in France, where it was grown over huge areas. Indeed, such was its popularity that Queen Marie Antoinette once wore a headdress of potato flowers to a fancy dress ball.

It has been suggested that the introduction of this staple food played a major role in the nineteenth-century population boom in Europe. At that time only a few varieties were known, and there was little genetic diversity. One variety, known as "the Lumper" (what a name!), was cultivated extensively in western and southern Ireland, where it provided cheap but nourishing food, and the Irish people depended on it heavily.

Unfortunately the Lumper had poor resistance to disease, and this led to disaster when a fungus, with the decidedly ominous name of *Phytophthora infestans*, began infecting and decimating the Lumper potato yields around mainland Europe. The fungal infection spread rapidly, and soon it crossed the sea to Ireland and attacked the potatoes there. Newly harvested potatoes were transformed into putrid masses, and hectare after hectare of Irish farmlands turned into smelly black rot. How well I remember reading about the terrible 1845 Irish Potato Famine, which lasted over three years. About a million people died, and another million, in desperation, emigrated to Britain, America, Canada, and other places. By the end of 1849 the population of Ireland had been reduced to about half its prefamine number.

Since those days, years of selective breeding have produced over one thousand varieties adapted to many environmental conditions. I was treated to a rare and delicious kind with a jet-black skin during my last visit to Spain. Until fairly recently it was assumed that these different varieties originated from a number of different wild ancestors, but DNA testing has now shown that all varieties are descended from an ancestor that grew in what is now south Peru and over the border into Bolivia. Today China and India are the main growers, but potatoes are the most important crop in Canada and still a major food source in Europe, especially in eastern and central Europe, where more potatoes per capita are produced than anywhere else.

It was, as I have said, our most important staple food during my childhood. Roast potatoes on Sundays, boiled potatoes on most other days, mashed potatoes (involving more work for my grandmother, who did most of the cooking) less often. Then there were new potatoes (harvested before fully mature), boiled with mint from the garden—the smell was mouthwatering. And my favorite, jacket potatoes slowly baked in the oven, cut open so that a little butter (or margarine) could be added, then closed again to keep everything warm. My mother did not like the skin, but it was the favorite part for Judy and me, and we used to get half of hers each. Finally, of course, there are the memories of cooking potatoes in the embers of a campfire—the only problem being that the skin was usually too charred to eat. We did not have tinfoil in those wartime years.

Today, Judy and her daughter, Pip, bring in bags of soil so that they can grow potatoes in the garden. It is a somewhat costly way of producing a few potatoes—but they really are quite delicious, and I know that the two potato growers, like the peasants in Vincent van Gogh's famous painting, feel a sense of accomplishment and satisfaction when they eat the fruit of their labors!

Potatoes are normally grown from "seed potatoes"—fully grown potatoes that, instead of being eaten, are stored in cold warehouses, cellars, and so on. Before having a license to sell, the farmer must submit his seed potatoes for inspection in order to ensure they are disease-free. In the United States only fifteen out of fifty states are permitted to sell seed potatoes, as they have the required cold winters as well as long hours of sunshine in the summer. In the United Kingdom, seed potatoes are mainly produced in Scotland, which has the overall coldest winters.

After their chilly winter sleep, the seed potatoes are planted, and roots and sprouts quickly appear (indeed, they often develop in the kitchen if you keep a potato too long). Some of the sprouts grow leaves and rise above the ground. Others, known as "stolons," grow horizontally just under the soil, and new potato tubers appear at their ends as small swellings. Like its poisonous relative deadly nightshade, which is also related to henbane and tobacco, the potato plant contains solanine—a toxin that affects the nervous system—in its leaves, stems, sprouts, and fruits. When a growing potato is exposed to light, concentrations of the toxin under the skin are increased and the exposed part becomes green. Sometimes stolons run along the surface of the ground instead of underneath it, and farmers must prevent "greening" by covering the new tubers with earth. Greening is also caused by aging and damage. When the soil temperature warms up, the plant stops growing and the tubers gradually swell. Eventually the plant dies back, the skin toughens, sugars convert to starch, and the potatoes are ready for picking.

Wisconsin is one of the states that is permitted to sell seed potatoes. I think of my drive through the farmland, past the potato farms, and of how the fields and woodlands were brightened by trees bursting with white or red blossoms—beautiful to look at, although the flowers were a couple of weeks early. The temperatures the week before, the driver said, had been up in the eighties—in March! And there had been no "proper" winter, he said. If our weather patterns continue to change, if winters overall continue to get warmer, I suppose that the nature of potato farming will gradually change too. Probably climate change will affect many crops in many ways all around the globe.

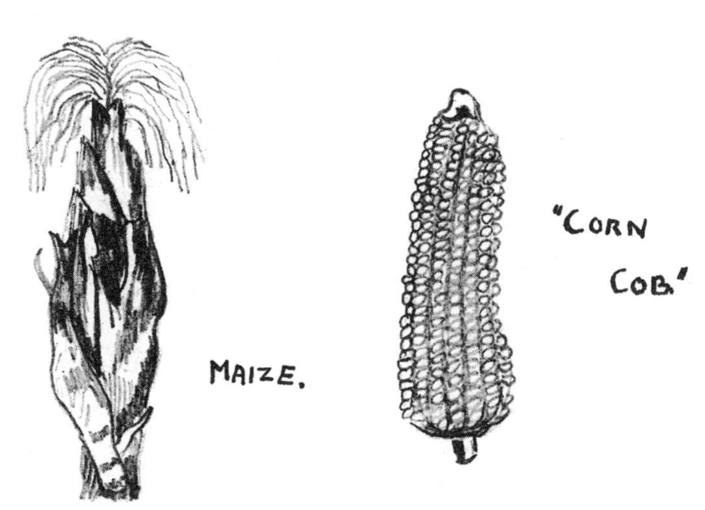

My mother saved this drawing of maize from my school notebook.
(CREDIT: JANE GOODALL)

Maize, Corn, Mealy Mealy—*Zea mays*

The maize plant—also known as corn or, in Africa, mealy maize or mealy mealy—has a tall, leafy stalk that produces an ear containing seeds known as kernels. When mature, this results in the familiar corncob. As you drive through the African landscape, you will see fields of maize growing near every little village as well as a few plants nestled up to the dwellings themselves. Yet maize is not indigenous to the African continent.

The most recent research suggests that it was first domesticated from its wild grass ancestor, *Balsas teosinte*, in the Central Balsas River Valley of Mexico some 7,500 years ago. And then, somewhere between 1700 and 1240 BC, it gradually spread into other parts of the Americas.

However, it wasn't until about 2,700 years ago that people succeeded in growing maize on the higher slopes of the Andes. This increased the caloric intake of the people, transformed the economy of the region, and provided the groundwork for the eventual emergence of the Inca empire. I learned about this from Alex Chepstow-Lusty. Alex was a student at Gombe in the early seventies, studying plants and not chimpanzees. I lost touch with him, but met him again in early 2012. Today he works for the French Institute of Andean Studies in Lima, Peru. Growing the maize at that altitude was "an extraordinary plant-breeding event," Alex told me. And it had only been possible through the application of organic fertilizers on a vast scale. The secret, Alex discovered, was llama dung! It is a fascinating detective story, which originated from Alex's careful study of pollen grains in the ancient sediments of a lake eleven thousand feet above sea level.

Throughout the fifteenth and early sixteenth centuries, after the arrival of the Europeans in America, maize began its travels to Europe and then gradually around the world, carried by explorers and traders. It is a good-natured plant, able to adapt successfully to a wide range of climates and soils, and its kernels have become a cereal staple in many countries.

Certainly maize is now a ubiquitous crop throughout many parts of Africa. In East Africa every village has its patch of maize, harvested when the kernels are fully mature, at which time roasted corncobs skewered onto wooden sticks are eaten around the fire at night or offered for sale at the side of the road. I have tried these mature cobs, but to my spoiled palate the grains are too tough and not sweet enough—though they look and smell delicious.

One variety, sweet corn, has a high sugar content, the result of a naturally occurring mutation in the genes that control the conversion of sugar to starch. It is harvested early when the kernels are soft, and eaten as a vegetable rather than as a grain. It was originally cultivated by several Native American tribes, and introduced to the white man by the Iroquois in 1779. When my son was small, we had a house outside Nairobi, and the previous owner had grown in the garden the best and sweetest corncobs I have ever tasted.

Then there is popcorn. Dried kernels heated with oil swell up—and pop. The result is the familiar crunchy, spongy snacks that have today—at least in the United States—replaced the chocolates and ice creams that were sold to cinemagoers in my youth. The smell of popcorn is an integral part of any movie you watch in America today. This can be bad news: one investigation into the popcorn sold by the largest cinema chain in America discovered that one serving of maize kernels "popped" with coconut oil and topped with butter or margarine contained more saturated fat than a bacon-and-egg breakfast, two Big Macs, and a steak dinner—combined! And although some changes were made, the same chain still serves portions containing 29 percent saturated fat, equivalent to three Big Macs—one and a half days' worth of the recommended daily amount. But the unhealthy part of popcorn has nothing to do with the grain itself, and when I read that report, I contrasted it with the corncobs eaten in the African villages, simply roasted over the coals—how we do manage to contaminate nature's gifts.

There is also increasing concern over the prevalence in our food of corn syrup, which is derived from maize kernels. It is cheaper than cane sugar, so it has increasingly replaced it in processed food products, especially in many of the packaged and fast foods. Not only are such foods linked to obesity, but a good deal of corn syrup is derived from genetically modified maize, which might cause health problems of another kind. Once again, we cannot blame the maize for the irresponsible way it is treated by those out to make money.

And there is another major concern. In North America fields and fields of arable land are given over to growing genetically modified maize to feed our modern hunger for meat and our modern hunger for fuel. To produce more and more food for more and more factory-farmed animals to feed more and more people around the world who want to eat more and more meat. Meanwhile other fields of arable land are given over to growing maize to fill empty fuel tanks rather than to fill empty stomachs. Thus despite statistics on the number of people who go to bed hungry, only about one third of the annual crop of maize is grown for human consumption. Poor, denigrated plant.

Maize represents so much of what disturbs me about industrial agriculture. We have transformed an ancient, graceful plant, one that has in its original form provided top-quality nutrition to millions over thousands of years, into a genetically modified demon, one of the major sources of industrial-farming pollution as well as a leading culprit in the growing obesity epidemic. And as a final twist, maize, instead of fulfilling its noble role of feeding people, is being used instead as a gasoline substitute to fuel our machines and as feed to fatten up our factory-farmed animals. Meanwhile, peasant maize farmers in Mexico, unable to compete with USA-subsidized farmers, have sunk into poverty.

Feeding the World

Agribusiness justifies intensive farming on the grounds that only in this way can farmers grow enough food to alleviate world hunger—but this, as we shall see, has by no means been proved, and is hotly disputed by many. And anyway, it is not only to feed the hungry, this relentless determination to grow more and more crops, never mind the consequences. Industrial agriculture cultivates plants for many purposes other than food, such as timber, clothing, and biofuel. And only too often, as agribusiness spreads its grasp over more and more land worldwide, it is the economic interests of individuals, institutions, and governments that drive such projects, ruthlessly eliminating the small farmers and peasants, taking over their land. Once-independent peasant farmers end up as beggars in the cities, for they have neither the skills nor the heart for this new way of life. Those who stay, paid to work on the land they once owned, are often exposed, along with their families, to harmful chemicals. People as well as the environment are the losers. Poverty and hunger are increasing, and thousands of farmers are committing suicide around the world.

The latest tool in the arsenal of modern agribusiness is the genetically modified plant, which, along with all its false promises and resulting disasters for the environment and for farmers, I shall be discussing in the next chapter.

Chapter 14

Genetically Modified Organisms

Greenpeace activists quarantining genetically engineered maize (corn) in Italy, July 2010. Test results showed that this maize is actually a patented Monsanto GE maize type, MON810, which has been linked to the tragic bee colony collapse disorder. Wearing safety equipment to protect against contamination, they are isolating, cutting, and securing the top of the GE maize plants, the part that contains the pollen.
(CREDIT: © MATTEO NOBILI / GREENPEACE)

The most recent monstrous crime against plants—at least in my view—is the tinkering with their DNA. One example is the insertion of bacterial genes into the DNA of plants so that they produce proteins toxic to insect pests. The era of biotechnology has begun. For me, born in 1934—before TV, before computers, before the landing on the Moon—the creation of genetically modified (GM) crops is another example of science fiction become reality.

Of course, when this new technology was introduced to the developing world, the gradual erosion of traditional farming methods—that began with the introduction of monoculture crops and agricultural chemicals—speeded up. When I was gathering facts for *Harvest for Hope*, I talked to many people about GMOs, people on both sides of what has become a hugely contentious issue. Proponents spoke of the benefits in glowing terms. Now there will be no need for spraying our fields with noxious chemical pesticides—the plants themselves will kill any pest that dares sample a forbidden leaf. Designer-crop plants are tolerant of chemical herbicides, so we can spray the fields and kill the weeds with those chemicals without harming our harvest. And as the globe heats up, GM drought-resistant plants will continue to thrive. Yields will increase. The farmers will benefit. The environment will benefit. Hooray! Science can solve the problem of providing enough food for the ever-expanding human population.

Alas! Such hopes have proved as insubstantial as the pipe dreams of the opium smokers—although the GMO giants such as Monsanto, DuPont, and Syngenta (the three largest) would have us believe otherwise. They clearly think that if we are told often enough that GM crops are the solution to the world's agricultural problems, we shall believe it. However, since 1996, when Monsanto first commercialized Bt corn, a growing chorus of voices has been pointing out the downside of this technology. In October 2011, a report titled *The GMO Emperor Has No Clothes* and coordinated by renowned environmentalist Vandana Shiva, expressed the findings and observations of a broad coalition of scientists, NGOs, traditional farmers, conservationists, and concerned citizens from Asia, Africa, Europe, Australia, and the Americas.

The report compiles and collates information from each region detailing the failed technology, false promises, and negative effects of genetically modified plants. It is based on years of personal

Scientist, lawyer, and environmental leader Vandana Shiva has vehemently fought the proliferation of genetically modified seeds and plants in India. Because of her efforts and those of other activists, awareness is growing, and more and more people are working to ban Monsanto's products.
(CREDIT: KARTIKEY SHIVA)

experience—GM crops have been grown in twenty-nine countries on a total of more than 3.5 billion acres of agricultural land. The information in this chapter is derived from that report, from many other scientific papers, and from talking with scientists, farmers, and concerned citizens I have met during my travels around the globe.

A Recipe for "Super Pests"

Monsanto has created insect-resistant crop plants (corn, cotton, and potato) by inserting a gene from *Bacillus thuringiensis* (Bt) into the DNA of the seed—the pest will then die when it eats the genetically modified plant. Here is an example of the sales hype of the industry: in Canada, Monsanto sells its Bt potato as "Nature Mark" and describes it as a plant using "sunshine, air and soil nutrients to make a biodegradable protein that affects just one specific insect pest, and only those individual insects that actually take a bite of the plants." In fact, this potato plant, like other genetically engineered crop plants, has been violated. The "biodegradable protein" is a toxin that is continuously formed during the entire growing season of the plant. And the natural "soil nutrients" on fields of GM monocultures have long since been exhausted and must be boosted by increasing amounts of chemical fertilizers—as in all monoculture-intensive farming.

And, like other genetically engineered (GE) insect-resistant plants, this Monsanto potato affects many insects other than pests, including beneficial ones, such as bees and ladybugs. A Cornell University study showed adverse effects of transgenic pollen on monarch butterflies: their caterpillars reared on milkweed leaves dusted with Bt corn pollen ate less, grew more slowly, and suffered higher mortality.

Meanwhile the insect pests themselves are, as was predicted, becoming increasingly resistant to the GM plants. As I write, in 2012, it seems that at least eight species of "super pests" have now become resistant to Bt toxins, in field or laboratory, including the diamondback moth, Indian meal moth, tobacco budworm, and the Colorado potato beetle. The most recent of these insects that have adapted to a diet of toxins is the tiny western corn rootworm, which, like the other super pests, is outsmarting the GE technology that was supposed to kill it.

Of course, the emergence of superbugs has forced farmers to resort to increased use of pesticides, since the plants designed to repel insects have to a significant extent failed. In India, for example, the use of chemical pesticides has increased thirteenfold since Bt cotton was introduced. As Bill Freese of the Center for Food Safety in Washington, D.C., said, "The biotech industry is taking us into a more pesticide-dependent agriculture, and we need to be going in the opposite direction."

Monsanto has genetically engineered agricultural plants to withstand its own Roundup herbicide, used to control agricultural weeds. But this meddling with nature has created an alarming infestation of more than twenty species of "super weeds" that can survive Roundup spraying. Weed scientist Jason Norsworthy has been studying the rapid rate at which herbicide-resistant pigweed plants can spread in a cotton field at the Arkansas Agricultural Research and Extension Center. This Palmer pigweed can grow two to three inches a day and damage harvesting equipment. (CREDIT: UNIVERSITY OF ARKANSAS SYSTEM DIVISION OF AGRICULTURE/FRED MILLER)

And Now "Super Weeds"

Monsanto has genetically engineered crops (soy, corn, canola, alfalfa, and sugar beet) that are tolerant of its own brand of herbicide, Roundup, now the most widely used herbicide around the globe. The first of these was sold as Roundup Ready soybean. It now seems that this may have been one of Monsanto's most ill-advised products to date because, like the insects that have adapted to a diet of Bt plant material, so a variety of agricultural weed species, as a result of frequent sprayings of Roundup, have gradually built up resistance.

The "super weeds" are now emerging at an alarming rate. In the United States, twenty-one species of agricultural weeds, some of which grow two to three inches a day, are now resistant to glyphosate, the key ingredient of Roundup herbicide. These plants have been reported in at least twenty-two US states, infesting over ten million acres of mostly soybeans, cotton, and corn.

Farmer Mark Nelson in Kansas writes that his soybean field has been invaded by one of these new super weeds, waterhemp (*Amaranthus rudis*). Towering above his beans, it is sucking up the soil moisture and nutrients that are needed by his crop.

"When we harvest this field, these waterhemp seeds will spread all over kingdom come," he said. And one waterhemp plant can produce a million seeds. So that even if only a few plants survive spraying, this can lead to a major infestation in a couple of years. Another farmer, Justin Cariker, in Dundee, Missouri, has an infestation of glyphosate-resistant Palmer pigweed (*Amaranthus palmeri*) on his farm. Looming above his cotton plants, it reaches heights of seven feet or more, and develops a stem as thick as a man's wrist. An infestation of this Monsanto-created monster can damage harvesting equipment.

The president of the Arkansas Association of Conservation Districts, Andrew Wargo III, described super weeds as "the single largest threat to production agriculture that we have ever seen" (*The New York Times*, May 2010).

All of this means that increasing amounts of herbicides are being used by farmers. In 2002, the global sales for glyphosate amounted to around $4.705 billion. There are more than seventy glyphosate producers in the world, but Monsanto is by far the biggest, with a more than an 80-percent share of the market. And agricultural weeds, resistant to glyphosate, have been reported in twenty-eight countries across the globe.

The response of Monsanto, the "GMO Emperor," to super weeds? It now instructs farmers to use a *cocktail* of other herbicides to deal with them. Dow, DuPont, Syngenta, and Bayer are all reviving sales of older herbicides, ones that may well be more damaging to the environment than glyphosate, probably hoping to challenge Monsanto's dominance in the business. And work is in progress to develop crops genetically modified to withstand the new massive spraying of the super weeds. Dow AgroSciences is, in fact, seeking the USDA's permission to sell farmers corn, soybean, and cotton seeds that are genetically altered to tolerate heavy spraying of glysophate as well as Dow's 2,4-D based herbicide "Enlist." When I read that, I felt a cold chill—2,4-D was a key ingredient of Agent Orange, the herbicide used to defoliate the Vietnam forests during that war. There is concern that this chemical may be linked to higher rates of non-Hodgkin's lymphoma among farmers, agriculture workers, and pesticide appliers.

Risks to Plants, Animals, and Human Animals

Here is another bizarre twist in the Roundup saga. I read a recent report from the Institute for Responsible Technology that glyphosate may actually encourage the growth of certain kinds of soil fungus, including *Fosarium*, which clusters on the roots of plants and has been linked to sudden death syndrome (SDS) in plants. This disease stunts and weakens plants, and enables various diseases to attack them. It destroys beneficial soil organisms, interferes with the plant's photosynthesis, reduces water-use efficiency, shortens root systems, and causes release of sugars, which changes the soil's pH.

Nor should we ignore the risks to human health. The American Academy of Environmental Medicine warns, "Several animal studies indicate serious health risks associated with GM food." These risks include infertility, immune problems, accelerated aging, faulty insulin regulation, and changes in major organs and the gastrointestinal system. The Academy even asked physicians to advise patients to avoid GM foods.

Evidence of various adverse effects on laboratory animals after eating GM foods comes mostly from studies on that poor victim of modern science, the laboratory rat. A 1999 study showed that rats fed on one variety of Bt potatoes suffered adverse effects on their intestinal tracts. The rats fed a different kind of GM potatoes had atrophied livers. After eating Roundup resistant corn, rats developed liver lesions. Liver damage also occurred when rats ate Roundup Ready soybeans.

And rats fed GM tomatoes displayed a peculiar incidence of stomach lesions. The FDA experts who saw the stomach lesion data agreed that it raised a safety issue—an issue they thought was never properly resolved.

It is not only the rat that has been tested: rabbits, after eating GM soybeans, showed altered enzyme production in their livers as well as higher metabolic activity; and eating GM peas resulted in an inflammatory response in mice.

Finally there is evidence that Monsanto's MON 810 corn may be at least partially responsible for the colony collapse syndrome (CCS) that is devastating bee colonies in different parts of the world. John McDonald, a United States beekeeper with a background in biology, decided to conduct his own scientific inquiry into a possible link. His study showed that bees foraging near Monsanto's corn did not gain proper weight and failed to put honey in the hive storage bins. At the same time bees who were not near GM corn put on weight normally and produced twice as much honey as they needed to survive the winter. After this study was released, Poland banned Mon 810 corn, specifically because the government is convinced it is linked to colony collapse syndrome.

The results of all these studies are challenged by the biotech industry and their supporters, but although I am not in a position to enter this particular debate, not having the scientific or medical knowledge, it seems very unlikely that *all* of them could be flawed. And if GMOs have adversely affected even some of the animals tested, it would be naïve to think that human beings would be any different. In 2001, a Centers for Disease Control and Prevention study found twenty-eight subjects had experienced apparent allergic reactions after ingesting GM corn. And there is substantial evidence that farmers face health hazards.

Contamination Threat to Organic Farmers

Organic farmers are threatened in a different way—economically. Pollen from GM crops is blown by the wind or carried by bees and can contaminate their crops, and birds drop seeds that can germinate in their fields. Many organic farmers have lost their organic status because GM plants are found growing in their fields—and in addition they may be sued by Monsanto for growing their patented plants without paying for them!

When writing *Harvest for Hope* I spoke several times with Percy Schmeiser, a Canadian farmer who fought Monsanto in court. His canola fields had been inadvertently contaminated with Monsanto's GE canola. Only a small roadside patch of Monsanto's canola was discovered—from seeds most likely blown into his fields (a nearby farm was growing GE canola.) It seems that someone from Monsanto snuck onto his property and tested this canola. Next Percy received a letter from Monsanto accusing him of patent infringement and threatening to sue him. Rather than buckle under to the corporate giant, Schmeiser decided to fight back in court. After six years of legal battles and $400,000 in Percy's court costs (which was offset by donations from concerned individuals and anti-GMO organizations worldwide), the Canadian Supreme Court ruled that since Percy didn't profit from "infringing," he didn't owe Monsanto any money. But it did uphold Monsanto's claim of patent infringement.

Since the mid-1990s Monsanto has filed 144 "patent infringement" lawsuits against farmers and won judgments against them. More than seven hundred *additional* farmers have settled out of court, according to the Organic Seed Growers and Trade Association. I can only assume many of these farmers settled just to avoid Monsanto's well-financed litigious actions.

Organic farmers are especially impacted by the fact that GM seeds can arrive in their fields, because accidental contamination of this sort means they will lose the organic certification that they worked so hard to obtain. And as if that wasn't devastating enough, they also have to defend themselves from a Monsanto-initiated patent infringement lawsuit. A consortium of more than eighty North American family farmers and organic-farming advocates has been formed to seek legal protection from Monsanto's patent-infringement lawsuits—but so far they haven't had success. The group is committed to fighting on, and I for one shall be wishing them luck.

A Reuters report of September 2011 points to the magnitude of Monsanto's grip on agriculture today. It states that in Canada the contamination of organic canola with GM canola is so severe that 90 percent of seventy certified *non*-GM canola seed samples tested were contaminated with the Roundup Ready gene or the Liberty Link gene—or both. Arnold Taylor, chair of the Organic Agriculture Protection Fund, said, "There is no organic canola in Canada anymore, virtually none, because the seed stock is basically contaminated... we've lost that crop." This, of course, is a huge blow, not only for organic farmers but for consumers who wish to avoid GM foods.

Nature: The True Maker of "Climate Resilient" Crops

Most recently, with concerns of climate change widely accepted, the biotech giants are working on designing GM crops that will be drought-resistant for planting in harsh climates. For example, in 2012 the USDA approved a new corn, genetically engineered by Monsanto to withstand drought. But is this really necessary? Hundreds of farmers and scientists around the world are insisting that it is not. All of those traits have already been evolved in the traditional way by peasant farmers—for when seeds are planted and saved annually, cross-pollination occurs, and plants continually adapt to changing environments. For instance, in the southwestern United States, this natural form of adaptation has resulted in native drought-tolerant corn.

Vandana Shiva summed up the situation regarding these climate-resilient traits nicely: "The biotech industry has simply pirated them from nature and farmers."

Deceit, Greed, and Arrogance

One of the most disturbing aspects of the whole GMO situation is the fact that the concerns of scientists and others are ignored, trivialized, or ridiculed. Misinformation is put out by companies with multimillion-dollar budgets for PR, and governments of developing countries are pressured to introduce GM crops into their agriculture. From 1999 to 2009, biotech firms spent over $547 million on lobbying Congress, and $22 million for political campaigns.

When I was reading through *The GMO Emperor Has No Clothes*, I came across an essay by Wendell Berry, a well-known writer and environmental activist whom I admire greatly. "GMO biotech science is involved directly with product-development, marketing, and political lobbying on behalf of their products," he wrote. "It is, therefore, subject to corruption as a result of personal self-interest and greed. For such a science to present itself in the guise of objectivity or philanthropy is, at best, hypocritical, at worst deceitful."

I couldn't agree more. Particularly shocking, to me, is the concept of *substantiated equivalence*, the core element of GM crop regulation worldwide. When the industry wants to avoid risk assessment and issues of liability, it argues that the genetically modified plant is "substantially equal" to its non-GMO parent. Yet when the company wants to patent a product, the *same* genetically modified plant is described as novel, or "substantially *different*" from the parent plant. I heard someone describe this as "ontological schizophrenia," commenting that it would be laughable if it was not so terrifying.

I've heard it said that substantial equivalence is a "pseudoscientific" concept. Some years ago I read an article in *Nature* magazine by the esteemed toxicologist and medical examiner Dr. Marc Lappé in which he wrote about Monsanto's Roundup Ready soybeans having levels of certain estrogens that were 12 to 14 percent different from non-GM beans. "To treat these differences as *insignificant* when it is a question of safety, and as *significant* when it is a question of patentability, is totally unscientific," he wrote.

Another article in *Nature*, in 1999, concurred saying that "substantial equivalence is a pseudoscientific concept because it is a commercial and political judgment masquerading as if it were scientific" and that "it was created primarily to provide an excuse for not requiring biochemical or toxicological tests." And I would add that it is also totally unethical.

How Can We Avoid Them If They Aren't Labeled?

I mentioned earlier that the American Academy of Environmental Medicine asked doctors to advise their patients to avoid GM foods. But unless governments force Monsanto and other biotech companies to attach a GM label to their products, it is not possible for people to choose not to buy them. In the United States the majority of corn, soybeans, cotton, sugar beets, and canola crops are genetically modified. This means that many of the ingredients you find in packaged foods—such as corn syrup, soy lecithin, sugar, vegetable oil, and cottonseed oil—are made from these crops.

As many as 70 percent of the processed foods in US supermarkets now contain GM ingredients, according to a study conducted by the California Department of Food and Agriculture. In Europe, where labeling is required, consumers make it clear they prefer not to buy food that comes from GM crops. In the United States, the demand for such labeling continues to be ignored by the federal government.

In June 2012 the US Senate voted overwhelmingly *against* legislation that would have allowed US states to choose to enforce GM labeling for food and beverage products. And this, despite the fact that two recent polls (MSNBC and Thomson Reuters) found that 93 and 96 percent of the American public believes genetically engineered foods should be labeled. The 2012 Californian initiative for labeling got almost a million signatures, and the FDA received 850,000 letters of support for labeling. Even the UN, that most cautious of organizations, finally concluded in 2011, after eighteen years of debate, that countries were free to label, as this would help inform customers about their purchases.

I found the Senate vote hard to understand until I learned that some of the very largest food and agricultural biotechnology firms and trade associations had spent ten years and millions of dollars on campaign contributions and lobbying. And the Organic Consumers Association reports that Monsanto had threatened to sue the state of Vermont if they voted *for* GM labeling.

We Must Not Give Up the Battle

I know only too well that this situation with GM foods can seem overwhelming. Multinational corporations such as Monsanto, with so much government support and financial power, can seem daunting and unstoppable. And the destructive industrial model of growing crops sometimes seems permanently embedded in our global infrastructure. But as I always emphasize, each one of us has the power to make a difference. We can all add our voices to the chorus of those shouting out that "the GMO Emperor has no clothes."

All is not lost. The resistance to GM plants and seeds is strong, and it is only getting stronger. Citizens are taking action all over the world. Some—in the United Kingdom, France, and Hungary—have even invaded the fields and torn GM plants out of the ground. Many were arrested, but the protests continued. In Hungary the people actually destroyed one thousand acres of GM corn. I know one of the protesters who took part in several such raids in the United Kingdom—he said he would go on with his acts of civil disobedience until Monsanto was driven out.

In March 2012 Belgium, Bulgaria, France, Germany, Ireland, Slovakia, and the United Kingdom blocked an effort by the Danish EU presidency to allow expanded cultivation of GM crops. And Peru has placed a ten-year ban on GM seeds and crops.

When I was in Argentina in June 2012, the papers were full of the five million Brazilian farmers who have engaged Monsanto in a lawsuit. When they planted their first Monsanto seeds eight years ago, they paid royalties on the harvest. In subsequent years they have continued to pay 2 percent per harvest and they claim this is unfair and that Monsanto should return that money. The Brazilian court ruled in the farmers' favor and ordered Monsanto to pay back their earnings from 2004—6.2 billion Euro! Monsanto is trying to overturn the ruling, but meanwhile it has temporarily stopped charging royalties on its Roundup Ready soybean seeds throughout Brazil.

There are even an increasing number of instances where Monsanto is being prevented from moving into a country, or actually being forced to quit. In March 2012, fifteen hundred beekeepers in full beekeeping suits marched through Warsaw and placed thousands of dead bees on the steps of the Ministry of Agriculture. It was their way of denouncing the apparent link between colony collapse syndrome and Monsanto's GM corn, MON 810—the one GM crop that's still allowed to grow in the EU.

There was a similar protest that same month when one hundred beekeepers and anti-GM corn protesters managed to storm Monsanto's administrative offices in Monbéqui, France, and occupy the building for several hours. It must have been spectacular: a couple of them drove a fake delivery van (their Trojan horse), and the moment the gates opened, the delegation, in full beekeeper suits, swarmed in behind them. That same March, France reinstated a ban on Monsanto's MON 810 corn. The government's justification of the ban was based on "significant risks for the environment" shown in recent scientific studies.

And finally, despite the Senate vote against allowing the states to demand GM labeling, the push for GM labeling is gaining traction in the United States. Thanks to the dedication of many citizen groups, individual states have introduced legislation to force labeling of consumer goods that contain GMOs. Some states, counties, and cities are even considering legally banning GMOs altogether.

What Does the Future Hold?

Thanks to a great deal of scientific research, and because of people like Vandana Shiva, Percy Schmeiser, and hundreds of concerned activists, things are beginning to change. I just read a really impressive and gripping book about the biotech industry, *Altered Genes, Twisted Truth: How the Venture to Genetically Engineer Our Food Has Subverted Science, Corrupted Government, and Systematically Deceived the Public*. The author, Steven M. Druker, is a public interest attorney who initiated a lawsuit that forced the FDA to divulge its files on genetically engineered foods. I encourage everyone to read it. The results are shocking.

Fortunately, people around the world are speaking out. The public is finally becoming aware of the terrifying effect of modern agribusiness, including GM foods, on environments, societies, and human health and there is growing support for organic and ethical farming.

A recent picture of The Birches garden in winter. I love the way snow creates a whole new magical landscape. (CREDIT: JANE GOODALL)

I love roses and was especially thrilled by the Jane Goodall Rose, created by the "rose poet" Christian Hanak and Guillaume Didier. When fully mature the inmost petals acquire a deep orangey color. The scent is glorious. How incredible that, wherever it grows, it will bear my name. (CREDIT: JEROEN HAIJTINK)

A new environmentally friendly gardening movement is underway in many developed countries. Gombe videographer Bill Wallauer and his wife, Kristin, transformed their backyard into a native plant habitat for bees, birds, and other wildlife. Just about the only thing that remained the same is the garden shed in the left corner. (CREDIT: WILLIAM R. WALLAUER)

I recently met with some of the traditional healers of the Waha tribe near Gombe. Mzee Mikidadi showed me where he now grows many medicinal plants behind his house, as it's becoming harder to find them in the wild. He purposefully grew this ntuligwa tree (*Flacourtia indica*) on a termite mound because he believes it makes the medicine from the leaves more effective. (CREDIT: © THE JANE GOODALL INSTITUTE —TANZANIA / BY DR. D. ANTHONY COLLINS)

In many Latin American countries, the leaves of the coca plant (*Erythroxylum coca*) are considered to have practical as well as spiritual value. A friend of mine took this picture of a Bolivian shaman (center) who is preparing to toss a bundle of coca leaves onto the cloth. He will then "read" the leaves to determine the success of an archaeological dig that is about to begin. (CREDIT: CHRISTIN M. JONES)

Amazingly, all 1,000 varieties of potato are descended from a single wild ancestor that grew in Peru and Bolivia. Potatoes were a staple food during my wartime childhood, and they still represent an important food in many parts of the world. (CREDIT: © INTERNATIONAL POTATO CENTER)

Fortunately, we can buy tea that has not been grown on an environmentally destructive, heavily sprayed monoculture plantation. This woman is harvesting tea from an ancient tea forest in China where no toxic chemicals, clear-cutting, or even weeding is permitted. Many of these trees are over 500 years old. (CREDIT: JOSHUA KAISER)

This is *Theobroma cacao*, the tree whose seeds provide us with that most delectable of all culinary delights, chocolate, the "food of the gods." The football-size seedpods produce almond-size seeds, surrounded by soft pulp. It takes ten or more seedpods to get one pound of cocoa. (CREDIT: DEBRA MUSIC)

With the help of caring landowners and committed volunteers, the endangered native grasses and other flora of the North American prairies are being saved and protected. A few years ago this beautiful blowout penstemon (*Penstemon haydenii*) was almost extinct, but it is now being lovingly restored in the Nebraska Sandhills. (CREDIT: ALAN J. BARTELS)

One of the most amazing restoration projects I know of. This is what's possible when humans and plants work together to restore a devastated landscape. The first picture shows the wasteland created by twenty years of quarrying by the Bamburi Cement Company near the Kenya coast. Next we see the same piece of land after the company's horticulturist, Rene Haller, spent years observing nature, planting different kinds of trees, and experimenting with plants. "Haller Park" is now a lush wildlife habitat, and until 2007 it was the home of Owen and Mzee—the famous hippopotamus and tortoise who befriended each other after Owen lost his mother during the tsunami. (CREDIT: RENE HALLER)

Only a series of miracles prevented *Kokia cookei* from becoming extinct. The extraordinary story behind this photo illustrates the strength of the "will to live." (CREDIT: DAVID EICKHOFF)

The Callery pear that amazingly survived the 9/11 attack after being buried in the rubble of the fallen Twin Towers. "Survivor" now blossoms each spring. You can see where the charred trunk ends and the branches of new growth begin. Even the darkest of times cannot crush the power of life. Always there is hope. (CREDIT: JULIE FELSHER)

PART FOUR

The Way Forward

Chapter 15

The Future of Agriculture

In the high hills above Gombe the soil and climate are ideal for growing good coffee. These little "cherries" will redden when ripe and the seeds within, when cleaned, become coffee beans. Over one thousand villagers grow shade coffee on their tiny farms. This type of sustainable organic farming is a recipe for the future of agriculture, providing good incomes without harming the land. (CREDIT: © THE JANE GOODALL INSTITUTE – TANZANIA / BY DR. SHADRACK M. KAMENYA)

The preceding three chapters, when taken together, present a pretty depressing picture of the many ways in which we have harmed the natural world, as well as ourselves and our children. Yet, at the same time, there is more than a glimmer of hope. More and more people are daring to stand up to Monsanto and the other biotech giants, expressing their outrage about the genetic tinkering with our food—with life itself. Those corporations are, indeed, immensely powerful—Monsanto in particular has a great hold over many of the governments of the world. But these companies are not invincible, and in the face of increasing scientific proof and increasing public anger—who knows. Let us never forget how David defeated Goliath.

Gradually the full implications of the harm we have inflicted on Planet Earth are seeping into different levels of society, in different parts of the world. An understanding of the connection between poisoning our fields and poisoning ourselves with agricultural chemicals is growing. And more people are beginning to realize what the world will be like for our great-grandchildren if we don't take action now. And soon.

As a wider section of the general public becomes more informed and understands the benefits of organic food, the markets are beginning to change, and more and more commercial farmers around the world are turning to organic farming. Also, more and more companies are sourcing and selling products produced in an ethical, sustainable way. Companies and farmers alike are part of a new movement that is beginning to heal some of the land that has been despoiled by industrial farming, to make some recompense to the peasants, who, since colonial times, have been so horribly exploited. Hopefully this heralds the dawn of a new era—ethical consumers demanding ethically produced products, and ethical CEOs who understand their responsibility to future generations.

Ethical Companies: Sustainable Farming

Quite apart from the obvious benefits to environment and our own health, the organic movement means that I can eat and drink the things I want without feeling guilty! I have selected three case studies that I know something about: coffee farming in Tanzania, tea farming in China, and cacao growing in the Democratic Republic of the Congo. And I hope to show that although these crops can cause great harm when grown with the agribusiness model, it is possible to reverse the damage. Which is fortunate for me, since I happen to be very partial to the products produced!

Coffee, tea, and cacao, when grown on conventional plantations, have resulted in a great deal of human suffering and environmental harm for hundreds of years. But today there are people and companies doing things right. Change is in the air.

Coffee—*Coffea spp.*

There are few smells more stimulating than that of fresh-ground coffee beans, and how delicious that first taste of good coffee in the morning. It helps the day get off to a good start. Johann Sebastian Bach not only had a mug of coffee every morning—he even wrote "The Coffee Cantata," which tells the story of a father who is chastising his daughter for her caffeine habit, which she, in turn, is hotly defending. It was first played in Zimmerman's Coffee House in Leipzig around 1732.

Coffee comes from plants of the genus *Coffea*. The two best-known species are *C. arabica* and the more robust *C. canephora,* both originally from Africa. About 90 percent of the coffee drunk globally is from the Arabica bean, thought to have originated in the cloud or "Coffee Forests" in the Kafa region of Ethiopia. This whole area, home to an exciting number of animal and plant species, has recently been designated a World Biosphere site, a major conservation success for Africa. And it is there that the last remaining population of wild-growing coffee can be found.

Gradually, since the first plantations were established in the 1600s, more and more coffee has been grown in order to supply the increasing global demand, and as might be expected, this has led to major environmental problems: Brazil, for example, has destroyed vast areas of forest for cultivating the plant, and there has been similar devastation in other Latin American countries. By contrast, Costa Rica, with no readily available supply of cheap slave labor and with many small farms instead of huge plantations, is one country that has managed to export excellent coffee without destroying its environment.

During the past decade, because of increasing environmental awareness among consumers, more and more farmers are producing "shade grown" coffee, planting noncoffee trees among the coffee plants, allowing regeneration, increasing biodiversity—and using fewer chemicals. And the coffee farmers around Gombe National Park are now following this trend, thanks to JGI's TACARE program, which works to alleviate poverty and secure the goodwill and cooperation of villagers. Without this we cannot hope to save Gombe's chimpanzees.

Our program started when I heard that really good quality coffee was being grown in the high hills outside the park, but that the farmers were not getting good prices due to their lack of marketing skills and lack of infrastructure. And, just about the same time, I received an invitation to give a keynote talk at the annual meeting of the Specialty Coffee Association of America. This was an unusual request—it seemed that it was meant to be!

I gave myself a crash course in coffee growing and its environmental impacts, learning about the benefits of shade-grown and organic coffee farming. The meeting took place in Seattle, and my talk went down really well.

At the end I said, "I believe we have a source of first-rate coffee around Gombe National Park. But I need some of you guys to come and taste it—and if it is good, buy it, create a specialty brand, give the farmers a good price, and help the environment and the chimpanzees in the bargain!"

That was why, within a month, a small group of senior executives from Green Mountain Coffee Roasters arrived in Kigoma, visited some of the coffee farmers, tasted the coffee, pronounced it excellent, and ordered a couple of crates. And that, in turn, led to a delicious coffee, which they market as "Gombe Reserve." The farmers got a better price than they had dreamed of—and, too, it helped to ensure a better future for the chimpanzees of Gombe.

Other roasters also came, tasted, and bought. With advice from experts, production per acre has greatly increased, and trees are being planted to provide shade, help control erosion, and restore moisture to the soil. This coffee is now regarded as the best in Tanzania, and last year the farmers were able to produce some four hundred tons.

The first time I went to the coffee-growing area high in the hills above Lake Tanganyika was to visit, with a small group of VIPs, one of the farmers, Lazeru. He had joined our Roots & Shoots program when he was a child in primary school, where he learned about TACARE and the importance of trees. He told us that he had inherited this tiny coffee farm when his uncle died, and at that time he had found it a depressing place. It was on a bare hillside, with a few sick "and sad-looking" coffee bushes, no trees, and all the animals and birds gone.

However, remembering his R&S training, the first thing Lazeru did was to plant some tree seedlings. Nature here is resilient. The trees grew. The ground, once shaded, regained moisture. And now his coffee plants look healthy, and surely "happy," laden with red "cherries" almost ready for picking. And now they are surrounded by trees, some of which are thirty feet tall or more. Lazeru told us that birds and small animals are coming back too. I was glad to be there with Lazeru, for he is dynamic, full of life and energy. And hope for the future.

After leaving him we drove a short way, then walked in the cool highland air, past a little boy herding huge-horned Ankole-Watusi cattle, and through another, longer-established coffee farm. In between the slightly "untidy" rows—because the plants each have their own individual growth patterns—banana plants were growing, and looking equally healthy and providing much-needed food. Here and there were tall *Grevillea robusta* trees that not only provide shade but also fix nitrogen in the soil, helping both bananas and coffee. (Four other tree species found on other farms do the same job.)

An old man was weeding the bushes. He seemed amazed to see us—he said he was just doing what he always did, and yet suddenly there were all these people taking photos of him. He was tickled pink, wreathed in smiles.

Close by was one of the "washing" operations of the region's coffee cooperative, where farmers such as Lazeru bring their harvest to be weighed, checked for quality, and entered in a logbook. The pulp surrounding the beans is cleaned in one machine, and all the waste goes as fertilizer to nearby fields. The wet, clean beans are then laid on giant drying racks. We saw the huge shed where the dried beans are stored before they are sorted and graded.

Once the farmer hands over his coffee, he no longer owns it—it becomes the property of the cooperative—which was why, at first, many farmers were reluctant to join the scheme. But the difference in price between the beans that they could individually offer for sale and the beans that had been cleaned and dried according to specific standards, then sorted and graded, was so great that soon more and more farmers were joining.

The headquarters of the cooperative is in the large building that houses the giant machine that cleans, sorts, and grades the dry

Our Tanzanian coffee farmers have formed a cooperative. They bring their harvest to be cleaned, sun dried on these huge racks, then graded for quality. They get their share of profit only after the coffee has been sold.

(CREDIT: © THE JANE GOODALL INSTITUTE / BY JENNIFER CROFT)

beans. We learned that it was purchased with a loan that had to be paid back in five years. The scheme was so successful they were able to pay it back in just two years—they are justly proud. They are proud, too, of their certificates: five years running they won the prize for Best Quality from the Tanzanian Coffee Board, and one year they got second prize.

This is a perfect example of successful production on a moderately large scale involving small family farmers rather than a big commercial operation. The current tally is 1,400 farmers, and the average size of each farm is an acre, with only one or two being as large as several acres. And because each farmer grows other crops scattered throughout and between the coffee-growing areas, they can still support their families even when the market price of coffee drops during a given year.

Tea: The British "Cuppa"

Now what about tea? It is made, of course, by adding hot water to the dried leaves of *Camellia sinensis*, and we Brits are known to be a nation of tea drinkers. My sister and I were given a doll's tea set when we were children—it was almost a mandatory gift for little girls back then, and it is still popular today. Tea was the first "grown-up" drink we were allowed—very weak and milky—long before coffee was permitted (we couldn't get coffee during the war anyway). In England, a cup of tea is a panacea for all ills. If you have a shock, a good strong cup of tea with plenty of sugar will steady you. If you are cold, a cuppa will warm you. If you are hot, a cuppa will cool you down.

My most favorite tea story I read in a small paragraph in a newspaper about eight years ago. A burglar was chased by three policemen, who finally caught him in an elderly lady's back garden in London. Two policemen sat on their captive while the third called for a car. The old lady came into her garden and stared in astonishment. Turning to the only solution she knew, she asked the policeman if they would like a cup of tea.

"You bet," they said, exhausted from the chase. The woman set off, then turned back and, looking doubtfully at the prostrate burglar, she asked, "Should I bring three cups—or four?" (She was told that three would suffice!)

Camellia sinensis is native to China. (There is another species, Assam tea—*Camellia sinensis* var. *assamica*—which grows in India, but this was not cultivated until very much later.) There are two versions of the legend of the discovery of tea in China. One story describes how an herbal-medicine practitioner, Shennong, when climbing a mountain to search for medicinal plants, picked up a leaf that fell on his foot, rubbed it between his fingers, and tasted it. Finding it bitter, he thought it might be medicinal, and subsequently infused some of the leaves in hot water. The second legend—my favorite!—attributes the discovery to the "Divine Harvester," Emperor Chen Nung, in 2737 BC. He was, we are told, very strict about hygiene and drank only boiled water. One day he apparently stopped to take a nap beneath a tree with a bowl of freshly boiled water beside him. A tea-tree leaf fluttered down into his bowl. He chose to drink the water anyway and was filled with inexpressible well-being. Thus, tea was born.

Although countless people still derive great pleasure from a cup of tea, it is unfortunate that unless they are drinking an organic brand, the brew is likely to be contaminated with a toxic mix of chemicals. This is because most tea plantations have been subjected each year to a positive barrage of poisons, being sprayed on average fifteen to twenty times (sometimes even more often), depending on the numbers of insect pests and weeds. Most of these chemicals—such as Aldrin 20E, Carbofuran 30, Endosulfan 35 EC, Malathion 50 EC, Tetradifon 8 EC, and Calixin 80 EC—are listed as hazardous and toxic, and a number of them are banned in Western countries. Despite the dangers of exposure to these poisons, the workers are frequently barefoot and in shorts rather than protected by recommended aprons.

According to Oxfam, a British nonprofit agency working to put an end to poverty worldwide, the spraying of pesticides on tea estates is often done by untrained, casual daily-wage workers, sometimes even by children and adolescents, who are illiterate and cannot read the warnings on the containers. And it's not just the workers but also the distant consumers who are at risk of chemical exposure—the first time you "wash" the leaves is when you brew the tea to drink it.

I was shocked to learn all this. The good old British "cuppa" suddenly did not seem such a good idea after all. At least, not unless it is an organic brand, and fortunately there are some great brands on the market. The Soil Association, an international organization for organic cultivation, notes that a typical organic field has five times as many wild plants, 57 percent more animal species, and 44 percent more birds. Without doubt, the human workers are many times better off as well.

Of course, the use of agricultural chemicals is not the only problem—thousands and thousands of square miles of tropical forest have been destroyed in India and China for tea plantations. Thus, I was excited to discover that it is possible to harvest tea—like coffee—from trees growing in the forest.

I first heard about this from Joshua Kaiser, founder and president of Rishi Tea, one of the companies that sources Fair Trade and organic certified tea from around the world. Joshua and his staff have personally visited many of the places to verify the conditions for themselves. One of the villages is Mannong Manmai in Yunnan Province of China. There 250 families have entered a Fair Trade Organic Co-op and contract with Rishi Tea to produce organic teas from a sustainable and biologically diverse environment. The tea is harvested from an old-growth tea forest established by ancient tea planters more than 1,500 years ago, and to pick the leaves, the local women climb into the trees.

These people protect their ancient tea forest fiercely, and have done so for generation after generation. No toxic chemicals, clear-cutting of trees, weeding, or soil-erosion-promoting actions are permitted in an ancient tea forest. Many of the tea trees are between five hundred and eight hundred years old, and some are thought to have lived for over a thousand years.

Before leaving the subject of tea, I must say that I am really grateful to those farmers and entrepreneurs who have taken the high moral ground and developed an organic tea standard. And especially to businesses such as Rishi Tea. Because it means that, without feeling guilt, I can once again enjoy a good old British cuppa.

Cacao—Food of the Gods

Chocolate!

Probably I am so addicted to chocolate because, during WWII, it was severely rationed. Just a few squares per week—which the grown-ups sacrificed for us children. And it really was a sacrifice for my mother—she was, I think, even more of a chocoholic than me, due, I suspect, to the deprivation of the war years. When I was spending months on end at Gombe, chocolate was one of the things I missed most, and everyone who came on a visit knew to bring me a supply.

Chocolate comes from the beans of *Theobroma cacao*, a tree that can grow to the size of a big apple tree. It matures when it is three years old and from then on, during its life of more than fifty years, continuously flowers and produces seeds all the year round. These seeds, the size of almonds, are surrounded by white soft pulp inside pods that, in some species, can be the size of footballs, and that are attached to the trunk of the tree. There are thirty to forty seeds per pod and it takes twenty to twenty-five pods to make two pounds of cacao.

Theobroma cacao is indigenous to South America, and was brought to Europe by Christopher Columbus. He was probably the very first European to set eyes on cacao beans, during his fourth and last voyage to the Americas. It was when he was sailing near what is now Honduras that he encountered the biggest native boat he had ever seen "as long as a galley, eight feet wide, and with twenty-five paddlers and with palm roof," he noted in his journal. Among the exotic fruits and other goods for trade were cacao beans. And he noticed the extreme value the natives placed on these "almonds," as he called them, since they so quickly gathered any that fell to the ground.

Indeed, cacao was a sacred plant for the Mayans. They believed that the Creator had given them the tree and that—perhaps because the liquid they made had the color of blood—it was the most important for the life force. This was probably why Linnaeus, when naming it, combined the Greek words *theo*, meaning *god* and *broma* meaning *food* with the Mayan name *cacao*—*Theobroma cacao*, "food of the gods."

The bean preparation is much the same as coffee, save that the cacao beans, when separated, are fermented before drying, roasting, and grinding. The result of these processes is known as chocolate liquor, which is bitter and sold in blocks.

Once the Europeans discovered the value of cacao, they established plantations in some of their African colonies. Throughout the 1930s and 1940s cacao growing increased in West Africa, especially in the Ivory Coast. Unfortunately for the environment, a great deal of rain forest was cleared—and this was unfortunate for the cacao trees too since in their original habitat, under the shade of the forest, they can live to be fifty years old, but out in the sun they age faster, and became nonproductive after thirty years.

As well, farmers often had to use a great deal of chemical spray to try to control the main problem with growing cacao in Africa, black pod disease. As the land in Ivory Coast became less fertile, farmers simply cut more forest down to start over again—or else left their impoverished land to seek work in the towns.

In the Cameroons, however, a more environmentally friendly method of production emerged—the cacao trees were allowed to grow in the shade of some of the original rain forest, and a mixture of other species were planted for fruit or timber. It was an environment rich in biodiversity and the soil remained fertile.

Then, in the 1990s, cacao prices fell on the international market. The Cameroonian farmers, unable to make a living by selling cacao, turned to maize, groundnuts, or oil palm, often clearing pristine rain forest. In Ivory Coast the desperate cacao farmers, in an effort to reduce their costs, resorted to exactly the same solution as that of the original European plantation owners—slaves. Only in this case it was a cheap labor force made up of children.

Most of them were lured from impoverished Mali, told that they would be able to earn money to help their families. In fact, they were seldom paid anything, and were mostly treated with extreme brutality. An investigation found that on a typical small farm, working hours were 6:00 a.m. to 6.30 p.m., the food provided was minimal, and the boys were often locked up at night to prevent them from running away.

At the time of the investigation there were some 600,000 small farms in the country, using roughly 15,000 children. When a child did escape, he usually reported his captor—the other slaves were then usually rescued and sent home. And once the international media began publicizing the situation, there was general outrage, additional inspections, and things improved.

Meanwhile consumers were beginning to understand more about the origin of their purchases. The Fair Trade label had been launched in 1988, bringing a lot of publicity to the issue in general. In 1994 Green & Black's (now owned by Kraft Foods) sold their Maya Gold chocolate, sourced in Belize, under a fair-trade label. Gradually other brands have followed suit.

It was also in 1994 that Joe Whinney, founder of Theo Chocolate, first pioneered the importation of organic cacao beans into North America. After witnessing the degradation of the tropical rain forests and the economic hardship endured by the workers, Joe became passionate about creating a more sustainable form of cacao growing, one that went beyond the organic label's requirements. He realized that it wasn't enough to teach cacao farmers about the advantages of long-term habitat protection. Unless the standard of living for the farmers, and especially their workers, was improved, the supply of cacao could never be sustainable. Theo started its program to improve things for these people at about the time that our TACARE program began in Tanzania.

Once JGI learned about Theo Chocolate, the first "bean to bar" organic, fair-trade chocolate manufacturer in the United States, we arranged a visit to their Seattle factory. Of course, being a lover of chocolate, it was a memorable experience for me. The mouthwatering smell of good chocolate, the abundance of bars and confections for sampling, and the chocolate-flavored story of the company's operations in Africa, nurtured both body and soul.

Theo has suppliers/farmers in Latin America, who have now enjoyed fifteen years of good, reliable income. They are protecting their forest environment and, knowing they have now created a sustainable environment, they are even planting hardwoods (which take many years to mature) as investments in their children's future—just as we are doing in Tanzania.

In Africa, Joe offers technical training and assistance to farmers about becoming certified as organic. This kind of information is eagerly sought after. He told me he ends up speaking in the largest spaces they can provide—schools and churches—and they are always packed.

When he asks his audiences why they have come, they often reply, "Because we want to grow cacao without chemicals. Whenever we grow with chemicals, we get sick. And we can't afford the doctor's bills."

Fortunately Joe can inform his farmers about organic solutions to common problems from pod-boring insects. The neem tree's leaves, munched by my son for protection against malaria, have antibacterial properties. The tree produces many seeds, and if these are collected and soaked in water, the resulting liquid becomes a natural pesticide that can be sprayed on the cacao trees.

Joe's business ethics exactly match those endorsed by JGI, which is why, in 2008, we decided to partner with Theo Chocolate to introduce "Cacoa Practices"—a program that brings together small-scale cacao farmers, larger producers, and nongovernmental organizations from the world's cacao-producing regions. The idea is to give farmers the tools they need to grow high-quality cacao beans while conserving indigenous wildlife and other natural resources in tropical rain forest ecosystems. At the time of writing, Theo is paying the farmers the top price for their cacao beans.

Cacao Dangers and a Buffer Zone for Chimpanzees

Joe's most recent venture is in the eastern part of the Democratic Republic of the Congo (DRC), where cacao is grown in the area that borders Virunga National Park, Africa's oldest nature reserve. The cacao trees provide a buffer zone for the home of the last mountain gorillas and a small population of chimpanzees.

The first time Joe tasted the roasted cacao beans from the DRC, he was astounded by how delicious they were—"they naturally taste like brownies," he told me. But until recently, it's been hard to source organic cacao from the DRC, since the region has been unstable and travel has been too dangerous.

Once things improved, Joe was able to travel through the cacao-growing area of the eastern part of the DRC, teaching farmers sustainable growing practices that are improving their crop production and quality. Joe also talks about child-labor issues to ensure there will be no exploitation of this sort. The project is moving quickly; some farmers have actually been able to triple their income; and it seems that cacao will be taking off as an export crop in eastern Congo. Already the first two containers, one from each of the areas where Theo is working, have arrived in Seattle.

Fortunately, Joe told me, cacao is a "safe" farming investment, because if a farm is attacked and pillaged by marauding rebels, they won't take the cacao pods. There is no use for them, because they are inedible unless they are processed and then sent to a cacao roaster, and rebels won't want to be burdened with all that work. So it is a highly favored crop for farmers who are seeking security for their income and families. Which is important in this volatile area of Africa.

Harvesting cacao pods in the eastern Democratic Republic of the Congo, where the cacao makes especially delectable chocolate. Cacao growing is considered a "safe" investment in this war-torn country because marauding militia passing through the area don't steal the pods—which are inedible until sent to a cocoa roaster for processing.
(CREDIT: EASTERN CONGO INITIATIVE)

Can We Feed the World Ethically?

Coffee and tea and chocolate have been important in my life, and I am deeply grateful to the leaves of *Camellia* and to the beans of *Coffea* and *Cacao*. And I find the changes that are beginning to impact the coffee, tea, and cacao industries inspiring. But we could (though I wouldn't like to!) live without them all. We must now ask whether similar sustainable farming methods can help to solve world hunger.

When the proponents of industrial and biotech agriculture are confronted with facts about the damaged land and the huge threats to human health, they invariably counter by telling us that large-scale industrial farming, especially with genetically modified crops, is the only way to produce enough food for our growing populations.

And this mind-set can result in some extraordinary reasoning—or lack of it. For example, the British government finally agreed to ban a certain pesticide when it was proved, beyond reasonable doubt, that it could cause cancer. Yet I heard a farmer, interviewed by the BBC, say that while he accepted that the product could cause cancer, it was important to use it in order to grow enough food to feed people.

Is it true? Must we continue to produce food that makes people sick in order to feed the world?

I recently read an article in the *Atlantic Monthly* by journalist Barry Estabrook. He was determined to find out whether it was true that we could only feed the world using our current industrial model for farming—the claim that has justified so much chemical poisoning and the zealous proliferation of GMOs. He couldn't find one scientific study to support this claim. But he did find numerous studies, including one conducted by that most conservative of bodies, the UN, that concluded that shifting our agriculture model to small-scale, sustainable farming is the *only* way we can successfully feed the world in the future.

The British Soil Association has conducted an exhaustive review of all the scientific literature—ninety-eight papers—published between 1999 and 2007 that addressed the question of whether or not organic agriculture could feed the world. And every one of these papers concluded that organic farming can, or at least has the potential, to feed the world's population. Yet still the powers that support *and benefit from* industrial agriculture continue to insist that their method is the only way to combat world hunger.

Perhaps the time has come when we should demand that the advocates of agribusiness prove to us that their model can feed a population of nine billion human beings. They will find it difficult, since after seventy-five years of their reckless experimenting they have so far failed. As I write this sentence, nearly one billion of the world's current seven billion people are still seriously undernourished. And the Union of Concerned Scientists in the United States reported that genetic engineering has not contributed to yield increase *in any crop*. Certainly not in the long run.

Thus it is encouraging to find that more and more businesses are not only doing things in an environmentally and socially responsible way, they are making it pay. Organic food is not a luxury, it is an investment in our own personal health, the health of the planet—and thus the health of future generations. So it is wonderful that the organic movement is growing.

Unfortunately, organically produced foods are often more expensive, but I find that if you pay more, you value the food more and waste less—and in the long run there will be a saving on doctor's bills. And unless GMOs are labeled, buying organic produce is one of the only ways to make a stand against the industry that creates them. The votes cast by shoppers in the developed countries will ultimately affect the practices of agriculture in the developing countries.

It is wonderful to hear of the growing popularity of sustainable, small-scale local agriculture. And it is inspiring to think of the number of family farmers who are holding out against agribusiness, surviving because of the support of their communities, the growing desire for organic food, and the growth of programs such as the Slow Food movement. Moreover, farmers' markets are flourishing and are becoming, among other things, gathering places for those who care about their food and the health of the planet, places where they can exchange views and support one another.

In the past two decades the Community Sponsored Agriculture (CSA) movement has become a popular way for consumers in the United States to buy local, seasonal food directly from farmers. The concept is simple: consumers pay the farmer in advance for a weekly share of his products—a box of seasonal vegetables and sometimes fruits, herbs, and cut flowers too. This is hugely beneficial to farmers who are trying to help communities to fight back against the agribusiness giants and take back some control over the quality and availability of their food. The government does not track CSAs, but

LocalHarvest, an Internet-based resource of local sustainable farms, has four thousand listed in its database. They say that in many places the demand for CSAs is greater than the supply, and this is encouraging more farmers to join in.

Of course, one of the best ways of ensuring that you are eating food free from harmful chemicals and GM plants is to grow your own.

Chapter 16

Growing Our Own Food

A proud Roots & Shoots member from the Tung Koon School in Sheung Shui, Hong Kong. This organic vegetable garden is situated in the middle of an inner-city school, surrounded by high-rise buildings and concrete. The Roots & Shoots leader told me that "before being involved with this garden, many of the students would not have gotten their hands dirty in the soil or even seen caterpillars and worms." (CREDIT: CHOW KAI-LEUNG)

I grew up reading about the vegetable garden of Beatrix Potter's crusty old gardener, Mr. McGregor, sworn enemy of Peter Rabbit, who, with his siblings, Flopsy, Mopsy, and Cottontail, was always crawling under the fence to steal carrots and lettuces—even though his poor father had been caught and cooked in a pie. Once, Peter almost met the same fate when he unexpectedly met the old man around the cucumber frame.

In England in the old days all the big country houses not only grew flowers in rich profusion, they also had extensive walled vegetable gardens. I remember going to stay for a weekend in one such place, and being amazed at the wealth of beans and peas, tomatoes, potatoes, cucumbers and marrows, and peach trees with their tortured, crucified branches spread out along the walls. There was a strong smell of horse manure mixed, interestingly, with that of mint and thyme and rosemary from the herb garden that was hiding away in a sheltered corner. Of course there had to be a number of gardeners to care for gardens of that sort. During World War II all the younger gardeners went off to fight for their country, and the older ones were on air-raid duty, so the flower gardens became invaded by weeds.

Only the vegetable gardens were saved—and often expanded, overflowing into some of the neglected flowerbeds. The reason for this is that everyone in England who had a garden was asked to help the war effort by creating a "Victory Garden," growing vegetables instead of flowers. This type of gardening was not only indirectly aiding the war effort but was considered a morale booster, as people on the home front felt they were making a contribution—"Digging for Victory."

Victory Gardens were also encouraged in the United States, Canada, Ireland—and Germany. Of course we wanted to do our bit, and my grandmother, Danny, planted runner beans and rows of lettuce and spinach, and we also had some gooseberry and raspberry bushes—but, as I have said, the soil in our garden was no good for most vegetables.

After the war Danny carried on with the garden. It was too much work for them alone, and an old gardener came on the weekends to help, mainly because he was devoted to Danny. The runner beans continued to thrive, but most of the vegetables were still unhappy when planted there. Judy's daughter, Pip, tried to grow turnips last year, and they were not much bigger than radishes when she finally released them from the inhospitable earth!

At the Birches most vegetables are not happy growing in the sandy soil, made acid by pine needles and rhododendrons. Pip, my sister Judy's daughter, tried to grow turnips one year—and this was as big as they would grow.
(CREDIT: JANE GOODALL)

A Kitchen-Garden Revolution

Many gardening experts believe that producing one's own food is the fastest-growing trend in American home gardening. I saw the results of the Garden Writers Association's "2011 Late Summer Gardening Trends Research Report." Their survey, representing at least a million US households, asked people with gardens to indicate which kind of gardening they were most interested in. Growing food was top for those questioned, with Earth-friendly gardening coming second. Next came native plants, and then organic gardening. I suspect that gardeners in Europe would also put food gardening high in their priorities. Growing vegetables among the flowers has always been part of European cottage gardening.

I also learned that about one million new food gardens were planted in 2010 in the United States, according to the National Gardening Association. That seems a lot until we learn that twenty million new gardens were planted in 1943 at the peak of the Victory Garden movement—when the US population was half what it is now.

Clearly the trend is growing, and more and more communities, especially in urban neighborhoods, are transforming land into viable food gardens. This rather rapidly increasing desire to reconnect with the earth, throughout at least parts of the developed world, has something to do, I suspect, with the fact that more and more people are realizing the extent to which so many of the vegetables and fruits we buy in grocery stores and supermarkets are contaminated by chemicals.

Only by growing our own food can we be certain it is pesticide- and GMO-free. It may not only be cheaper than buying from the grocery store, it may also save on doctor's bills in the future. And it tastes better, too!

There is another advantage: just as we grew food during my childhood to help the war against the evil of the Nazis, by growing our own food today we are fighting another kind of evil. We are beginning to stand up against the corporate/industrial agriculture giants that control so much of how our food is grown and distributed. It is a form of activism—doing our bit, along with the small family farms and organic farmers, to create an alternative to a system that is poisoning the world.

The New Urban Landscape—Food Gardens

Across the globe, from Russia to Argentina, from Cuba and Haiti to Tanzania, in almost every city, people are growing food. In some cases it is for pure pleasure, the joy of being connected to the land, of picking and eating a sun-ripened tomato, cooking your own runner beans. At other times it is for economic reasons. Or it may be because you are in need of spiritual healing. Urban food gardens are like the daisies that push through cracks in the sidewalk. They show the way of the future for cities where concrete mixes with compost and nourishing plants are as integral to the landscape as skyscrapers and parking lots.

And as more and more people move from the countryside to urban areas, so there is a greater need for real farming in the city, and the practice grows. In some cities you have to wait for two years or more to get a vacancy for a space in an allotment. The Urban Agriculture Network, founded by Jac Smit, collects information on what is going on, but there are many websites out there describing the various projects, large and small, on disused plots, roofs, and balconies and terraces.

*Members of the Lehae Youth Roots & Shoots group working on their "Food Garden" at the Lehae Primary School close to Soweto in South Africa. I was really impressed when I visited this project, now a 600-square-mile-plot providing vegetables for the school and needy families. The gardeners are (*left to right*) Sphiwe Genge, Steven Mabasa, and Lebo Mantsho. They told me their group planned to introduce home gardens in the community, and within the past couple of years they have created 50 small (20 x 13 foot) plots for the neediest of families, crèches (childcare centers), and the* goggos *(grannies).* (CREDIT: © THE JANE GOODALL INSTITUTE – SOUTH AFRICA / BY JULIET PRICE)

There are organizations helping refugees, unemployed inner-city youth, and bankrupt farmers who have been forced to move into the cities, to start growing some of their own food. As small projects grow, surplus food is sold in farmers' markets and the food security of an area is increased. Gradually, too, the need for trucking food in from faraway sources will decrease.

Of all these hundreds I have only been able to visit just a few—in the United Kingdom, America, Canada, China, Hong Kong, Singapore, Tanzania, and South Africa. I have met people who told me about wonderful projects, or read accounts that grabbed my attention. It is from that list that I have chosen the following ones to share.

"Urban knights" is new term to describe the people behind this exciting horticultural force in the world's cities. These commoner knights are helping to create food gardens in all sorts of places—from city rooftops to alleyways and balconies and tiny backyards. Susan McCoy, of the United States–based trend-spotting Garden Media Group, describes them as "the urban grit influence to protect the Earth's resources."

After reading about the wartime Victory Gardens, Taja Sevelle was inspired to start the Michigan-based project, "Urban Farming." It began in 2005 with three gardens and a pamphlet. Seven years later her organization has facilitated the planting of over 43,000 community gardens around the world. The goal is to create an abundance of food, especially for people in struggling communities, by planting, supporting, and encouraging gardens on all available unused land and space—including on a rooftop in the Bronx and helping a school in Los Angeles create an "edible wall." Sevelle hopes her project will create a "paradigm shift" and enable people of all economic means to have access to healthy food.

I have a most innovative and imaginative friend, Gary Zeller, who embodies the spirit of an urban knight. Every time I meet him, he has some new invention to show me, and always it is something that will help us reuse, reduce waste, and live in greater harmony with nature. One of his latest, and most delightful, is the "Garden Up" tower. "It's perfect," he told me, "for the urban gardeners who sometimes only have a window seat or balcony to work with." He has received requests for information about these vertical gardens from Jordan and many other countries where people are desperate for pesticide-free, locally grown produce that uses very little water.

Commercial Farming in the City

Meanwhile, there is increasing understanding among city planners that food gardens are helpful to the city in many ways. They contribute to improved health and economic stability, adding a rustic element that is attractive to so many people—and they reduce crime.

In light of this, city planners across America are changing zoning regulations to encourage urban farms, run by private companies, to supply the demand for locally grown and organic food. Let me share a few examples.

In Cedar Rapids, Iowa, an NGO is working with city planners to build a 2.5-acre urban farm on vacant lots in an area devastated by the 2008 flooding. At present most food must be trucked in from up to one thousand miles away. In Columbia, Missouri, an enterprising farmer has developed a thirteen-acre urban farm and is now allowed, by the city, to sell his produce. In Boise, Idaho, new regulations have been created that encourage the growing of food in the city in order to help the tough economy. Salt Lake City has voted to allow the sale of food without a business license, and has eased rules prohibiting greenhouses and plastic hoop houses in the city.

I just learned about a project called Growing Power, in Chicago, which was launched in 2002 with the aim of bringing the city's various small and dispersed farming projects together and integrating them with other food-related activities. This way the wider issues of city food security and nutritional, ecological, and public health could be tackled. There are two farms (2.5 acres and 0.5 acre, respectively) on the South Side, a twenty-thousand-square-foot lakefront area in the heart of downtown Chicago and, most recently, a seven-acre site in the Bridgeport neighborhood. From its office, Growing Power addresses nutritional, ecological, and public health problems and, best of all, provides education in farming methods and training for jobs. Many citizens volunteer in these programs.

And now I must discuss the extraordinary events that are taking place in Detroit. It was one of the places where I gave a lecture a few years ago, and even though I was only there for a day, I noticed, from the taxis that took me to and fro from hotel to lecture venue, that many stores were boarded up, the train station was closed, and the whole place seemed run-down and dejected. The recession had hit hard and many people had left, my cabdriver said. And when a house was damaged, he told me, it was torn down.

I was soon on my way to the next city and the next lecture, and thought no more about Detroit. Until very recently when I heard about the exciting developments that were taking place because a group of citizens, whose unofficial meeting place was a coffee shop, began to make new plans for their city. And growing food was at the heart of these plans.

The very fact that there are so many vacant plots in Detroit means that urban farming and gardening can truly thrive. The chairman of Detroit Food Policy knows that farming empowers people as well as providing much-needed fresh and local food, and today urban farming is driving the city's economy.

Townspeople can "adopt a lot" for free—and there is so much scope, so much space. One young man has eight plots already and is planning to get three more, and he is training young people to work on his farm. In one neighborhood where thirty houses were torn down, leaving just three standing, people are growing vegetables, fruit orchards, and flowers, and one of the remaining houses is being turned into a community center. In this new Detroit, farming is unifying the community, drawing African Americans, Asians, and whites together, all growing food to contribute to their future. Citizens ages ten to sixty are volunteering, giving their time to the greening of their city. There are gardens everywhere. And the city has plans for greening one area of three hundred acres that will include tree farms and the restoration of a forest.

I read about one enthusiastic citizen, Jackie Victor, who told a reporter, "Imagine a city rebuilt block by block, with a gorgeous riverfront, world-class museums, and fantastic local food. Everyone who wants one has a quarter-acre garden and every kid lives within bike distance of a farm."

Community Harvests

As I have said, the urban farming revolution is happening all over the world. In April 2007 I was invited to participate in the official opening of the Bukit Panjang Community Garden, a four-thousand-square-foot plot close to one of the universities in Singapore. Once, the whole area had been agricultural land, but as part of the plans for city development the farmers had been moved from their land and put into apartment flats. There they were not happy.

They missed the land, I was told, and many of them began planting vegetables in any vacant spaces they could find—such as underneath the new expressway. The same sort of thing was happening in other parts of the island nation, and the government had decided, in 2005, that allowing them access to vegetable plots in assigned areas would be better. Especially if they could be persuaded to work together rather than in "individual secretive locations." And so Community in Bloom, a national garden movement, was launched "to foster a gardening culture in Singapore." The community garden I was visiting is one of some four hundred that have been established on residential estates, schools, hospitals, and commercial places, such as the rooftop herb garden of the Fairmont Hotel.

It was a sunny day. I met some of the old residents. Someone gave me one of the traditional straw hats. I wandered through the area—a typical allotment, each gardener with his or her plot where they were growing the vegetables of their choice. But Allan Lim, chief executive of Alpha Biofuels, and fourth-generation farmer Kenny Eng, hope that they can persuade the residents to join ComCop, a project they have devised to try to increase productivity of the area through cooperative farming in an environmentally friendly way. Both Allan and Kenny are young men, both were bubbling over with enthusiasm. They took me to see the communal herb garden that stands outside the enclosed gardens, where any member of the apartment blocks is free to take the produce—the resident troop of rhesus monkeys fortunately do not seem to care for dill, mint, and other herbs planted there.

Allan and Kenny have persuaded Starbucks Coffee Company and the downtown microbrewery Brewerkz to donate and deliver their waste products for compost. Indeed, it would be hard to refuse them.

The government is behind ComCop—officially it was announced as a project designed to create "a meeting place for residents to interact and elderly residents to get some exercise while gardening." But there is another reason—to encourage urban farming as an economically and environmentally sustainable source of food throughout the island. If everyone grew at least *some* tomatoes (or any other crop) over and above what they themselves need, the community as a whole could make money by selling their combined tomato harvest. This is exactly what the coffee farmers are doing around Gombe, in Tanzania.

Food Gardens for Refugees in Tanzania

When JGI started our youth program in Lugufu, the big Congolese refugee camp in Tanzania, one of the first projects that were introduced was a vegetable garden. Our goal was to try to involve the young people in activities that would bring meaning into their lives, for so often there is a dearth of hope in the camps.

Producing one's own food is a great tonic, to watch it grow, then harvest and cook it—and finally eat it. It provides exercise, knowledge, and skill, and all this improves self-confidence and self-esteem. Over time, the gardens prospered. Chickens, from our chicken-incubation project, flew over the fence, fertilized the ground, and consumed insect pests. A little Congolese boy of about twelve showed me around when I first visited, so proud of the beans, peas, tomatoes, and maize that his group was growing.

Many of the elder refugees were delighted with our food-growing projects and were eager to share their knowledge. During one of my visits an old farmer from Congo was demonstrating, to our Roots & Shoots group, how you could make insecticide from papaya (pawpaw) leaves. He explained that you cut them small, added some salt, and boiled them. The residual liquid made a strong insecticide that could be used, at different strengths, for different kinds of pests. When the refugees were forced back to the DRC, our groups took with them not only their chickens but also seeds from their vegetable gardens. That was their one comfort as they faced an uncertain future.

Refugees in America

Conditions were not easy in Lugufu for the Congolese refugees, but at least they were still in Africa and many of them could speak to each other in Kiswahili. Nor are the foods very different in Tanzania from what is grown on the other side of the lake in the eastern part of the DRC.

It can be very much harder for people who have been forced to leave their countries and who end up in a very different part of the world. Some refugees, from many parts of the world, have ended up in the City Heights neighborhood of San Diego. Here you will find people from many countries, including Somalis, Cambodians, Liberians, Congolese, and Latinos from Central and South America. There are Burundian mothers with babies on their backs and produce on their heads, Latino men with wide hats and chaps, Muslims, and Christians.

Half the residents of the City Heights community lived at or below the federal poverty line when they first arrived. But it was not only poverty that made them so often unhappy. They were housed in apartments, which was hard for those who came from rural areas—very different from the openness of village life. And they were homesick for the traditional foods of their homeland. Most could not afford fruit and vegetables, and gave them up for cheap fast food.

One day, in 2006, a conversation took place between a Somali Bantu refugee, Bilali Muya, and a group of people from the International Rescue Committee, an organization that helps refugees. It would lead to a project that provided new hope and new life to hundreds of refugees. Muya talked with passion about the need his people felt to grow their own food. Together they conceived of the idea of an urban farm. Needing more support, they reached out to the Cambodians, who had arrived in numbers in the 1980s, escaping the Khmer Rouge. One of them, Bob Ou, was very excited by this, and a search began for suitable land.

Eventually the perfect place was found, a vacant lot of 2.3 acres, and after two years of negotiations with the city, permission was finally given. During this time Muya and Ou frequently met at meetings, but although each of them was working to raise money and organize their communities, they had never spoken to each other. However, when the New Roots Community Farm opened, Ou and Muya had neighboring plots, and as the weeks went by, a friendship developed. As they worked among their tomatoes and beans and cabbages, they sometimes shared stories about the violence that had forced them to leave home, the terrible conditions in their refugee camps, the disappointments they had faced on arriving in the United States of America.

*In San Diego refugees from many countries have created the New Roots Community Farm where they can grow many of the foods that they grew back home. Bob Ou (*left*), a refugee from Cambodia, and Bilali Muya from Somalia are leaders in this venture. As they worked on their plots they gradually struck up a close friendship.* (CREDIT: ALLEN J. SCHABEN, COPYRIGHT 2013, LOS ANGELES TIMES. REPRINTED WITH PERMISSION)

Now both men are leaders in their communities and both, of course, are passionate about the farm, which enables eighty-five families from twelve countries to grow food—right there in the heart of the city. Many of them were farmers before they fled, and the work helps to reconnect them with the land, feed their families, and, like Ou and Muya, become friends. Food surplus to their wants is sold each Saturday in the City Heights farmers' market, which has become a meeting place in the heart of the community.

New Roots Community Garden in City Heights, San Diego, is one of about fifty such community farms for refugees that are spreading across the United States. Courses are offered in farming techniques suited to the new environment in which they find themselves. Some of these farms are very successful: Hmong Min and Lao refugees who settled in Fresno County, California, in the late seventies are now growing and selling Asian crops. At least 1,300 farmers are taking part in this program, and they can earn from $5,000 to as much as $50,000 per year. Some refugees have made the leap from working in community gardens to their own independent farms.

Saving Our Food by Saving Our Seeds

Here is another homegrown movement that is a direct way of fighting back against the industrial control of our food supply—saving your heirloom seeds. An heirloom plant is a cultivar that was commonly grown in a bygone era, one that has been pollinated naturally—by insects, birds, and the wind—and that is not used in modern intensive agriculture. Many have been grown from seeds handed down, generation after generation, through a family or community for hundreds of years, although not all have such an ancient lineage.

It was after World War II that so many heirloom seeds began to disappear, and this was the same point at which agriculture became more centralized and big companies began advertising commercially packaged seeds that often consisted of hybrids. This was also when markets were being developed by the larger corporations to make the most profit and as quickly as possible.

Fortunately many individuals and organizations are working to preserve, collect, grow, and distribute heirloom seeds. The largest in the United States is Seed Savers Exchange in Decorah, Iowa, founded in 1975. Each year they publish a book with the names and addresses of their growing membership (more than nine hundred in 2012) along with lists of some six thousand heirloom vegetable and heritage fruit varieties that they are offering to gardeners. And there are countless other smaller organizations throughout North America and around the globe.

Another, in Canada, is the Salt Spring Seed and Plant Sanctuary. It has built up a large, properly stored collection of most local food and herb seeds, comprising currently some nine hundred mostly heirloom varieties in their living gene bank. These seeds are distributed to many custodians across Canada, who test the performance of different varieties in different parts of the country.

Communing with Nature's Bounty

Just as people can share seeds, so too can we share nature's bounty with one another. As children we used to go to Richmond Hill Church—a big and very beautiful church in Bournemouth, with a tall spire, glorious stained-glass windows, and a picture over the altar that I loved of the Good Shepherd holding the lost sheep under His arm and a shepherd's crook in the other hand. As I relive the occasion in my mind, He seems to be smiling down on us as we gathered to celebrate Harvest Festival.

Almost everyone has brought something from their garden or from a nearby farm. I begged some potatoes from the farm where I had helped to dig them from the ground. There are baskets and baskets of large polished tomatoes, and cucumbers, radishes and cabbages, and a couple of giant squashes. And what a bounty of apples and pears, plums and gooseberries. There are two sheaves of golden corn propped up at the base of the pulpit, and autumn flowers are everywhere, ranging from roses and dahlias in elegant vases to bunches of wildflowers in jam jars picked by Judy and me!

All of the lessons, hymns, and the sermon celebrate and give thanks for the bounty of nature.

It is sad, but true, that today people seldom give thanks for their food. Some families still say grace, but many families no longer even sit around the same table to eat and talk in companionship. How often do we thank nature, think of the plants that have provided our food, or offer gratitude to their plant spirits? How often do we even think of the people who grew and harvested them?

Some time ago I was a participant in a workshop organized by Satish Kumar, a follower of the teachings of Gandhi and editor of *Resurgence* magazine, which publishes articles about the environment and sustainability. Afterward we moved into a simple room that opens onto a small garden, shaded by plane trees. It was late summer, and the evening sun lit up an amazing array of food that awaited us on the rough wooden table. It was all, of course, vegan and organic and homegrown.

It was a veritable feast, and not only for the eating. The colors were a feast for the eyes: crisp lettuce leaves and spinach and cucumbers, different shades of green, in giant salad bowls, with splashes of red radishes and small orange-red tomatoes and sliced peppers. Apples, red and green and yellow, pale-golden brown pears, dark-purple plums and grapes, and almost-black avocadoes.

Now I close my eyes (lucky I learned touch-typing!) and I am smelling the amazing fragrance; there is parsley, the tang of the stems to which some of the tomatoes are attached, the mint leaves that are being crushed and mixed into a fruit punch, and over all the scent of roses and honeysuckle wafting in from outside.

Then comes the tasting, the different flavors—I always like to keep the different tastes separate—to enjoy the fullness of each one, so special. There is indeed much to enjoy, for people have worked hard to cook their special dishes in order to honor Satish and his guests.

And tonight we experience not only the delicious tastes but a very rare opportunity to become familiar with all the different textures, for we eat just as a huge percentage of people around the world eat, using our fingers only as we put the food onto plates made of recycled cornstarch. And so we *feel* the food with our fingers, and the crunchiness or smoothness in our mouths, and the sliding down into our stomachs. (I am sure, though, that we shall not feel the process of digesting such wholesome, healthy food!)

But before we load our plates and find a chair, we make a circle around the table, and Satish bids us to hold hands while he gives thanks for the food and thanks to the Great Spiritual Power that has provided for us, and for the companionship we enjoy. And he gives thanks to Mother Nature, too. He is well qualified for this prayer, for he was a Jain monk before he realized he needed to be out in the world to spread Gandhi's teachings.

Many people have become separated from their food and from the beingness of plants in our modern, high-speed materialistic society, but it is my belief that as more and more of us turn to growing our own food and harvesting it for our own table, some of the old connectedness with the plant world is returning to our lives.

Indeed, I pray that this is true, for so many of the world's plants are endangered and desperately needing all the help we can give them. Fortunately there are those who do care, very much, and who are working passionately to save them.

Chapter 17

Saving Forests

Richard St. Barbe Baker (1889–1982) was one of the earliest foresters to realize the terrible harm that was being done to the planet through deforestation. He saved and restored forests all over the world, including in many parts of Africa. It's estimated that at least 26 trillion *trees were planted during his lifetime by organizations he founded or advised.*
(CREDIT: BARRIE OLDFIELD)

When I arrived at Gombe in 1960, the forests, home to the chimpanzees, stretched for miles to the north, south, and east of the park (the west is bounded by Lake Tanganyika.) But by the early 1990s, when I flew over Gombe and the surrounding area in a small plane, I realized with dismay that outside the tiny, thirty-square-mile park virtually *all* the trees had gone. Only in the really steep-sided ravines, where even the most desperate people could not farm, could I see a few small forest remnants. Chimpanzees and most other animals bigger than a mongoose had gone. Humans were struggling to survive on the overfarmed, eroded soils. It was clear that there were more people settled there than the land could support, people too poor to buy food elsewhere, cutting down the last of the forest in their desperate struggle to grow crops to feed themselves and their families.

The Gombe forest is just one among thousands worldwide that survive as fragments, cut off from other forests or fragments of forests by human activities. Nature's bounty is depleted as a result of poverty, on the one hand, and, on the other, the unsustainable lifestyle of a growing number of the elite and the middle class. It is the consumer-driven, materialistic lifestyle, exported from the West to the developing nations, that creates the market for products from the forests and that encourages our greedy desire for more and more stuff that only too often we don't really need. As Gandhi famously said, "Nature can supply human need, but not human greed."

Huge areas of forest are being destroyed or degraded by the extraction of timber, minerals, and oil; by monoculture tree plantations, ranching, and farming; and by commercial developments. The list is long, and we are shocked when we hear of the number of animals and plants that become locally or totally extinct each week, the spread of the deserts, the shrinking supplies of freshwater. It strikes terror—and anger—into the hearts of all of us who care about the natural world and the future of our children. Even "protected" forests are often at risk.

In fact, it is all so grim that some people who start off fighting to save forests, or a particular piece of forest, simply become too depressed to carry on. While I can well understand the depression, we must not, must not, must not give up. Instead, we have to fight harder and support the efforts of those who are working tirelessly, from various perspectives, to save what is left.

Of course the destruction of our forests is not a new phenomenon. Since the dawn of history, people through the ages have sought wood for building cities and warships, and cut down forests to have access to the fertile forest soils for growing crops.

It is not my intent to delve deeply into these stories of past destruction but simply to point out that the onslaught of "man" against "tree" is as old as the hills. Back in 1875 that remarkable priest Père Armand David recorded what was going on in China. "From one year's end to another," he wrote, "one hears the hatchet and the axe cutting the most beautiful trees. The destruction of these primitive forests, of which there are only fragments in all of China, progresses with unfortunate speed. They will never be replaced. With the great trees will disappear a multitude of shrubs which cannot survive except in their shade; also all the animals small and large which need the forest in order to live and perpetrate their species."

He went on to write, "It is unbelievable that The Creator could have placed so many diverse organisms on the Earth, each one so admirable in its sphere, so perfect in its role, only to permit man, his masterpiece, to destroy them forever."

About the same time the redoubtable plant hunter E. H. "Chinese" Wilson, when collecting in Japan, came upon the stump of a huge yakusugi cedar that had been felled in 1586, when it was estimated to be over three thousand years old. They measured the tree that had been killed—the circumference of the base was 32 meters (104.9 feet), and the stump, at waist height, was 4.39 meters (14.4 feet) across. The stump was hollow, and men could stand inside it. When I read about the felled giant, I felt a surge of anger. Was not the tree, quite as much as the *Homo sapiens* who destroyed it, a "masterpiece of the Creator"?

Another massacre took place in the ancient redwood and Douglas fir forests along the west coast of the United States. I had firsthand experience of the devastation that was wrought, and that is still continuing today, when Mike Fay invited me to join him and environmental activist Lindsey Holm for two days during their walk through the past range of these forests. It was truly a marathon undertaking—they told me the forests had once covered some two million acres (5,033 square miles) along America's west coast. Heavy logging began in 1880 after a gold rush brought countless people to the region who, when gold was not found in great quantities, turned to exploiting the forests for the rapid development of San Francisco and other cities.

Just being in the forest with those giant trees, and with the stumps of so many that had been felled, was humbling. I felt I was in the presence of an ancient wisdom. Sometimes I sensed a sadness, as though the trees were dreaming of times past—when the world was young, before the white man invaded and raped their forest; at other times I sensed an anger because of all the terrible destruction. But most strongly of all I sensed a vast endurance.

Inexorably, century after century, the vandalism of the world's forests has continued. In 2002 I attended the fiftieth-anniversary meeting of the International Tropical Hardwood Association in Rome. One speaker, reviewing the history of the organization, described how, after World War II, it was clear that the European forests could not provide enough timber to rebuild the cities and towns destroyed by the years of bombing. And so, he said, the European timber companies got together and planned how they would divide up the forests of Asia, South America, and Africa so that they would all have access to the necessary resources.

I listened with mounting horror to this account of premeditated plunder—it was a terrifying new chapter in the sorry litany of rich nations stealing the natural resources from other parts of the world. An early indication of the dark side of globalization, when giant and ruthless multinational companies would gradually seize ever-greater control over governments, economies, natural resources, small businesses—and lives. Moreover, our human populations are growing everywhere, so that forests are increasingly cut down to provide fertile soil for growing crops and feeding livestock, and for space to live. So while it is true that humans have been exploiting forests for hundreds of years, the situation is now infinitely more challenging. We must strive, on the one hand, to alleviate poverty and help billions of peasants to find environmentally sustainable lifestyles, and, on the other hand, we must encourage the growing well-to-do societies to do well with less, for it is this "consumer society," with its desire for ever more "stuff," that gives such power to the big corporations.

And make no mistake, this is the hardest battle—fighting vested business interests, powerful and unscrupulous multinationals, and corruption.

Today, a huge threat for any tropical forest that is not fully protected is China's voracious appetite for timber for building materials to feed her rapidly growing economy. And because of the migration of rural populations seeking new livelihoods in urban areas—said to be the greatest migration in human history (four hundred new cities need to be built!) China is buying timber (and mineral) concessions in Asia, Africa, Latin America, Canada—wherever forests have been left standing. Western countries did exactly the same thing—but China is very much larger.

Of course, China is not alone. The Canadian government is allowing the exploitation of the tar sands in Alberta that is leading to the desecration of thousands of square miles of pristine forests. American agribusiness is persuading African governments, with false promises of the wealth it will bring, to lease (or sell) hundreds of square miles of their precious rain forests for the growing of monocrops or biofuel. And on and on.

Let me give just a few examples of the massive scale of some of the operations that are destroying our forests that must be tackled—and somehow stopped. Or that must be conducted in a much, much more responsible and sustainable way.

The Problem with Tree Plantations for Our Paper and Timber

Countless old-growth forests have been destroyed to make way for industrial plantations, especially for growing pines, firs, eucalyptus, and teak. Plantation wood is sold for timber. It is also destined to become wood pulp for paper. This book is written on paper, and the better it sells, the more paper it will use—which is why we insisted it be printed on recycled paper. It is a fact that the world uses an enormous amount of paper. How many pause to think where this paper comes from? Most of it started as trees that we cut down and ground into pulp. Incalculable damage to forests around the world is caused by our use of paper.

Most people assume that although using old-growth forests is clearly a bad thing, if trees are specially grown for paper, it should be okay. In some cases this is undoubtedly true, but sadly this is often not the case. A group of NGOs, including WWF and Greenpeace, along with local groups, carried out case studies in seven countries to document the negative environmental impact of industrial tree plantations for pulpwood. They found in many cases that natural forests had been destroyed and replaced with monocultures of fast-growing species that, only too often, needed large amounts of water. This had caused streams and rivers to dry up.

Despite promises by the companies involved, rural poverty had not been alleviated but had actually increased, and far fewer jobs had been created than the villagers had been led to expect. Moreover, the paper mills built to process the wood not only used a great deal of energy, they were also very polluting. (I know, from driving past a paper mill in Maine in the United States that the smell is truly terrible: I asked a local how he could stand it and he replied, "We tolerate it because it is the smell of money"!)

In all seven countries the investigators found that the introduction of pulpwood plantations had led to protests (sometimes violent ones) from local communities. The Landless Peasants' Movement, in Brazil—the largest land-rights movement in the world—has repeatedly targeted pulpwood plantations.

One company in particular has caused enormous environmental and social damage: Asia Pulp & Paper (APP), part of the giant Sinar Mas Group (a Chinese/Indonesian conglomerate). It has been a focus of environmental and human-rights groups for years, and George Monbiot, writing in the *Guardian* newspaper (2011), suggests that it is one of the most destructive companies on the planet.

The Hidden Cost of Oil

Then there are the often rapacious operations of the petrochemical companies. I learned a little bit about the situation during a visit to Ecuador a few years ago. Groups of indigenous people were uniting as they tried desperately to prevent oil companies from operating in their ancestral lands. Unless there was some miracle, I was told, their rain forests would be invaded and many of them would be forced to leave.

I met with several tribal leaders of the Achuar and Shuar people, and they told me of past persecution and present fears for their future. I was so upset and moved by their story, I agreed to join them for a press conference, during which we made a passionate plea to protect the forest and its indigenous people. But the hold of the petrochemical companies over the government was strong—and the explorations and destruction began anyway.

Our thirst for oil in the developed world is leading to untold destruction in the developing countries. Everyone knows what this has meant for the Middle East, the US Gulf, and Alaska—these things are always discussed on TV. But few people think about the devastation that is ongoing in Africa—except, perhaps, Shell's operations in Nigeria, which has received a great deal of coverage.

In the early 1990s I flew in a small plane over parts of the Republic of the Congo (Congo-Brazzaville), Gabon, and Angola. We flew quite low over the rain forest canopy and I was shown some of the concessions made by the governments of those countries to different petroleum companies, including Shell, BP, and Elf. I was horrified by the devastation that had been inflicted on the environment: the straight paths that had been slashed through the green virgin forest for seismic-drilling operations, and in one place a huge treeless clearing that had been hacked out of the forest where the workers of one of the companies were based. It showed a complete lack of respect for the integrity of the forest and its people.

Those of us who know what is going on are deeply concerned that oil deposits have been discovered in the so-far-unspoiled Albertine Rift area of Uganda where JGI is working to protect chimpanzees and their forests.

Nor should we forget the monstrous threat created by the runaway desire to grow more and more crops for biofuel. Too many people believe biofuel is the answer to our energy needs. I just wish there was more TV coverage of the vast areas of African forest that have been destroyed in order to grow monoculture crops to be transformed into energy so that Ms. X can drive her car to the supermarket every time she forgets a packet of potato crisps rather than walk or take a bus, or Mr. Y wants a new, fast gas-guzzling car to impress his new girlfriend.

More and more Africans are protesting, at the local level, as they begin to understand how their land is being stolen for profit—and sometimes demonstrations can pay off. When President Museveni of Uganda approved the clear-cutting of a forest block for conversion to sugarcane for biofuel, he was forced to cancel the deal when the citizens of Kampala took to the streets to protest. It was a protected forest and, they argued, it was protected for the good of the people of Uganda.

Forests and Food

I've already talked about the shocking impact of industrial farming in forested areas around the world. Here let me just mention the consequences of the desire of more and more people to eat more and more meat. Millions of acres of forest in many parts of the world are destroyed each year just to provide grazing or to grow corn for feeding cattle or other livestock.

I have seen this devastation with my own eyes in parts of Africa and Central America. It is just one more example of short-term thinking, illustrating the unscrupulous dealings of those who see the chance of making a quick buck. Not only will undisturbed forests continue to provide medicines and food for generations to come but, as we shall discuss, they also play a vital role in regulating global climate.

Another threat to many forest ecosystems is the bush-meat trade—the *commercial* hunting of wild animals for food. In a number of forests in the Congo Basin this trade has boomed, in part due to the presence of logging companies, since even if the loggers strictly follow the prescribed code of conduct, they nevertheless make roads deep into the heart of the forest.

Hunters follow the roads, often riding on the logging trucks, camp at the end of the road, and shoot everything edible. This slaughter, so different from the subsistence hunting that has been a way of life for forest people for centuries, is unsustainable. Truckloads of smoked meat from elephants, apes, monkeys, antelopes, pigs—and in fact any creature that could be sold in the markets or sent overseas—are being taken out of the forests.

And when the balance of an ecosystem is upset like this, things begin to go wrong, since all life-forms are interdependent in ways we are only just beginning to understand. In Africa and Southeast Asia, the great apes, along with many other mammals and birds, play a critical role in dispersing seeds. Recently it's been determined that there are fewer seedlings in forests where there has been a lot of hunting, especially where primate numbers have been greatly reduced.

In other words, to ensure the health and long-term survival of a natural forest, we must preserve the whole complex mix of animal and plant species in the ecosystem. So even if a timber company practices "sustainable" logging—taking out only trees above a certain size and then moving on to a new concession, leaving the area to regenerate over the next twenty or more years—if animals are being slaughtered indiscriminately, the forest will become increasingly unhealthy.

Illegal Logging

Toward the end of the 1990s I spent a few days visiting Birute Galdikas in the forests of Kalimantan National Park in Indonesia. We followed a river that wound through the trees, and from our small boat I saw a wild orangutan for the first time, and an old male proboscis monkey looking down at me over that long bulbous nose that makes this species one of the most extraordinary of all the monkeys. It is a wonderful rain forest—an area of great biodiversity. But everywhere I heard stories of the illegal logging that was going on—even within the park. And the river that we followed to reach the orangutan camp was sometimes all but impassable because of the sheer volume of illegally logged tree trunks that were being floated out of the park. And now the forests of Indonesia have also been harmed by raging fires, often lit to clear huge areas for palm oil plantations—which are all too often used for biofuel. Because of all this, the orangutans are being driven to extinction.

Warriors Fighting for the Forests

I remember hearing, in 1972, about a group of women in India who were desperate to save the forest, on which they depended for their livelihood, from being cut down. So they went and joined hands around some of the trees. I was inspired by the story, and though I didn't know much about it, I talked about these women during some of the lectures I was giving while teaching at Stanford University.

Since then I've learned more about it. That first spontaneous action was initiated by two village women, Dhoom Singh Negi and Bachni Devi, and involved about twenty others whom they persuaded to join them. Gradually more people took part, and it led to what became known as the Chipko movement. *Chipko* means "embrace," and its philosophy was rooted in satyagraha, the form of nonviolent protest policy practiced by Gandhi during his successful campaign to force the British to leave India.

News of that first protest spread, and soon there were hundreds of decentralized and locally autonomous initiatives, led mostly by village women. Some men also became involved, and one of them, Sunderlal Bahuguna, played a major role in the campaign. It was his personal appeal to Mrs. Indira Gandhi, then prime minister, which led to a major victory—the 1980 green-felling ban. This prohibited all cutting down of trees for fifteen years throughout the Kumaon

Himalaya in Uttar Pradesh. Bahuguna was instrumental, too, in spreading the message to the villages he passed through during his extraordinary five-thousand-kilometer (over three thousand miles) walk across the Himalayas in the early 1980s. Eventually the Chipko movement spread throughout India and led to a ban on clear-cutting also in the Western Ghats and the Vindhyas. What a triumph.

It is clear that there is something about ancient trees that rouses deep passions in those who care. And this is fortunate, because some of these people then dedicate their lives to protecting the forests and the humans and other animals who live in them. They are many, but some stand out because of their passion, their courage—and their persistence.

Richard St. Barbe Baker (1889–1982) was, without doubt, one of the greatest advocates for the protection and restoration of forests ever. His love for trees began when he was a small child growing up near a pine-and-beech forest in Hampshire—I described the special childhood relationship he developed with a beech tree in chapter 3. After serving in World War I he became a forester, and for the rest of his life worked to help protect forests around the globe, starting in Kenya, and then working in Tanzania and Ghana. He also helped reforestation efforts in all the countries bordering the Sahara. And he extended his efforts to parts of the Middle East, Europe, North America, Australia, and New Zealand. It is estimated that during his lifetime at least twenty-six trillion trees were planted by organizations he started or advised and assisted. He himself planted his last tree—in Canada—when he was ninety-seven years old, just days before his death. The NGO he started, the International Tree Foundation, has programs in many countries around the world. An amazing man with an amazing life.

John Seed, a real warrior of the forest, fights in a different way. He became one of the first Westerners to take direct action against the timber industry, starting in his native Australia, but subsequently initiating and assisting campaigns in many parts of the world. He is one of the more inspirational and successful people in the forest-conservation scene—as a result of his interventions, hundreds of thousands of square miles of rain forest have been protected around the world. In June 2011 I was lucky enough to spend a few hours with this amazing man. We walked along the tamed beach of a Sydney marina, then climbed just up off the path and sat on the grass under a tree overlooking the water. And talked. I could have listened to his stories for days. Tales of his hippie youth, when he first began his tireless efforts to save the rain forests of the world, tales of the many extraordinary experiences that have enriched his life—and ours—since.

His hair is gray now, but he radiates peaceful vitality and quiet strength. During his years working for the trees he has clearly absorbed something of their stoic endurance.

John began life as a sculptor in metal, taking steel from metal stamping machines and transforming it into a "spiritual cornucopia of organic shapes." In his old hippie days he moved into a commune,

Forest warrior John Seed is one of the first Westerners to take direct action against the timber industry. He has saved huge areas of rain forest in many parts of the world. (CREDIT: TRISH ROBERTSON)

thinking he would organize meditation retreats and grow organic food. Then one day a timber company moved in and started logging the rain forest next door. The chainsaws were so loud, he told me, that he couldn't meditate anymore—and that spurred him to take action.

In 1979 John joined one of the first groups of idealistic Westerners determined to actually *do* something to try to prevent the destruction of a forest. They followed Gandhi's philosophy of nonviolence, putting themselves in the path of bulldozers that were approaching to fell trees, or actually climbing into the trees themselves. Tactics very familiar today—though at that time nothing like this had ever been done to protect a forest.

The loggers still managed to cut down some trees, but were nonetheless hindered in many ways, and police were sent in to arrest the protesters. First they had to get them out of the trees. TV crews followed both sides, and there was growing sympathy for the activists among the general public. When the Australian premier finally called for a suspension of logging, it was a pivotal moment for the environmental movement in both Australia and the world. Known as the Terania Creek Campaign, it achieved international prominence.

For the next two years there were further successful direct actions on behalf of the subtropical rain forests of New South Wales. Then John turned his attention to the temperate rain forests of Tasmania—it was easy to get the attention of the media at that time, and newspapers ran photos of people chaining themselves to bulldozers or climbing up the trees that were in their path. But gradually the public lost interest in these images—or, as John puts it, "society developed antibodies" against such actions. Which meant that when the protesters were delaying the building of a road in the far north of Queensland that would give loggers access to the pristine tropical forests at Cape Tribulation, the media was no longer interested. John remembers "calling a newspaper and being told 'ring us back when there's some blood.'"

Still, they managed to stop the road building until the rainy season prevented further work. And then, in John's words:

"The following year, while waiting for the road builders to arrive, we found a place where there was only a narrow space between the mountainside and the ocean, and here we dug holes in the ground and when the bulldozers arrived, people buried themselves up to the neck in the path of the machinery so that they had either to be dug up or crushed, there was no way to get around them.

"At first the police used shovels to try and dig people out but eventually called in a backhoe. Pictures of these huge metal buckets digging inches from protestors faces when they could not even protect their heads from flying rocks, gave us the image that we needed—a nonviolent equivalent of "blood," and it was these images at the top of the news around the country that finally put the issue into the national spotlight and led to the protection of hundreds of thousands of hectares of tropical rain forests as World Heritage national parks."

Thanks to John's tireless efforts, large areas of forest have been protected also in Papua New Guinea, Ecuador, and India. His Rainforest Information Centre in Australia, launched in 1981, was the first organization in the world with the mission of rain forest protection. The US Rainforest Action Network was the second, and he has started many similar organizations in different parts of the world since. He has worked to provide sustainable development projects for indigenous forest dwellers tied to the protection of their forests.

Knowing how desperately important it is to reach the minds and hearts of as many people as possible, John began to take his "Forest Roadshow" from country to country, showing the films he has worked on, making CDs of his songs, and giving talks. He is now deeply involved in helping people to understand the importance of climate change. In my mind he is one of the greatest heroes alive today. His efforts have saved hundreds of thousands of hectares of forest.

At about the same time as John began his work in Australia, another defender of trees was tackling the shocking deforestation in Kenya. Professor Wangari Muta Maathai—what an extraordinary woman: dynamic, inspirational, and enormously courageous. She was born in a small village in Kenya, got a scholarship to study in the United States, and was the first woman from East Africa to get a PhD. She became involved with environmental and women's issues on her return to Kenya, and in the mid-1970s, which is when I first met her in Kenya, she planted her first tree nursery. This led to her famous Green Belt Movement to combat deforestation, the water crisis, desertification, and rural hunger.

She began traveling around the country and encouraging rural women to plant indigenous trees from seeds they collected in the forest.

Wangari Muta Maathai (1940–2011), founder of the famous Green Belt Movement. Despite being beaten and arrested for her efforts to combat deforestation in Kenya, she never gave up. Eventually her movement led to the planting of hundreds of thousands of trees around urban areas in many parts of Africa. (CREDIT: JEFF HOROWITZ)

She gave workshops on the importance of protecting and restoring watersheds and riverbanks. She found funds to give the women a very tiny stipend for each seedling that was planted out, and even managed to give a little money to husbands or sons who could read and keep accurate accounts. In effect she was using tree planting as an entry for improving livelihoods and self-determination for women, one of her main issues.

In 1998 the government tried to take over an area of public forestland, which they planned to give to their supporters to develop. Wangari was outraged. She organized a group of supporters to go there and plant trees. When she arrived with a few members of parliament and some media, she found the area closely guarded by a group of men, who attacked them. Wangari, several dignitaries, and members of the media were injured. Fortunately Wangari's supporters had filmed the event, and the TV coverage triggered international outrage. Eventually the international investors, mostly from the United Kingdom and the United States, pulled out, leaving Wangari and her supporters the victors.

Wangari's programs became ever more successful, and eventually, with funding from UNEP (the United Nations Environment Programme), she was able to establish the Green Belt Movement throughout Africa—people came to Nairobi from fifteen different countries to find out how they could start similar initiatives. Thus was the Pan African Green Belt Network born.

Wangari never gave up—not when the government closed down some of her programs, nor when, at least twice, she was beaten and arrested. It only made her more determined. For her work she received countless invitations to speak at international conferences, where she and I often met. And she was given many prizes and awards, culminating in the Nobel Peace Prize in 2004. During her lifetime thirty to forty million trees were planted in Kenya alone. The forests lost a true defender in 2011 when she died from cancer.

Just recently I met another outstanding defender of the forest, Chief Almir of the Surui people, who dared to stand up to illegal loggers in Brazil. As a result there is a price on his head, and he is carrying on his fight from outside, speaking movingly and eloquently at international conferences.

It is the same in India—the renowned environmental activist Vandana Shiva wrote, "Every forest area has become a war zone. Every tribal is defined a Maoist by a militarized corporate state appropriating the land and natural resources of the tribals. And every defender of the right of the forest and forest dwellers is being treated as a criminal."

My friend and National Geographic explorer Mike Fay has raised awareness and helped protect forests by undertaking marathon treks through the world's most precious and endangered forests. Here Mike is crossing the Goualougo swamps with Pygmy guides in 1999. The photographer Michael (Nick) Nichols told me that Mike confiscated the shotgun days before from a poaching camp; and the men in the team were so proud of the weapon they refused to destroy it until they finally grew tired of carrying it.
(CREDIT: COURTESY MICHAEL NICHOLS, NATIONAL GEOGRAPHIC SOCIETY)

Mike Fay, like Sunderlal Bahuguna in India, decided to raise awareness by walking. As a result of his walk across Congo and Gabon, which I mentioned in chapter 4, some wonderful forests have received protection. He and Nick Nichols met with President Bongo of Gabon and talked to him about the magic of the forest world in his country. They showed him film and slides taken by Nick, and Mike told me that President Bongo had been moved to tears—and, more importantly, was moved to create thirteen new national parks in the rich, unlogged forests of his country. He even withdrew some concessions already committed to logging companies.

And after my visit to the pristine forests of the Goualougo Triangle, Mike and I were able to meet with President Denis Sassou Nguesso of the Republic of the Congo to seek protection for the "Last Eden." Our mission was successful, and as a result those trees that so inspired me have a chance to remain standing, perhaps for hundreds of years to come.

Of course, much money is needed to create infrastructures and properly protect these new parks. And there is always the danger that another president might overturn the legislation. It is the same everywhere: even when forests are protected by law, economic interests often take precedence over conservation interests—in many of America's great national parks, for example, mining and petroleum companies have been permitted to carry out their destructive operations.

Fortunately, there are a growing number of people in governments and NGOs around the globe working on introducing new legislation to better protect our forests and the indigenous people living in them. On several occasions I have lobbied on Capitol Hill and written letters in support of Save America's Forests.

Best Forestry Practices

There is no doubt that it is desperately important to fight for the protection of old-growth forests. And it would be wonderful if we could save them all. But as, in the short term, this will not happen, it is necessary that we also push hard for the best forestry practices in the timber companies themselves. Many foresters I have met care deeply about sustainable logging and are as shocked by clear-cutting as we are. Sometimes this is only to ensure the continuation of their own industry, but a great many have a true respect for the forest itself. Unfortunately the extraction of timber today involves huge sums of money and there are many opportunities for corrupt politicians to make tidy sums on the side.

About fifteen years ago I organized a private meeting with the heads of several of the biggest European timber companies to discuss, among other things, their "code of conduct." This specifies that a given section of forest can be logged only every twenty or thirty years, and then only trees of a certain size may be felled, with a strict limit on how many can be removed from a given area. They told me of one problem they were facing: government officials in Zaire (now known as the DRC) would not allow the loggers to follow the code—they demanded that smaller trees be felled, and closer together, so that there would be more timber and more money. (One good outcome of that meeting was that these big companies agreed to add rules relating to the protection of endangered species to their "code.")

Sustainable logging is one thing—but is it possible both to protect the soul of a forest and also to extract timber? One forest in British Columbia has been logged for some forty years and still retains much of the essence of a wild forest. Aptly named "Wildwood," it was managed by an inspirational forester, Merve Wilkinson, until his death in 2010. As a young man he had borrowed money to buy the land in order to save it from developers. He had refused to construct paved roads, and felled trees were often dragged out by horses to the little mill that he had constructed on his land.

I was thrilled to meet Merve when I was visiting British Columbia about ten years ago. We walked through the forest on the dirt trails, and he explained that he knew all the bigger trees individually and never felled one until it was just past its prime. He used only natural methods to control tree diseases, he told me. "And" he said, "there are more species of mammals and birds today than there were when I first started."

He had never felled the ancient trees in his forest, and they still stood, reaching way up into the sky, the guardians. That was why, I believe, Wildwood, although it had been logged for years, retained that sense of timelessness that is, for me, one of the most important attributes of a forest.

Merve's modest logging operations made quite enough money for his unassuming way of life, and for years he provided many people with jobs. And he passed his knowledge on—forestry students came from all over the world to learn about his successful and sustainable methods. Except students from the nearby university, for whom Wildwood was forbidden territory—the university received a good deal of funding from the timber industry and forbade their students to attend Merve's workshops.

It is difficult to imagine that the timber industry as a whole, in today's cutthroat world, would adopt Merve's way of doing things, but as more and more forests are maintained on private land, it becomes an attractive possibility.

Even a petroleum company can work in a forest in an environmentally sustainable way. In the early 1990s I had extensive dealings with Conoco—before it was affiliated with either DuPont or Phillips. Back then my friend Max Pitcher was Vice President for Exploration at Conoco—meaning he was in charge of finding new places to exploit. Max flew me in a small plane over the forest to show me how different companies worked. We flew over the whole of the Conoco concession near Pointe-Noire in Congo-Brazzaville, and Max explained that seismic exploration does not have to be conducted in straight lines.

He showed me a grove of trees, sacred to the local people, that had been directly in the path of the Conoco exploration team. They had gone around and not through the grove. But the seismic lines were not visible—the Conoco teams, back then, walked through the forest, and had equipment dropped from helicopters, so that bulldozers were not necessary. If they needed to make a temporary road, they used roll out "carpets" of logs so that the soil would be less impacted, and they removed the carpet afterward and even had botanists to study the vegetation before disturbing the soil and to replant it afterward.

Of course, if a commercially viable oil deposit had been found, a proper road would have been constructed. We spent a lot of time discussing how an oil well could serve to protect all the forest in the area around it and provide benefits to the people. Conoco did not find a commercially useful oil deposit, so we could never put our plan into action. But they did leave a team and some equipment behind when they left to build our Tchimpounga Sanctuary for the infant chimpanzees we were caring for who had been orphaned by the bush-meat trade.

We Need Our Forests

One tool that can be helpful to those fighting to save the forests is the fact that we really do *need* our forests. They provide us with clean water, protect the watershed, and prevent erosion. They also provide food and medicinal plants, and support a very wide range of different animals and plant species, thus protecting biodiversity. Moreover, forests are often referred to as the "lungs of the world," as they take in CO_2 from the air around them and release oxygen. The CO_2 is stored not only in the leaves of the trees but also in forest soils, especially peat soils.

All of these benefits are referred to, in conservation and development circles, as "services" provided by the forests. And although this is clearly accurate, it always angers me—forests are not there to "serve" us. Rather we need to be wise enough to understand how they work and gratefully accept the benefits they offer. However, in this greedy, materialistic world it is useful to be able to point out that it makes more economic sense to protect rather than to destroy the trees—in other words, to assign a monetary value to living trees, particularly those in an intact forest.

My first intimation that this was possible was during one of my visits to Costa Rica, when I learned about the Payment for Environmental Services, a program, launched by the farsighted government in 1979. Under this scheme, payments were made to owners of forests and forest plantations in recognition of the valuable role played by these forests in maintaining clean air and pure water in the country.

In 2005 the British government commissioned the most comprehensive review ever carried out of the economics of climate change. I happened to be at the conference in Paris when the principal investigator, Sir Nicholas Stern, presented the conclusions of the countless scientists and economists involved. And I still remember how thrilled I was to hear him saying that the cheapest and most efficient way of slowing down global warming was to save and restore our forests.

For a very long time I had been trying to think of a way to convince governments and villagers that it was in their best interests to preserve their forests. Ecotourism, while it would provide long-term economic benefits and was an exciting prospect for villagers, could not hope to provide the kind of money that governments received in return for handing out forest concessions for logging and for mining, oil, and gas operations. But if the developed countries, in an effort to compensate for their ever-increasing levels of greenhouse-gas emissions, would agree to put monies into the protection of "carbon sinks," as forests have been described, this might be the answer.

By this time scientists around the world were working on ways to be able to estimate, quite precisely, the amount of CO_2 sequestered in different kinds of forests and forest soils. From the start it was clear that tropical forests, along with the great boreal forests of the Northern Hemisphere—known as taiga in northernmost parts—play the most important role in this respect. The boreal covers most of inland Canada and Alaska, most of Sweden, Russia, inland Norway, and northern Kazakhstan, Mongolia, and Japan. These vast and wonderful forests store huge amounts of carbon, especially in their rich peat soils—more, it is estimated, than that which is stored in the remaining tropical and temperate forests combined, and second only to that stored in the oceans of the world.

Like the tropical forests, the boreal forests are increasingly being logged and this is obviously having a big effect on the production of greenhouse gases. The most recent estimates suggest that deforestation and forest degradation account for about 15 percent of global CO_2 emissions—about the same as the transport sector.

Thus it really was important to create financial incentives for governments and villagers to preserve the remaining forests and restore trees to cleared or degraded land. Lengthy deliberations in many countries resulted in a UN program—Reduction in Emissions from Deforestation and Forest Degradation, or REDD—to compensate governments of the forested nations that protected their forests. Initially, this concept was flawed, since it was almost impossible to monitor its effectiveness. A government, or village leadership, could accept money to protect their forest but continue to cut down the trees undetected. Nonetheless, gradually new technology was making it possible, in cooperation with DigitalGlobe, Google Earth, and Esri, to monitor the situation from space using satellite imagery.

Another criticism of REDD was that it showed a lack of concern for the welfare of villagers: if they were suddenly deprived of their livelihood—not allowed to cut down trees for charcoal or make new clearings to grow food for their families, for example—they would suffer. Moreover, tree plantations might be introduced, and although these might sequester CO_2, they lead to loss of biodiversity.

So a new version of this program, spearheaded by the Norwegian government with support from Germany, Finland, and the United Kingdom, was created—REDD+. This recognized the importance of poverty alleviation, sustainable forest management, especially by local communities, and the conservation of biodiversity, *as well as* forest protection per se for carbon sequestration. I was immediately enthusiastic, for our JGI TACARE program, which has been so successful, was based on exactly this kind of holistic vision.

Tanzania was one of five countries selected for piloting REDD+ programs—and JGI was successful in acquiring a grant from the Norwegian government to work on one of these programs. Already we had funding from USAID for our TACARE program in the degraded land around Gombe. This new grant has enabled us to move south and use similar methods to protect still-intact forests.

It is very exciting, for not only does it enable us to help the villagers living around the forests to have better lives, but it also helps us protect the chimpanzees that live there, as well as their habitat. The total area covered by our various projects is 4,633 square miles, a mixture of protected forest and degraded forestland, home to approximately 1,100 chimpanzees.

JGI is working in a total of fifty-two villages (which involves around 350,000 people). In each village we have trained forest monitors who, with the aid of new Android smartphones and tablets, can accurately and instantaneously record forest fires, any tree felled illegally, or houses being built in protected areas. The important thing is that these forest monitors have been empowered—it is they who have selected what should be recorded, based on their indigenous know-how. They have chosen thirty different types of human activity that they believe can be threatening to the forest. And there are twenty species of animal that they monitor. Of course they note every time they see or hear a chimpanzee, or see a chimpanzee nest. It is in this way that we know there are almost as many chimpanzees outside as there are within protected forest areas—vital information for us as we devise plans, along with the villagers, to protect these endangered apes.

All this information is collected in a standardized way and is sent immediately to the DigitalGlobe cloud, from where JGI can download it for analysis. The program is changing lives. The forest monitors are very proud of their work, and it increases their standing in the village. They are helping to make accurate maps of village land, recording the sacred sites, including sacred trees. And they are providing invaluable information, not only for science but to help the village leaders. JGI has a similar program in Uganda and will be developing one in the eastern part of the DRC.

If such initiatives can be developed around the world, especially where there are forests rich in biodiversity, then indeed we can have hope for the future. Hope that we can slow down climate change while the global community works out new ways to live in harmony with nature. Hope that our children's children will know and marvel at the amazing diversity of life in the forests of the world.

Spiritual Value of Forests

Let us never forget that forests are beautiful in their own right. They have, for me, a spiritual value that makes them the most enchanted places on earth.

I want to share something that was one of my inspirational stories for my book *Reason for Hope.* It happened when I was walking along a trail through a glorious old-growth forest on the slopes of Mount Hood in Oregon. Suddenly, from the trail, I saw an amazing tree. It had been in a forest fire—about a hundred years ago, apparently—and only some forty feet of the trunk remained. I walked over to it and found it was completely hollow. I entered through an opening, almost like a small door into a chapel, pointed at the top.

The remaining outer shell of the tree, straight and tapering as the spire of a church, directed my eyes up and up, through the surrounding green of the forest, to the sky high above. I stood there, awed and humbled, and sent up a prayer for the survival of the remaining forests of the world.

I was with Chitcus, my Native American "spirit brother," and a small group of Roots & Shoots children. I wanted to share my experience, and as the tree only held six people at a time, we held several ceremonies during which I stood inside the tree with four children at a time. We faced one another, holding hands, and gazed upward to pray for the forests while Chitcus knelt in the middle and chanted an Indian blessing and made smoke from the sacred Kish'wuf root that seemed to carry our prayers up and up and up, and out into the blue playground of the clouds.

It was an extraordinarily moving and significant experience, and now, when things seem particularly grim, I relive that sacred memory and somehow find the strength to go on.

Chapter 18

Hope for Nature

These before and after pictures show the restoration of prairie grasses and flora on the grounds of the US government atomic accelerator facility "Fermilab" in Illinois. The first picture was taken in 1976. The second one shows what the prairie looks like now. At one time this was the largest reconstructed prairie habitat in the world. (CREDIT: FERMILAB)

A couple of years ago I went back to Cambridge to give a talk at my old university. The weather was perfect and I decided to go for a walk in the country. So a friend and I drove to one of my old haunts. But it was only because of a little church I remembered that I could find the place. Where there once had been trees and bluebells and a small clear stream, there was now churned-up earth, a bull-dozer, and some muddy pools of filthy water. And there was a notice board—"SOLD"—and the name of some developer. I don't think I shall ever forget the shock of seeing the destruction of what had once been so beautiful. I felt pain, anger, and, perhaps most, a deep, pervading sadness.

The truth is that when corporate greed and public demand for a better and better lifestyle are pitted against the health of the environment—and the health of people for that matter—it is the bottom line that wins. Have we totally lost the wisdom of the indigenous people who made decisions based on how they would affect their people in years to come? How many more supermarkets or luxury apartments do we need?

It is not only avarice—there is a shocking ignorance too. Some people simply do not understand, or do not want to understand the consequences of environmentally destructive actions. Others understand only too well, but are overwhelmed by feelings of helplessness and hopelessness.

The other experience I cannot forget is when I flew in a small plane over the area around Gombe, in the early 1990s, and saw what had been pristine forest in 1960 reduced to bare, eroded hills. Here was the result of poverty. Too many people living on land that was not large enough to support them, too poor to buy food from elsewhere, cutting down the last trees in their desperate need to feed their families.

And so, relentlessly, the planet is being desecrated in the name of "progress," on the one hand, and as a result of poverty, ignorance, and apathy, born of hopelessness and despair, on the other.

So long as never-ending economic growth remains the goal of our governments and our major financial institutions, and the corporate bottom line continues to put immediate profit above the future of our children, and so long as so many of the world's inhabitants continue to live in unalleviated poverty, the crimes against the natural world will continue.

We who care, we who understand, must use every means at our disposal to fight back. We shall lose some of the battles—but we must not give up. And we have a powerful ally, for nature, ever resilient and resourceful, will, given time, clothe a devastated landscape with green growing things, so that it becomes a place where animals once again can thrive. Of course it can take a very long time indeed for such an area to become a well-functioning ecosystem with diverse flora and fauna. But when the right people work along with nature, the healing process can be speeded up. People who truly understand the dynamics of a healthy ecosystem, who have learned by watching, and who are prepared to accept that nature may know best.

For instance, I know about the resurrection of the countryside around Sudbury in Canada, which was so devastated by reckless logging followed by relentless nickel and copper smelting that the whole region became a vast panorama of dead tree stumps and blackened rock faces. It looked so much like a moonscape that the National Aeronautics and Space Administration (NASA) used Sudbury's barren landscape as its rehearsal area for lunar-surface landings in the 1970s.

When I visited Sudbury in 2002, it was hard to believe it had ever been damaged. In the late 1970s, community members began planting trees, shrubs, herbs, and grasses in order to heal the land. They had to try many tests and listen carefully to nature so that they could figure out ways to help plants grow in soil that was compromised by so much metal toxicity. Eventually the mining companies started to join the restoration effort, hoping to improve their impact on the environment as well as their reputation. Now Sudbury is a lush, thriving, highly vegetative region, and the wildlife is thriving in healthy fields, forests, and waterways.

I often think of Sudbury as an example of a place that seemed hopelessly ruined and has returned to full vibrancy. We have to remember that it's possible. We have to keep telling ourselves these stories and sharing them with others, and we have to keep hope alive—and go on fighting. For the planet. For our children and theirs. The wonderful thing is that there are so many great examples of habitat restoration that it was hard to decide which ones to include.

Listening to Mother Nature

But here is one that I really want to share. I learned about it from one of my "Forest Warriors," John Seed. We were sitting under a tree on that Australian beach when he told me about an amazing initiative that is restoring a landscape, honoring the culture of the people, and demonstrating John's huge vision and the determination, energy, and skill that makes it happen. This project is known as "Restoring Shiva's Robes."

The Hindus believe that one of their supreme gods, Shiva, was so dazzling in his original form of pure light that the other gods pleaded with him to tone it down a bit. And so Shiva, in his compassion, agreed to do so, and appeared as the sacred mountain Arunachala. This has been his only form ever since. At the foot of this mountain is a huge temple honoring him. The temple covers acres, and is one of the largest in India.

This mountain is, of course, considered a very holy place, and millions of pilgrims flock there each year. In 1988 the Rainforest Information Centre in Australia, where John Seed works, received an appeal from an Australian nun who had lived at the base of the mountain for twenty years.

"She seemed desperate and despairing," John told me. She explained how, when the temple was originally founded, Shiva was clothed in a lush jungle and even tigers could be met walking along its flanks. But gradually the trees were felled until only thorn scrub and goats remained of "Shiva's robes." She ended with this final request: Would John and his group help to reforest this so-special mountain?

John wrote to her saying that they were only interested in *protecting* forest—but somehow he could not post that letter. Instead, he listened to his heart, sent her some money, and told her how to start an NGO. And as time went by, he couldn't help collecting and sending more money. He also started visiting as often as he could, and encouraged other people to go there and help.

The act of reforestation turned out to be tremendously difficult work. The only suitable time for planting out seedlings was after the monsoon. But conditions were hard, as great rivers of mud poured down the deforested mountain slopes.

To make the most of the planting season, some five hundred local villagers, both men and women, were employed each year. It was time-consuming work, since almost every seedling had to be surrounded by its own rock wall, and the little trees had to be protected during the summer months, when blistering heat blew in from the deserts.

Meanwhile, millions of pilgrims continued to walk, clockwise, around the mountain to get spiritual enlightenment. And this gave John Seed an idea. On his visits to Arunachala he started telling some of these pilgrims that although Shiva could have appeared as an "eroding, muddy, barren piece of rock, he had chosen one covered with a mighty forest," and if the people took good care of the trees, perhaps they would get enlightened faster. For surely it would be a spiritual task to help in the reweaving of Shiva's robes.

It worked. Word spread and more and more people began volunteering their time to help with the reforestation effort. But suddenly John was seized with doubt. Was he not being arrogant to think that he could speak like this, as though he had some kind of authority to speak for Shiva? He climbed the mountain to ask forgiveness and seek the truth in the spiritual energy of the place. As he sat there, a troop of monkeys came to spend time close by—the most powerful wildlife experience of his life. He felt it was a sign that he was doing the right thing.

The next breakthrough occurred when they got permission to establish a tree nursery on the temple grounds. Once the temple got involved in reforesting Shiva's robes, things really took off. Soon other village temples began to help in the reforesting, and before long they were growing up to three million infant trees each year for planting up on the mountain and the surrounding area, along the roads and riverbanks and around the lakes.

Some of the trees that robe the sacred mountain are now over twenty years old, and the trail up the mountain is shaded by thick foliage that is home to monkeys and other small animals—though the original tigers have not returned. Today the program is self-sustaining, with tree planting and tending carried out by local NGOs. There are environmental education programs, and villagers are helping with sustainable farming and sustainable livelihood options. And most significantly, John told me, the local people are beginning to understand and honor the connection between the new ecological awareness and the ancient spiritual traditions—a shift in consciousness that he hopes will continue to grow and expand.

"Mop Crops"

One of the things I have been fascinated by as I gathered stories for this book is the way people have turned to the plants for help. Indeed, some species have been conscripted into armies—armies to help us as we try to right the wrongs we have inflicted on Mother Nature. These are powerful armies, able to extract impurities from the soil and the water. They are known as "mop crops."

Using plants to clean soil and water is not a new idea—it was first proposed as a way to treat wastewater in Berlin three hundred years ago. And by the end of the nineteenth century two species, pennycress and a small violet, were being used for this purpose.

"Phytoremediation" is the fancy term that describes the use of various plants in cleaning up different kinds of soil and water pollution. Most plants in heavily contaminated areas will get sick and die, but some are resistant, and even fewer actually thrive. These plants "mop up" and accumulate high levels of toxin in their bodies, thus bringing contaminants up from the ground. The plant, its job done, can then be cut down and the toxins safely destroyed. Gradually, after successive plantings, the soil is cleansed.

A major threat to human health and the health of ecosystems is the high level of poisons and heavy metals that have contaminated soils and waterways. Through careful research, a growing number of mop crops have been identified to help in the job of purifying this contaminated land and water. In 1999, for example, it was found that various species of fern were able to remove arsenic (which is a metalloid) from the soil. And since then at least twenty other indigenous American plants have been identified that, between them, can remove lead, copper, nickel, and other metals. Poplar and willow trees are being used to clean up a heavily contaminated area around an oil refinery.

Some plants can even help to clean up radioactive contamination. The increasing desire for nuclear energy poses very real risks to environmental health—that such concerns are justified was amply evident after the Chernobyl explosion and was brought home again, forcibly, by the 2011 Fukushima nuclear reactor disaster after the Japanese earthquake and tsunami. In addition to these headline-grabbing incidents there are countless leakages (usually downplayed by the industry) from nuclear facilities around the world. I know because there is one not too far away from where I live in England.

Hemp, that innocent and actually benevolent plant, was used in the cleanup effort after the Chernobyl disaster. In fact, Slavik Dushenkov, a research scientist with the company Phytotech, said that hemp was proving to be "one of the best phyto-remediative plants we have been able to find." Among others are two varieties of mustard, and hydroponically grown sunflowers.

A couple of years ago I saw a powerful demonstration of the purifying power of plants when I visited an ongoing effort in Taiwan to clean the waters of the Lujiaoxi Stream, heavily polluted with domestic waste, before it flows into the Dahan River. The stream has been diverted: and now some 1,200 tons of filthy, stinking water per day are exposed to the cleansing, healing influence of a variety of carefully selected plants before joining the river again.

First I was shown an area where pollution-tolerant native vegetation has been planted: the area looked dull and lusterless, the water that flowed through it dark and lifeless. After this first cleansing, the stream, less murky but still without visible life, passed through another type of vegetation.

Next I walked through a region of tall grasses and other plants, some in flower, where already the water was much cleaner, and I saw insects, some crabs, and a few birds.

Finally we came to the 150-acre, human-made wetlands, where

many species of birds were feeding. There were more insects and crabs. Dragonflies darted above us and butterflies fluttered. From there the cleansed water, shining and alive, flows into the Dahan River.

Other Ways of Cleaning Water

All those plants press-ganged into helping us to clear up our filth. We owe them a great debt of thanks. Fortunately, "mop crops" are not the only way to clean water polluted by industrial, household, and agricultural runoff and by acid rain. Most other techniques involve pumping out the water, cleaning and returning it, and/or removing accumulated sediments. And while this is most often for our own good, here's a story about the huge efforts made on behalf of endangered water plants.

Imagine small, shallow lakes with crystal-clear water. It is spring, and they are covered by a blue haze that dances in the breeze. We are in the Bergvennen area in the Netherlands, and the lakes are habitat for a number of unique plants, one of which is the water lobelia (*Lobelia dortmanna*). It spends its life completely under the water until the spring, when its beautiful pale-blue flowers rise up above the surface on slender stems.

My botanist friend Rogier Van Vugt had fallen in love with this little plant after reading about it as a child, and he was devastated to learn, years later, that agricultural fertilizer from the surrounding farmlands had increasingly contaminated the lakes. Sediments had built up, algae had proliferated, and the water had become murky. The lobelia's rosettes of underwater leaves were not receiving enough sunlight for efficient photosynthesis, and it seemed doomed for extinction.

But then, thanks to the efforts of conservationists, the local authorities agreed to remove the sediment and then pump in well water to reduce acidity. The result was spectacular.

Rogier told me that he drove across the country to see the renewed lakes for himself. What he found there blew his mind. The number of lobelias had exploded. "The blue of literally thousands, maybe millions of water lobelia flowers hung like a mist over the crystal-clear water of the shallow lakes," he said.

From that moment, Rogier told me, he realized that while human action can destroy, it can also restore "and create the most breath-taking nature." And that knowledge led to his lifelong dedication to protecting plants. Meanwhile, the water lobelia and a number of other species have been taken off the list of endangered species in that area.

Some of the Most Endangered Plants in the World—North America's Grasslands

The grasslands with which I am most familiar are those of East Africa, particularly the Serengeti Plain of Tanzania, but I have also come to know some of the places in the United States where the North American prairies used to stretch. Every year I spend a few days in Nebraska visiting wildlife photographer Tom Mangelsen in the cabin on the Platt River built by his father. Here I can recharge my batteries during the migration of the sandhill cranes. They arrive every spring, along with many other kinds of waterbirds, to fatten up on the grain left over from the harvest. In the evening they fly in from the fields to roost along the river, hundreds of thousands of them filling the sky.

One day Tom and I were driving along the long, straight roads cut between huge cornfields, and we began talking about the unsustainable industrial agriculture that had so changed the area since he was a boy. Today almost every field has its sprawling and somehow sinister center pivot that relentlessly pumps water for irrigation from the great Ogallala Aquifer deep down below. And the aquifer is already depleted and polluted from the runoff from the chemicals sprayed on the corn. Our mood grew somber.

Then Tom said, "Let's go to our special place," and he turned off onto a narrow grass road where almost nobody ever goes. We rolled down our windows as the car moved slowly along the bumpy surface and in a few moments we had entered another world—a little oasis of original prairie, with the spring flowers and grasses, butterflies, and a small, startled quail. The air smelled different, and when Tom cut the engine, there was a stillness. Tom didn't know who owned this precious stretch of a time gone by, but we breathed a prayer that it will stay this way forever.

It was almost painful to realize how beauty of this sort once stretched for thousands of miles across North America. And I found myself envying a young woman named Eliza Steele, about whom I had just been reading. In 1840 she traveled to Illinois and saw, for the first time, the tall grass prairies as they once were. Entranced, she wrote, "A world of grass and flowers stretched around me, rising and falling in gentle undulations, as if an enchanter has struck the ocean swell, and it is at rest for ever."

At that time these grasslands, stretching across 35,000 square miles of Illinois, and the prairies, like the pristine one I visited with Tom, covered nearly one third of North America, stretching from Canada to Mexico, from the Rockies to Indiana. When the white man arrived in North America, things began to change as more and more prairieland was converted to agriculture. Today less than 1 percent of the original grasslands remains, and this habitat, like the grasslands of Australia, is one of the most endangered in the world.

Native prairie grasses have adapted to the environment of the windswept plains by developing very long roots that stabilize the soil and trap moisture even during dry times. Once this grass has gone, the topsoil is vulnerable to erosion from wind and rain and is eventually blown away. As I mentioned earlier when talking about how important roots are because they keep soil in place, the early settlers' deep plowing of mile after mile of native prairie led to the horror of the Dust Bowl of the 1930s. Vast black clouds of dust were swept across the country—much of it actually landing in the Atlantic. It affected some 400,000 square miles of the Central Plains, and caused 2.5 million people to leave their homes.

The relentless plowing of the Central Plains removed the prairie grasses that had adapted to the environment by evolving very long root systems, which served to hold the soil in place. This led to the disastrous Dust Bowl of the 1930s. Over 400,000 square miles was affected and 2.5 million people were forced to abandon their homes.
(CREDIT: U.S. DEPARTMENT OF AGRICULTURE)

The first project dealing with prairie restoration, in 1935 (when I was one year old), was initiated by Aldo Leopold at the University of Wisconsin Arboretum in Madison, Wisconsin. Seventy acres were successfully planted with native prairie plants, but at that time conservationists were mainly interested in protecting existing wilderness rather than restoring that which was damaged.

It would be nearly thirty years before a horticulturist from Nebraska, Ray Schulenberg, started work to restore one acre of native prairie on a farm in Illinois. From the seeds collected and planted, five hundred species grew. The success of this project triggered other initiatives, the first of them being at a highly unlikely spot—Fermilab in Illinois, which happens to be on the US government atomic accelerator lab ground. With the help of volunteers from the lab, the community, and the local university, one thousand acres of prairie was restored. The incredible difference in the landscape before and after restoration is illustrated in the color section of this book.

Individual landowners are getting into the act too, voluntarily working to restore the original prairie to their properties. They understand that diversity is important and that it is necessary to introduce as many as possible of the original endemic species. There is also growing realization that controlled fires are important for the health of the prairie ecosystem. These efforts on a series of ranches are helping to create corridors for butterflies, birds, and other wildlife.

I learned about this when I went with my good friend Alan Bartels to stay at the ranch of Bruce and Sue Ann Switzer and their family. They have joined forces with two neighbors and are successfully combating the invasive eastern red cedar trees on their combined holdings of more than fifty thousand acres. They have restored cultivated rye fields (that needed irrigation) back to native grassland so that the original prairie plant and wildlife is returning. I was particularly interested to learn about the restoration of the blowout penstemon—a few years ago it was almost extinct. But thanks to the work of local scientists, and with the help of Alan and a group of local children who have been planting seedlings on the Sandhills, including the Switzer family's property, this beautiful and fragrant flowering plant is now making a comeback.

Another exciting development is prairie ecotourism. Increasing numbers of the visitors who come to explore the unique flora and fauna of the area are hosted by the Switzers at their ranch. And because of this they are able to stay and work there as a family. The grown-up children of Bruce and Sue Ann have moved back. One of them, Sarah, told me of the plans they are making, with other ranchers, for further restoration of the land. Sarah's five-year-old son, Emmett, solemn under his giant cowboy hat, idolizes Grandpa Bruce. He follows him everywhere, learning more each day about the prairie habitat and about good stewardship. The family hopes

I recently spent a day with the Switzer family—three generations working together to restore the local Nebraskan prairie lands. Their ranch also has an ecotourism business where they can show visitors the unique endangered flora and fauna of the American prairies. (Back row, left to right: Adam Switzer [Bruce and Sue Ann's son], Bruce Switzer, me, Sue Ann Switzer. Front row, left to right: Ella Switzer, Emmett Sortum, Sarah Sortum, Henry Sortum). (CREDIT: ALAN J. BARTELS)

he will stay, even after he is finished with school, and help them look after this beautiful land. It is people like this who are, truly, my "seeds of hope."

Wildlife Corridors

One important way to fight and even reverse the increasing fragmentation of wilderness areas is by creating wildlife corridors. Usually, these are only possible when NGOs, private landowners, and government agencies join forces to create contiguous plots of land that link major conservation areas.

One of the goals of JGI's TACARE program in Tanzania is to create a leafy corridor that will link the hundred or so surviving members of the Gombe chimpanzees population with other remnant groups. For they cannot survive indefinitely without the benefit of new genes from outside. We have no way of knowing whether they will use it, and there are those who do not believe corridors of this sort can be effective, but there is a lot of evidence showing that, at least in some cases—and particularly for plants—corridors can be crucial.

Just this spring (2012) I was driving from Turin to Florence in Italy, and I noticed that the edges of the road were brilliant with red poppies. Occasionally a whole field blazed with glorious color, and these reminders of the fields of my youth were linked by the populations along the roadsides. It made me think of Lady Bird Johnson's legacy in Texas, where she had wildflower seeds scattered along the medians and strips of land along many of the major roads.

Such wildlife corridors are now policy in the United Kingdom, where there are efforts to conserve not only roadside "verges," as we British call them, but also hedgerows that are either ancient or species-rich, disused and current railway lines, and cycle trails. Even the old stone walls of northern England are protected, as the stones were carefully laid without cement, and in the crevices all sorts of plants and animals thrive.

Banks of rivers and canals can also serve as corridors linking protected areas. Conservation groups are working with city councils as to time of year and method of managing the vegetation along these corridors. It is considered of special importance for the dispersal of plants because of climate change, since, just like animals, they may need to move to new, more suitable habitats, and corridors will play a vital role in their ability to survive. An intensive study in North Carolina showed that wildlife refuges connected by corridors had 20 percent more plant species than those, with the same habitat, that are isolated.

Children and the Future

I have often heard the Native American saying "We have not inherited this planet from our parents—we have borrowed it from our children." Unfortunately, this is no longer true. We have not borrowed it, but stolen it. We are still stealing their future. And more and more young people know this—no wonder I meet so many, on every continent, who are apathetic, depressed, or bitter and angry. They tell me they feel that way because we older generations have compromised their future and there is nothing they can do about it.

I have grandchildren, and when I think how we have harmed the planet since I was their age, I feel a kind of desperation. Indeed we have compromised the future for our children. But I do not believe it is too late to turn things around, and it was for this reason that I initiated our Roots & Shoots movement. Almost everywhere I go during my three hundred days of travel each year I hear about a project where our children are lending willing hands to the task of putting to rights places that we have despoiled. They are helping to restore wetlands, clean creeks and streams, remove alien vegetation, and encourage native plants to grow again in habitats from which they had been driven.

Sometimes, when there is a free space in my schedule, I ask if there is some R&S group I can visit. I know that this often serves to motivate the young people, and to remotivate those who may have become less involved, so I feel it is important, even if I am feeling too tired for such an effort. But there is a good reward, because the enthusiasm of the young people so often helps to restore me.

One day I visited a group of youth who helped to restore a unique ecosystem in a Chicago suburb that had been seriously harmed by storm/wastewater pouring from a newly constructed shopping mall. This had created an artificial canyon and enabled a thick growth of invasive buckthorn to colonize the area. Finally the contractors blocked the illegal flow and burned off much of the brush. The Roots & Shoots group then cleared away more of the buckthorn as well as a great deal of charred material, and planted woodland grass seeds that they had collected, in readiness, the previous fall. Now the wildlife has benefited, and the general public is becoming increasingly aware of the potential of this area and more willing to contribute toward protecting it.

One of the things I love about R&S is that the children learn, through hands-on action, that they really and truly can make a difference. Some accomplishments are outstanding, and I can use those stories to inspire others. Such was the case with the R&S group of ten- and eleven-year-olds in Illinois that decided to protest a plan to build a Perrier water-bottling factory upstream from their school. And they conducted and presented such a good study that the EPA realized that they should do a proper environmental impact study! In the end, the proposed factory was vetoed.

R&S began in Tanzania, where many groups now have tree nurseries on their school grounds. In some instances I have seen, over the years, depressing areas of trampled earth gradually transformed into "Roots & Shoots Forests." One school is growing five thousand seedlings of native trees, in a school nursery for tree-planting programs in seven villages. Two schools are adjacent to national parks, and the children are trying to protect their young trees from various animals: they discourage elephants by smearing crushed red pepper and elephant dung on the trunks and branches of young trees.

Several groups are learning about the importance of protecting mangrove forests. One group is working on Pemba Island planting nonindigenous pines as pioneer species on an abandoned coral quarry. And I just visited an exciting project on the outskirts of Dar es Salaam, where Roots & Shoots groups are working to restore the original trees and other vegetation on land devastated by the operations of Twiga Cement—an effort initiated and encouraged by the company itself. There are hundreds more Roots & Shoots restoration and tree-planting programs around the world.

The R&S Green Thumb program in Taiwan encourages schools to replace ornamentals on their school grounds with indigenous flora to try to create a linked network of natural habitat for butterflies. After all, Taiwan was originally called "Formosa"—the land of the butterflies. And in a recent effort, R&S groups waited at each station along the route of the high-speed rail that links the north and south of Taiwan and handed seeds of indigenous plants to the passengers, asking them to plant them wherever they could.

There are still some people who wonder why I devote so much time and energy to working with young people. It is pretty obvious, really. Of course I care desperately about conservation of chimpanzees and their forest habitat. Indeed, I care about all wildlife and wild places. But it would be of little use to spend my life working to protect those animals and those places if we were not, at the same time, raising new generations to care for what we have saved.

And there is another reason. Young people can influence other family members. I know so many parents, and grandparents also, who tell me that they do things differently now because of their children. Also, there is a vital energy in our youth that comes alive once they understand the problems and are empowered to take action. They see the difference they can make, and it feeds their determination and their energy. And it feeds mine, too.

Chapter 19

The Will to Live

One of the two 500-year-old camphor trees that survived the atomic bomb dropped on Nagasaki that ended World War II. Only about half the trunk and a few leafless branches remained. It was designated a national monument in 1969. Prayers written on strips of parchment are hung from its branches in memory of the thousands of Japanese who died. (CREDIT: MEGHAN DEUTSCHER)

Well, dear reader, we have come to the end of our wandering through the wondrous Green Kingdom, the world of plants. Together we have traveled along well-trodden paths, turned aside to explore small lanes, and ventured into places unknown even to me before. We have been up in the strange world of the rain-forest canopy to meet life-forms that never leave the trees, and delved into the eerie world under the ground, where roots and fungi live their fascinating connubial lives.

We have traced the origins of some of the garden plants that we love today, and investigated those plants that have medicinal qualities, and those that, when treated and used unwisely, can harm us.

We have learned a little about the long-ago days when nations established colonies overseas and shackled slaves in order to make their masters prosper, and we have been shocked by the harm that agriculture has wrought on humans and the environment alike by those who think only of making money and care not for the future of the planet—or, it seems, of their children.

We have stared aghast at the harm that our species has, for centuries, inflicted on the natural world, and been stirred by the actions of those brave green warriors, standing up to the might of ruthless governments and corporations.

These explorations have been dictated by my own travels, have happened because of the people I met who told me wondrous tales or as the result of one of those Internet sessions where one thing led to another to another, until I ended up in places I never knew existed and was so inspired I had to call or e-mail those who were connected to the amazing stories I found.

I am fortunate. I have spent time in wild places where people live in harmony with nature, taking from the land around them only so much as they need. Places where trees and plants are not just valued for the food, healing, and clothing they provide but are also truly appreciated and respected. And where they grow freely, expressing their plant natures fully and magnificently. I have also spent time among the tortured plants, plants with limbs cut and twisted into growth patterns dictated by their human masters, neglected in little office pots, sickened by applications of agricultural chemicals, lined up along busy city streets where they are exposed to all the pollution of the passing cars. Yet still they do their best, absorbing CO_2 from the contaminated air, drawing sunlight through leaves coated with grime or poisons, producing oxygen for the rest of us. And, so often, brightening our day with flowers.

Indeed, nature is resilient. Therein lies our hope. And I want to end this book with three of the most extraordinary stories of survival that I have come across. They all concern trees. After all, trees are my first love.

The Grandmother Tree Who Refused to Die

Every time a particular species of tree becomes extinct, the distinctive murmuring of its leaves in the wind is lost forever. Fortunately we are waking up to the situation, and there are people and organizations working to save species after species. This first story is about a most singular tree. It describes the persistence and tenacity of people who worked and never gave up, determined that this one tree and its lineage should be saved, so that the impossible should come to pass.

Cooke's koki'o (*Kokia cookei*) is a Hawaiian tree that was "discovered" in the 1860s by Mr. R. Meyer on the small archipelago island of Moloka'i. Though he searched everywhere, he found only three individuals of this charming new species, with its delicate star-shaped leaves. Several years later when botanists went back there, they failed to find even one, and it was assumed that Cooke's koki'o was extinct.

But not so—about thirty years later one tree was found in the same general area, probably the last survivor of the original trio. As I read about her, I found I was thinking of her as Grandmother Koki'o, and that is how I introduce you to her! Five years later, when another group of botanists returned to the site, they found that Grandmother Koki'o, although still living, was in very poor shape, and three years later she was dead. In 1918 Cooke's koki'o was *officially* listed as extinct in the wild.

However, that old tree, sick though she had been, had managed to produce a few seeds before her death. And at least one of those precious seeds must have germinated, because twelve years later, in

1930, a young tree—the offspring of Grandmother Koki'o—was found near the site of its dead parent. It was taken to the Kauluwai residence on Moloka'i so that it could be better looked after, and there it took root, grew, and produced seeds. From those seeds more than 130 seedlings grew—the future of the species seemed assured.

Imagine their dismay when botanists who went to see how the seedlings were getting on found that not even one seemed to have survived. Their parent, seeded from Grandmother Koki'o, was still living—but died in about 1950. This time, surely, Cooke's koki'o was finally extinct.

But there was something magical about Grandmother Koki'o's lineage. I can almost imagine the spirit of that original tree hanging around and breathing new life into dormant seeds. Because, almost twenty years later, in 1970, one more single adult tree was found—at the Kauluwai residence! And so, yet again, the Cooke's koki'o had risen, like the phoenix, from the ashes.

But that is not the end of the story! Eight years after it had been found, in 1978, that one lone survivor, grandchild of old Grandmother Koki'o, was caught in a fire. Unable to escape, it burned. But by an amazing stroke of good fortune, before the mostly charred remains of the tree had lost all life, someone removed a still-living branch.

One branch, the last link in an unbroken lineage that stretched back over more than a hundred years to the tree's ancestor in the Hawaiian forest. That one special branch was grafted onto a related species at the Waimea Arboretum on Oahu. And there, with expert care, the graft took. And grew. True, there was sap from a different species in its veins—but the life force, surely, was inherited from Grandmother Koki'o.

As time went on, more and more plants from that original graft were distributed all over Hawaii. They seemed to prosper. But—and it was a very big but—not one of them set seed. For almost a quarter of a century those young trees grew without producing, between them, even one seed. Not even one.

Not until a horticulturist on Oahu finally managed to get viable seeds from one of the young koki'os. Those seeds grew, and one of the precious seedlings—now the great-grandchild of Grandmother Koki'o—was sent to the local Audubon center, where it grew, but reluctantly. The others died.

Alas, it was not strong, this miracle tree. How fortunate, then, that at this point Nellie Sugii, director of the Hawaiian Rare Plant Program, was asked to help save it. She was determined to succeed, for she knew the extraordinary history of its ancestry. Nellie worked with tender embryonic plants grown from seeds, trying to find a way to get more vigorous seedlings.

I asked her how she felt when given this awesome responsibility. She replied that in the beginning it was quite frightening, but thrilling at the same time. "The procedure was new, and tried only a few times," she told me. And on those occasions the seedlings had not survived.

But although she felt apprehensive, she was excited to try. And "totally elated" when a few tiny seedlings started to turn green and began to grow. Perhaps she succeeded because she has a connection with the plants she grows.

One of the Cooke's koki'o seedlings nurtured by Nellie. One day, with luck, it will return to its ancestral homeland in Hawaii. (CREDIT: NELLIE SUGII)

"I watched them every day," she told me, "and talked to them and bossed them to grow... and be strong. And they did." She also used to play a lot of Hawaiian classical music to Grandmother Koki'o's great-great grandchildren, and sometimes rock 'n' roll. "I like to think they enjoyed it as much as I did," she said.

It is because of Nellie's painstaking (and ongoing) efforts and her dedication that Cooke's koki'o can, at long last, produce viable seeds that will develop into strong, healthy individuals—a growing number of great-great-grandchildren of Grandmother Koki'o. And soon some of these seedlings will be planted back in the home of their ancestors in the Hawaiian forests.

I would give anything to be there when that happens.

Surviving the Atomic Bomb

This is the incredible story of three trees that survived the atomic bombs that were dropped in 1945 on the unsuspecting citizens of Hiroshima and Nagasaki in Japan. Although the deployment of these bombs almost certainly played a major role in ending World War II, it also led to the immediate deaths of hundreds of thousands of innocent Japanese civilians. The contamination of the environment with radioactive materials led to the suffering and death of thousands more Japanese for years to come. And vast areas of human habitation and the natural world were laid waste. Indeed, the creation of those bombs represented one of the most monstrous tools of war ever unleashed by the human species, and as we know only too well, the threat of nuclear war still hangs over the world today.

The first of the three survivor trees was a *Gingko biloba* that had been planted in 1850 as a temple tree. It survived the destruction of Hiroshima, although the temple itself was destroyed. Eventually, as life returned to the shattered city, there were plans to cut the survivor down to make way for a new temple building. But thousands protested such a heartless plan, and in the end the plan for the temple was reconfigured. I have not been there, but I have seen pictures that show how the steps up to the entrance pass on both sides of that tree, and seem to hold it in their embrace.

In 1990 I went to Nagasaki to give a lecture. I found the city lush and green—which startled me, as I had been looking, in dismay, at photographs taken forty-five years earlier that showed the lunar landscape that was the aftermath of the second atomic bomb.

My hosts filled me in on some of the history. Two months after the explosion, they told me, a group of scientists and military had visited Nagasaki to assess the impact of the bombs. One of them, Lieutenant R. Battersby, wrote an account of what he saw. Everything, he said, was destroyed. Trees had lost all their leaves and branches or been uprooted. Sometimes a great trunk had been snapped in half. It must have been like a scene from Dante's Hell.

To his amazement he found two five-hundred-year-old camphor trees that were still alive. The upper part of their trunks had been ripped off, and the remainder had lost many branches and all their leaves. Once, they had been very tall trees—now, mutilated, they were only some thirty feet high.

Those two trees in Nagasaki are still living. I was taken to see one of them—it had been designated as a national monument in 1969. This survivor, like the gingko in Hiroshima, had prayers, written in tiny kanji on strips of parchment, hanging from its branches, placed there by those who will never forget. It is revered, a holy shrine and memorial to all who died and suffered. I stood there a long time, humbled, in tears.

One of my most precious possessions is a leaf from this tree, given to me by my Japanese host, a powerful symbol of nature's resilience.

The Tree That Survived 9/11

My last story comes from another dark chapter in human history. A recent horror, which all but young children will remember. A day in 2001 when the World Trade Center was attacked, when the Twin Towers fell, when the world changed forever.

I was in New York on that terrible day, traveling with my friend and JGI colleague Mary Lewis. We were staying in mid-Manhattan at the Roger Smith Hotel. First came the confused reporting from the television screen. Then another colleague arrived, white and shaken. She had been on the very last plane to land before the airport closed, and she actually saw, from the taxi, the plane crashing into the second tower.

Disbelief. Fear. Confusion. And then the city went gradually silent until all we could hear was the sound of police-car sirens and the wailing of ambulances. People disappeared from the streets. It was a ghost town, unreal. There were times when I felt I was living in a dream.

It was eight days before there was a plane on which we could leave. Eight days during which the city remained quiet, and fear gave way to grief, anguish—and eventually, as the facts emerged, anger. Mary and I met with our Arab and Muslim friends, desperate to try to help them face the terrible backlash that we predicted would be directed against hundreds of innocent people. And all the while we could see the haze over what had been the Trade Center, and we could smell death.

Ironically, when Mary and I finally left, we were flying to Portland, Oregon, where I had to give a talk, to a boys' secondary school, entitled "Reason for Hope." It was, without doubt, the hardest lecture I have ever had to give. For where was hope at that time? Only when I was actually talking, looking out over all the young, bewildered faces, did I find the things to say, drawing on the terrible events of history, how they had passed, how we humans always find reserves of strength and courage to overcome that which fate throws our way.

Just over ten years after 9/11, on a cool, sunny April morning in 2012, I went to meet "Survivor," a Callery pear tree, and the three people who had most to do with her survival, Bram Gunther, Ron Vega, and Richie Cabo. We met outside the new 9/11 Memorial at what was once known as Ground Zero, and went through the tight

*"Survivor," a Callery pear, was the only tree at World Trade Center plaza to survive 9/11. Horticulturist Richie Cabo (*right*) helped nurse the decapitated and mutilated tree back to health, and Ron Vega (*left*) made sure she had a place of honor back on the plaza of the 9/11 Memorial site in New York City.* (CREDIT: MARK MAGLIO)

security together. I could hardly believe that, finally, I was going to meet this incredible tree.

In the 1970s she had been placed in a planter near Building 5 of the World Trade Center and each year her delicate white blossoms had brought a touch of spring into a world of concrete. In 2001, after the 9/11 attack, this tree, like all the other trees that had been planted there, disappeared beneath the fallen towers.

But amazingly, in October, a cleanup worker found her, smashed and pinned between blocks of cement. The discovery was reported to Bram Gunther, who was then deputy director of forestry for the NYC Parks Department, and when he arrived, he initially thought the tree was unsalvageable. She was decapitated and the eight remaining feet of trunk were charred black, the roots were broken, and there was only one living branch.

Bram told me how, as he looked at the stricken tree, he was skeptical at first, but ultimately the cleanup workers persuaded him to give the tree a chance. And so he ordered that she be sent off to the Parks Department's nursery in Van Cortlandt Park in the Bronx.

Ron Vega, now the director of design for the 9/11 Memorial site, was a cleanup worker back then. He smiled as he thought back to that time. "A lot of people thought it was a wasted effort to try to rescue her," he recalled. "So she was taken out of the site almost clandestinely—under the cover of night."

As we walked toward this special tree, on that special April day, I felt as much in awe as if I were going to meet one of the great spiritual leaders or shamans.

She is not spectacular to look at—not until you realize what she has been through and understand the miracle of her survival. We stood together outside the protective railing. We reached out to gently touch the ends of her branches. Many of us, perhaps all, had tears in our eyes—my own were too blurred to be sure.

Richie Cabo, the nursery manager, who became one of Survivor's principal caregivers, told me that when he first saw the decapitated tree, he did not think anything could save her. But once the dead, burned tissues had been cut away and her trimmed roots deeply planted in good, rich soil, Survivor proved him wrong.

"In time," said Richie, "she took care of herself. We like to say she got tough from being in the Bronx!" But in the beginning, with all the fertilizing and pruning, it was hard work. And during this time all the staff became very attached to Survivor, for she symbolized endurance and resilience. In particular a special bond grew up between the tree and Richie. "She became dear to me," he said.

In the spring of 2010 disaster struck Survivor again. Richie told me how he got news that the tree had been ripped out of the ground by the terrible storm that was raging outside, with hundred-mile-per-hour winds. He rushed there at once with his three young children. They found the roots completely exposed, and he and the children and the other nursery staff worked together to try to rescue her.

At first they only partially lifted the tree, packing her in compost and mulch so as not to break the roots. For a long while they gently sprayed the tree with water to minimize the shock, hoping she'd make it. A few weeks later they set to work to get Survivor completely upright.

"It was not a simple operation," Richie told me. "She was thirty feet tall, and it took a heavy-duty boom truck to do the job."

But, yet again, Survivor survived.

It wasn't until six years after Ron Vega had witnessed the mangled tree being rescued from the wreckage that he heard that Survivor was still alive. Immediately he became passionate to bring her back and incorporate her into the design—and with his new position he was able to make it happen. Finally the day arrived, the day when Survivor finally came home. She was planted near the footprint of the South Tower.

It was an emotional ceremony for her planting. One of those taking part was Keating Crown, who had escaped from the seventy-eighth floor down the last usable stairwell of one of the towers. He said, in his remarks, that the survival of the tree was symbolic of the endurance of the human spirit.

There was a lot expressed that day. "For personal accomplishments," Ron said, "today is it. I could crawl into this little bed and die right there. That's it. I'm done... To give this tree a chance to be part of this memorial, it doesn't get any better than that."

As Survivor stood proudly upright in her new home, a reporter said to Richie, "This must be an extra-special day for you, considering it's the ten-year anniversary of the day you were shot."

Before he started working at the Bronx nursery in the spring of 2001, Richie had been a corrections officer at Green Haven, a maximum-security prison in New York. He had left the job after nearly dying from a terrible gunshot wound in the stomach, inflicted not at the prison but out on the streets when he tried to stop a robbery in progress.

Until the reporter pointed it out, Richie hadn't even realized the date was the same, and then, he told me, he couldn't even speak for a moment. "I could hardly even breathe," he said. And he thought it was probably more than a coincidence that the tree would go home on that special day. "We are both survivors," he said. "We healed together. And somehow it seemed only fitting."

"Survivor" before (above) and after (next page). The first picture was taken just after the terrorist attacks. The next one was taken ten years later. She is a testament to the resilience of nature and the ability of humans to help if they will only understand how important it is. (CREDIT: MICHAEL BROWNE)

(CREDIT: PHOTO BY AMY DREHER, COURTESY 9/11 MEMORIAL)

While overseeing the design, Ron had made sure that the tree was planted in such a way that the traumatized side faces the public. One of the branches was low-hanging, and Ron said ordinarily they would have removed it, but instead they simply raised it slightly with a support cable so that people wouldn't bump into it. "It took it ten years for her to grow that branch, so there is no way we would lop it off." He stroked the branch lovingly as he spoke.

Some people, Ron told us, weren't pleased to have the tree back, saying that she "spoiled" the symmetry of the landscaping, as she is a different species from the other nearby trees. Indeed, she is different. For one thing she is much older, and wiser. And on the tenth anniversary of 9/11, when the memorial site was opened to survivors and family members, very many of them tied blue ribbons onto Survivor's branches.

One last memory. Survivor should have been in full bloom in April when I met her. But, like so many trees in this time of climate change, she had flowered about two weeks early. Just before we left, as I walked around this brave tree one last time, I suddenly saw a tiny cluster of white flowers. Just three of them, but somehow it was like a sign.

It reminded me of a story I read in a newspaper. In the aftermath of the horrifying tsunami and Fukushima nuclear plant disaster in Japan, a TV crew went to document the situation. They interviewed a man who had just lost everything, not only his house and all his belongings but his family also. The reporter asked him if he had any hope.

He turned toward a cherry tree beginning to bloom. "Look there," he said, pointing at the new blossoms. "That's what gives me hope."

Gratitude

This book has taken three years to research, write, cut, and edit. Looking back—oh, the people with whom I have corresponded, talked to on the phone, met, exchanged views. People from whom I have learned, who have enriched me, educated me. And we are all united by a love of the natural world.

At times I thought the book would never be finished—and indeed, it could have gone on and on as I found more and more fascinating stories that I wanted to include. And of course the manuscript got too long! Some of the stories could be shortened. Others were so full of important details that it had to be all-or-nothing. Those that have been cut from the book will soon be posted on my blog at the Jane Goodall Institute website, www.janegoodall.org.

"To begin at the beginning." With my family! At least in part I am the person I am due to genetics—I inherited my father's constitution. How else could I have maintained my insane schedule, on the road three hundred days of the year, giving lectures around the world, *and* found the energy to gather information about the plant kingdom and write this book. But storytelling—that gift comes from my Welsh forebears on my mother's side, or so I'm told.

But genes are only part of it, and environment and upbringing most assuredly played a major role in molding my clay. My childhood experiences at The Birches, as well as the mix of wonderful characters who made up my immediate family, had a huge influence on the adult I would become. My grandmother Danny (Elizabeth Hornby Joseph) and her daughter, Olly (Elizabeth Olwen), both loved gardening. My mother, Vanne—pronounced Van—(Margaret Myfanwe) was a writer, and when my school essays came back covered in red *x*'s because of my poor spelling and handwriting, it was she who told me that the substance of the essay was by far the most important and had me read my essays and stories and poems aloud to the family. And my brilliant Uncle Eric (William Eric), who came home most weekends from war-torn London, always encouraged me to go one better than my best. Rusty, my constant companion on all my wanderings in the cliffs and chines. My beloved Beech—always when I get home, I spend quiet time with him, feel the energy under the bark.

And, too, my childhood was surrounded by books—so many books in every room. And they, and their long-dead authors, influenced me too. I can never forget the plants that Hugh Lofting described that lived on the Moon, especially the vain lilies that talked to each other. And there were the jungles of Rudyard Kipling and Edgar Rice Burroughs. And there was that book that shaped and channeled my scientific curiosity about the natural world, *The Miracle of Life.*

O Vanne, how can I ever thank you. And Danny, Olly, Uncle Eric. All of you—up on that cloud—will love this book. You sang the first notes of it when I was a child, and I have not forgotten. Without my family and my wonderful upbringing, this book could not have been written. My sister is still very much alive and will be thanked later.

Let me not forget those crazy seventeenth- and eighteenth-century plant hunters who ventured into remote parts of the world to bring back species that were new and exotic then, many of which are a normal part of our gardens and parks today. And just wait, dear reader, until you can read on my blog the almost unbelievable story of David Nelson and the breadfruits, the true raison d'être for the mutiny on the *Bounty*, and the full story of the indomitable Ernst Wilson and how he acquired his "lily limp." I salute you all. I admire and thank you for your indomitable spirits, for enriching us with stories of deprivation and danger, and for the pure joy you have given all of us who love plants.

It will have been obvious to anyone reading this book how much I love trees. I learned something about their strange prehistoric ancestor, *Eospermatopteris*, commonly known as Wattieza, from Dr. William E. Stein, professor of Biological Sciences at Binghamton University. Thank you so much.

Several people have shared with me their special relationships with individual trees, and I am so very grateful that they did so. Dana Lyons—your song, "The Tree," is so hauntingly beautiful, and I shall share it on our blog. And Myron Eshowsky and Chiu Sein Tuck, your stories are wonderful. I would never have met Tuck had it not been for Andy Brown and Andrew McAulay, who allow me to stay in the little bungalow in the middle of Kadoorie Farm & Botanic Garden, where I am surrounded not only by marvelous trees but also by wild boar, porcupines, and other wildlife. Thank you, thank you. And thanks also to Julia Butterfly Hill, for reading and adding to my account of your marvelous relationship with Luna. I hope people will read your book, *The Legacy of Luna*, and learn more about the weeks you lived in her branches, the storms you endured, the love that grew between you.

I am eternally grateful to a number of people who have helped me to travel to the forests of the world. First, of course, Louis Leakey, who taught me so much about the plants of Olduvai on our Sunday adventures, when we took a day off from the hard work of digging for fossils and set off to explore different places. Then there is the intrepid Dr. Michael Fay. Mike, not only have you done so much to help save forests, but you have made it possible for me to visit some of the most beautiful of them. I remember with delight when I spent two days with you during your marathon walk throughout the historic range of the great redwood forests. You even added my little tent and extra supplies to your already weighty backpack, since I was unfit from a life of airplanes and hotels! We sat in the dark after supper, wrapped in our sleeping bags against the cold, while you told me more about the history of forestry there, the many people who had lost their lives, the thousands of giant trees that had been killed. And outlined your hope for the future.

And then, Mike, you persuaded the National Geographic Society to fund an expedition to the forests of the Goualougo Triangle—that last Eden hidden in the swamps of the Congo Basin. There I met ancient forest giants that had never heard the sound of ax or chainsaw. One night was special: the leaves on the forest floor gave out phosphorescent light when we disturbed them with our feet. You told me that this phenomenon was rare and how one night you had sat spellbound as the Pygmies, one by one, disappeared beyond the light of the fire, covered themselves with these leaves, and ran back, each one magically seeming to be a different animal.

There were other people involved in that Goualougo adventure. Michael "Nick" Nichols was the *National Geographic* photographer. I have known Nick for more than twenty years, and we have worked together on stories about chimpanzees—revealing their plight in the wild and their exploitation for the live animal trade, medical research, entertainment, and the pet industry. When working on those issues, Nick, you even persuaded my son, Grub, to go with you to the forests of Sierra Leone—where both of you nearly died from some terrible tropical fever! And thank you, Nick, for donating that amazing picture of Mike Fay trekking through the swamps with the Pygmy guides.

David Quammen, you not only wrote up the *National Geographic* magazine story "Jane in the Forest Again," but also tended my blistered feet, advising me to bind them up with camera tape—it worked! Dr. Crickette Sanz and Dr. Dave Morgan, I shall always be grateful to you for the way you welcomed me to your forest paradise, introduced me to your chimpanzees, and shared your camp and your stories. It is like a dream now, as I look back. And an integral part of that dream are the Pygmies—I wish I could thank each of you in person. You shared your knowledge about chimpanzees, told me stories of their life, and cooked me a fantastic meal of brilliant-orange forest mushrooms and green forest leaves.

Dr. Don Jacobs, you are indeed a true friend. You organized my trips to Costa Rica and made it possible for me to see something of the forest there. We went together on the canopy walkway, and we had dinner with President Óscar Arias, who has done so much to save the environment. And, as if that was not enough, you also arranged for me to go with you to the rain forest of the Mamoni Valley Preserve in Panama, where you introduced me to Nathan Gray and Lider Sucre of Earth Train, and Colin Weil of EcoGroup. Nathan, you really looked after me, bringing hot coffee to my tent early in the morning when the night calls of the howler monkeys were still ringing in my ears. I got to know some of the local indigenous tribe, the Kuna, who work for Earth Train. And we survived one of the most dramatic river crossings ever—the cars were submerged almost over their bonnets (hoods) and the current was strong. I shall always remember how two of the Kuna tested the depth, riding across on their horses—what superb horsemen they are.

Special thanks to Panta Kasoma, executive director JGI-Uganda, and Peter Appell, manager of Field Programs, for several wonderful walks in Kibale and Budongo forests, where we have a snare-removal program and are helping to protect chimpanzee forest habitats and link them along the Albertine Rift by means of a leafy corridor. And to Rebeca Atencia, executive director JGI–Congo-Brazzaville and her husband, Fernando Turmo, for incredible explorations of the canyon forests and the Kouilou River, which flows through enchanted forests in a faraway part of the world.

And I must also thank my good friend Randall Tolpinrud of Pax Natura Foundation. I received a most unusual award from your foundation: a Native American blanket, presented by Forrest Cuch, which adorns my bed in Bournemouth. This is the place where I have written almost all of this book (and the one before)—sitting on that very blanket! You told me about the amazing Paul Rokich, who reforested the Black Mountains—initially working all on his own. I have not met Paul, but you persuaded him to send me a leaf from one of the first trees he planted, all those years ago. Randall, you even hand-carried a homemade meal on a plane from Utah to Tom Mangelsen's cabin in rural Nebraska so I could have a special birthday dinner while working on the book last April. How you got it all through security was a miracle!

And, Randall, you also put us in touch with your friend, public-interest attorney Steven Druker, executive director of the Alliance for Bio-Integrity. Steven, it was so kind of you to fact-check our GMO chapter. I am greatly looking forward to reading your book about GMOs, *Altered Genes, Twisted Truth*. It promises to be the definitive work on the subject.

Dr. Hugh Bollinger, you, almost more than anyone else, have provided me with so much fascinating information about the kingdom of the plants. From the time when we first met, in Costa Rica, you have kept me up-to-date with everything you feel will interest me—throughout the time I was writing the last book, as well as this one. You are a true friend.

I am grateful to Howard Bernstein. You located the photo you had shown me years ago of your son, Isaac, entranced by the flowers on his narcissus. Thank you so much.

I have always been fascinated by the medicine men and women, or traditional healers, in Tanzania. Here I want to thank Mikidadi Almasi Mfumya and Yusuph Rubondo, who welcomed me into their homes and shared information about their work. Yusuph, I loved your sense of humor. You shared that dramatic story about how you were seized by a python when you were a child and dragged toward the river—fortunately some villagers rescued you in the nick of time. The way you told it to us made it very funny. And Mikidadi, you were so delighted to show us around your forest garden, telling us stories of where the different medicinal plants came from.

Dr. Shadrack Kamenya, of our Gombe Stream Research Centre, helped to arrange those visits. You were with me and helped with translations and photography. And it was you who told me that two of our staff at Gombe are also skilled in the use of medicinal plants. One, Shaban Mbwama, is a close relative of Mzee Rubondo. The other, Madua Mbrisho, is a friend of my son—as small boys they swam and fished together in Lake Tanganyika.

Forester Aristides Kashula, for years you have been working with traditional healers, gaining their trust, persuading them to pass on their ancient herbal knowledge. You and botanist Grace Gobbo of our TACARE staff were eventually able to gain the trust of eighty-six medicine men and women in the area, and I thank you both for all the information you have shared with me.

Revocatus Edwards, in charge of Kigoma region Roots & Shoots program, I must thank you for introducing me to the teachers and students of the Sokoine Primary School, where the students are protecting their forest and learning about medicinal plants. And Smita Dharsi, you generously shared your experiences at that school, teaching the children to draw those plants, providing them with their very first computers. You told me that when they first received them, they carried them as a mother cradles her infant, so precious were they.

Dr. Mark Plotkin, you have done so much to help protect the Latin American indigenous people and their forests, and you helped me so generously with information and photos for the chapter on the use of plants for healing. We have known each other a long time—sad that we have only met and talked in hotels when it is our passion for the forest that brought us together in the first place. You have taught me so much about the evil theft of medicinal plants, and you have fought so hard to address this wrong.

And Vandana Shiva, too, is a tireless crusader on this issue. Why have we never met, Vandana? But when we talk on the telephone, it is as though we are old friends—and that is how I feel, having heard so much about your life and work. I have such admiration for all you have done and am so grateful for the help you offered me for this book.

Other people provided wonderful material for the chapter about medicinal plants. Dr. Alison Jolly, it seems that you always have stories about everything I ask you about! We have known each other for so many, many years and become such friends. This time you told me about the rosy periwinkle. And Terrence Brown, my Native American friend Chitcus, you have shared so much information about the healing plants, for you are a medicine man and use the knowledge you acquired from your mother, herself a skilled medicine woman. What amazing times we have shared, what stories you have told me about the history and culture of your Karuk people.

Dr. Mike Huffman, another old friend, how fortunate that you decided to study the ways in which chimpanzees, and other animals, use medicinal plants. Thank you so much for so freely sharing your findings and photos.

I also want to thank Michael Crook, who was born in China and loves the old traditions and the history of places. We have known each other since my friend Greg MacIsaac invited me to China seventeen years ago, to visit the school (Western Academy of Beijing) where you both teach. Michael, you have taught me most of what I know about how a Westerner should behave in China, introduced me to key people, and with Greg served on the board of JGI-China since it began. It was you who organized the visit to Jane Tsao's organic farm, and told me about the famous herbalists of long ago, whose faded pictures were pinned to the wall of the old foresters' hut in the woods.

Now, in my mind's happy wandering, I am visiting botanical gardens and thinking of the extraordinarily talented and passionate people working there. Carlos Magdalena, master horticulturist of Kew Botanic Gardens, I know about your childhood in Spain and your botanical exploits around the world. You have shared with me many stories of plant rescue. Your enthusiasm brings those stories to life, and I am so very grateful.

Dr. Lourdes Rico Arce—or Lulú, as you like to be called—I have to thank you so much for the time you spent taking me around Kew's Herbarium, showing me some of the type specimens sent back by those crazy plant hunters. It brought back memories of Gombe in the early days when Vanne was helping me with the collection of chimpanzee food plants. I told you how we had sent them to our great friend, Dr. Bernard Verdcourt at the Coryndon Museum herbarium—and how calmly he had accepted and identified those mildewed specimens. It turned out that he was a great friend of yours, too. He would have loved this book.

I had a wonderful time when I visited the Millennium Seed Bank at Wakefield, Kew's sister organization. Dr. Tim Pearce spared no pains and gave up the best part of his day to show me around that amazing place, explaining all the processes that the seeds go through after arriving from the field. I feel so grateful to you, Tim, for teaching me so much. And that day I also met Wolfgang Stuppy. You have been more than generous, sharing information and contributing the stunning photographs of seeds in this book. Some of them are like images from a fantasy world. They seem unreal, and you have captured all this with your camera. I treasure the short time we spent together and look forward to seeing you again when we celebrate the publication of *Seeds of Hope*.

Dr. Dawn Kemp, you were so gracious when I visited the Chelsea Physic Garden on a cold January day with my sister Judy, and Mary Lewis. I could sense your love for the place when you showed us the old rare books and talked of the history of the wonderful old institution. You showed us around the garden and the greenhouses, giving up a lot of precious time. Thank you, Mary, for suggesting that this visit would provide rich material for my book—how right you were. And I want to thank David Lorraine also. You not only drove us to the Chelsea Physic Garden but, together with Mary, organized my trip to Cambodia during which we went to see the incredible temples of Angkor Watt. Indeed, you took the photograph that appears in this book.

A very special thank-you to two of my best friends, Rick Asselta and his wife, Nelly. You welcomed me to your home in Puerto Rico, you took me to the wonderful botanical gardens and introduced me to the director, and organized a meeting at the International Institute of Tropical Forestry, where I met Frank Wadsworth and heard about his dream to save Puerto Rico's endangered trees—with which some of our R&S students are now involved. At ninety years of age, Frank has not given up the fight—people like this inspire me and help me to keep going.

Rick also took me to visit an organic, shade-grown coffee farm up in the hills, where we met the farmer, resplendent in his elegantly cut jacket made from a coffee sack! I could write a whole book about our relationship, for it goes back to the very start of Roots & Shoots in America. You tailored a wonderful relationship with the Western Connecticut State University, and now you are coordinating the R&S program throughout Latin America.

Now I come to Dr. Rogier V. Van Vugt of Leiden Botanical Garden. You have been unbelievably helpful—sending me the story of the water lobelia and other stories about endangered plants. And not only did you provide photographs to go with the stories, but you actually took some especially for this book. It seems I have known you forever—yet we only met that one time when you gave me the little bunch of special flowers. And I wished there had been time to sit down and talk about the things we both love. Instead we have had to make do with e-mails and the occasional telephone call.

Dr. Sarah Sallon, of Hadassah Medical Organization in Jerusalem: you and Dr. Elaine Solowey, from Kibbutz Ketura, nurtured and loved that two-thousand-year-old date-palm seed. You recorded the magical appearance of the little shoot, then watched Methuselah slowly grow to maturity. And you brought all this to life when you visited me in Bournemouth and left me with such rich memories. Thank you so very much.

Nellie Sugii, tissue-culture expert, your work is almost magical, coaxing new life and energy into lethargic, reluctant seeds and seedlings. You helped with my last book—and lo and behold, you turn up again, playing a crucial role in the almost-unbelievable story of Cooke's koki'o. This time you have not only shared scientific facts but also given away one of the secrets of your success—your love of the plants you work with.

I met Paul Scannell for the first time in the Governor's House in Melbourne, Australia. Paul, your love of orchids is matched by the love you have for the environment where they grow, the boxwoods. And your love for the Aboriginal people, and for your family. You have been unfailingly helpful to me right from the start—thank you.

And another very special thank-you to journalist, photographer, and friend Alan Bartels. You introduced me to the very beautiful blowout penstemon and your enthusiasm is contagious. You also introduced me to Bruce and Sue Ann Switzer and arranged for me to stay overnight at their ranch, to see the prairie chickens. And over breakfast the next morning their daughter, Sarah, explained how they are gradually, together with neighboring ranchers, restoring the original prairie in the area. It is a very successful project, about which I hope to write more later. Before we left, you also introduced me to a blowout-penstemon seedling, part of a project involving the Roots & Shoots group you started. To give and receive energy, I kissed it—the plant, not the children (although they give me energy too)—and I have just received your letter saying it is planted out in a special place on the Switzer Ranch.

Now let me thank Dr. Stewart Henchie for sharing information about the reintroduction of the interrupted brome in the United Kingdom. And David Aplin, I am very grateful for all that you told me about the brome of the Ardennes, the fascinating sequence of events that led to saving this little grass from certain extinction.

Joshua Kaiser of Rishi Tea, not only did you and your staff share information with me, but I was invited to your offices and given a chance to talk with all your staff. And you made a special tea to benefit JGI. Thank you so very much.

And thank you also to Debra Music and Joe Whinney of Theo Chocolate. You answered all our questions and provided us with many wonderful photographs. And Joe, you taught me so much about the growing of cacoa and the work you are doing to improve the lives of the local villagers—including in the politically unstable DRC, one of the areas where JGI is working to protect the forest.

I'm not sure quite whom to thank when it comes to our JGI coffee-growing project in Tanzania. It all started when Green Mountain Coffee Roasters came to test the quality of the beans. Our TACARE team, under the leadership of Emmanuel Mtiti, worked with the coffee growers and encouraged the development of the cooperative. Mtiti and Mary Mavanza, thank you both for enabling me to visit the project on several occasions.

I am, of course, overwhelmed by the fact that Christian Hanak, known as a rose author—or "rose poet," as he calls himself—and Guillaume Didier, a rose breeder, created, between them, the Jane Goodall rose. You arranged for me to "baptize" it, closely collaborating with David LeFranc and Jeroen Haijtink of JGI-France, and I was so terribly grateful for all that happened on that so-special day. As a bonus, we visited the gardens of Versailles, where the director presented me with a pair of secateurs (pruning shears)—for, he said, you will need them to prune your rose. And these were no ordinary secateurs—each handle was inset with polished wood taken from an ancient oak, a much-loved tree that had blown down in a terrible storm. It had originally been planted, along with many others, for Marie Antoinette in 1786. Most of the tree was left to lie where it fell, a historical monument. But some of the wood had been harvested and used, sparingly, for very special purposes. What a gift!

Whenever I think of the gardens that have been planted on the Lakota Pine Ridge Reservation, I am deeply moved, and I have the utmost admiration for Jason Schoch and Patricia Hammond, who, against all odds, have succeeded. You have involved not only the Roots & Shoots children but their parents and a number of the elders. You are bringing back new understanding of the plants that are part of the food and medicine culture of the people. And this, along with the many other projects you have started, is bringing new hope to the reservation. I thank you so very much for providing me with all the information I needed for the book and the inspiration I get from your work.

Indeed, gardens are good for the spirit. Thank you, Revocatus Edwards, Shadrack Meshach, and Japhet Jonas, for giving me the facts about the gardens in the Lugufu refugee camp. And I am grateful, also, to Mary Raphaely, coordinator for the Natural Growth Project, for checking the facts in my story about the torture victims and making corrections and suggestions.

And thank you too, Bill Wallauer and Kristin Mosher, for helping us with photos of your garden—both before and after you transformed it into a miniparadise for wildlife.

Gary Zeller, as always you are involved in all manner of "eco-innovations." Thank you so much for sharing information about "Garden Up."

John Seed. My word! You have contributed hugely to this book. I close my eyes now and I am back, in my imagination, sitting with you on the grass under a tree in Sydney. And you are telling me about how you got involved in activism and the many successful campaigns you have led. As we talked about the urgent need to protect our forests, there was a seagull listening to us, not knowing about the world we are trying to save. His world needs help too, desperately. But fortunately for him, he does not know about that either.

I learned about Richard St. Barbe Baker from Lord Eden. John, I am so grateful to you for giving me a copy of *My Life, My Trees*, one of the many books he wrote. From it I learned so much about the history of forest protection. Why have we not all heard of this extraordinary man? I thought it was just ignorant me—not true. I have asked many, many people if they knew about Baker—almost nobody did. I am amazed by his life and his accomplishments, and plan to share some of this in our blog.

Our efforts to protect the forests to the south of Gombe in Tanzania, described in chapter 17, are proving extremely successful, thanks to the tireless work of our team on the ground under the overall direction of Emmanuel Mtiti. Mtiti, you have been with us since our TACARE program began, you and Aristides Kashula and Mary Mavanza, and I cannot begin to thank you for all you have done for me and all I have learned from you.

We are really grateful for funding from the EU, USAID, and the Norwegian government that is helping us to restore and protect a total area of more than 4,600 square miles, which encompasses the home of almost half of Tanzania's remaining chimpanzees. And over the lake, in the Democratic Republic of the Congo, or the DRC, we are involved in protecting 103,125 square miles of prime chimpanzee habitat.

Special thanks to Dario Merlo, executive director of JGI-DRC, and all our staff for doing such a remarkable job there despite the political instability. I am really grateful to the Arcus Foundation for your support, and to Jane Lawton of JGI-Canada for making a successful application to CIDA (Canadian International Development Agency) for additional funding. Other JGIs have helped with our forest programs—Diederik Visser from Netherlands, David Lefranc and Jeroen Haijtink from France, Ferran Guallar from Spain.

Dr. Lilian Pintea, JGI's vice president for conservation science, I am so very happy that you joined our team. By using the most up-to-date GIS, GPS, and satellite-imagery technology you are mapping those areas where JGI is working so that government agencies and villagers can determine which areas should be set aside for conservation. Much of this work is made possible thanks to the generosity and support we have had from Jack Dangermond, founder and president of Esri. And it is not just the contributions from your company, but your personal commitment and friendship for which I am so very grateful. You even agreed to join our JGI board.

Chuck Herring, you opened the doors of DigitalGlobe to Lilian back in 2005. And Chuck Chaapel, I know you have spent hours and hours during weekends and at night pre-processing thousands of images for JGI forest projects all around Africa. I am overwhelmed by your contribution, and it was wonderful to meet you both and actually see some of the extraordinary work that is going on at DigitalGlobe. As I told you, I don't pretend to understand the sophisticated technology, but I certainly understand how it helps us in the field.

And Rebecca Moore, of Google Earth Outreach program, you have been a staunch supporter ever since we first met and you told me how you had used satellite imagery to show your local community that plans to log a pristine forest would endanger the community's children, since helicopters carrying huge tree trunks would have to fly right over the school. And this saved the forest. I was so impressed—and from there you have gone on to give us huge support. Google Earth, thanks to your efforts, is providing the Android smartphone tablets and cloud technology to help local communities monitor their forests around Gombe and Masito-Ugalla in Tanzania. I value our friendship, too.

I learned a great deal about REDD+ and carbon trading from Jeff Horowitz, founder of Avoided Deforestation Partners. Jeff, your tireless efforts on behalf of saving our forests are astounding, and it was thanks to you that I was able to take my message to a number of international conferences, including the climate conferences at Copenhagen, Cancun, Durban, and, lastly, Rio+20. Disappointing outcomes overall, but with a good deal of positive momentum for our efforts to save forests.

It would indeed be remiss if I did not express gratitude to government agencies and officials, particularly in departments of Natural Resources, National Parks, and Forest Reserves, in Tanzania, Uganda, DRC, and the Republic of the Congo, for their cooperation and support for our various JGI projects, including our efforts to protect forests and biodiversity and to encourage sustainable farming in communities around wilderness areas.

I shall never forget meeting the Survivor tree, the Callery pear who survived the 9/11 attacks on the World Trade Center. I also met Bram Gunther, Ron Vega, and Richie Cabo on that special day, three people who helped her live. It was an intensely emotional time, and I thank you, all three, for sharing your amazing stories and spending time with us that day. And, too, for helping us get the photos we needed for the book. And thank you, Vickie Karp, director of Public Affairs, NYC Parks & Recreation, for I know how hard you worked behind the scenes to help us get in touch with all the people involved.

Now comes the hardest part of these acknowledgments, for I must thank all the wonderful people who shared stories that are not in the book.

I want to tell you how very much I appreciated all of you who answered our e-mails and shared information about your work. I have to be honest—I got carried away doing research for this book, utterly fascinated by all that I was learning. I wanted to write about all of it—alas, as with my last book about endangered animals, this one was getting way too long. Cuts—many cuts—had to be made.

The good news is that the cut material will appear on my blog on the janegoodall.org website. And I am assured that it will be an exciting and interactive blog—a place where I can tell so many other wonderful stories and where everyone can share their own comments and updates about the kingdom of the plants.

When I met Dr. Robert Robichaux, I knew there could never be a more passionate advocate for the flora of Hawaii. I had an unexpected free evening during a 2011 tour, and Rob joined me for a picnic supper in my hotel room somewhere in California. You had already shared with me details of the successful program to restore the beautiful Mauna Loa silverswords. (I wrote about it in *Hope for Animals and Their World.*) Now you have told me about another of Hawaii's most critically endangered plants, the stunningly beautiful lobelia—*Clermontia peleana.* The story is ready for my blog.

Valente Souza, I want to thank you for sharing information about your amazing, ongoing efforts to reforest 40,000 hectares (100,000 acres) of forest in the western mountains around Mexico City. And for involving Roots & Shoots in the program. You also sent me a marvelous story about a lawyer who went to defend some old trees, and won the case. People will love that tale!

Rick Asselta, you told me how the students and faculty of all eleven campuses of the Inter American University of Puerto Rico, under the leadership of Myraida Anderson and her partner, Alejandro, have organized the biggest tree-planting program in the country's history—64,000 trees are already planted by families around the country with a goal of having 12.2 million trees planted by the end of 2012. And now some of our Roots & Shoots members are helping with this effort. I am really looking forward to sharing this story.

So many people, friends, and colleagues have contributed by telling me about projects they feel would add value to the book. Many of them are written up and ready to be posted on my blog as soon as it opens. At this point in time I just want to send all of you a really big thank-you.

Polly Cevallos, you wrote to so many botanists who are doing fascinating work, telling them about my book—and you introduced me to many of them also, during my visits to Australia. Annette Debenham of JGI-Australia, you too have contacted your friends—one of them, Jenny Stackhouse, has sent me a list of people doing marvelous things, and I really look forward to contacting some of them.

Dr. Jim Begley, of the Goulburn Broken Catchment Management Authority, is involved in a project to restore the Australian grasslands in Victoria. It is a wonderful program, as is the Grassy Groundcover Research Project of Dr. Paul Gibson-Roy, also in Australia. And on the other side of the world, Dr. Mike Forsberg is working on protection and restoration of the Great Plains ecosystem. And when we post all that material on the restoration of the world's grasslands, I so look forward, Matilda Essig, to sharing some of your exquisite artwork depicting the prairie grasses. I was so grateful that you offered to contribute some to this book.

Thank you, Mark Fountain, for telling me about the fascinating and successful efforts to save the Davies' waxflower (*Phebalium daviesii*) in Tasmania.

Ferran Guallar, of JGI-Spain, introduced me to his friend Dr. Martí Boada, and Sònia Sànchez, a member of his group, told me of a really interesting project they are doing—restoring genetic strains of apples in Spain. I look forward to learning more about that.

And Dr. Rod Morris sent me some terrific stories about endangered trees, including the *Sophora toromiro* on Easter Island. I was especially pleased to hear that you believe that it may indeed have been the extinction of the dodo that prevented the germination of the forest tree, *Tambolo coque.* (An ingenious theory that someone debunked.)

I first knew Alex Chepstow-Lusty as a student at Gombe. You told me an extraordinary detective story. As a result of analyzing a sediment core that you took from a small lake in Peru—painstaking work counting pollen grains and identifying the plants that had produced them all those years ago—you were able to piece together the story of how llama dung enabled the Inca to grow corn at a higher altitude than had been possible before. The whole story is absolutely fascinating and I am dying to share it on our blog.

Robert Eden—I am particularly saddened that I could not include the amazing story of how you gradually built up your organic vineyard in France, the wonderful benefits of buildings made with hemp bricks, the use of a horse rather than a tractor for plowing, and all the other fascinating aspects. Best of all is the fabulous organic wine that you produce. I have so much to thank you for, over and above information to help this book, such as your taking on, pro bono, the huge task of incorporating JGI-Global as a bona fide NGO.

Will Raap, you were so very generous with your time and gave us fascinating information about your wonderful Intervale community garden project in Vermont. People will definitely benefit from reading about it on our blog.

A big disappointment—it simply was not possible to include all the Roots & Shoots projects that involve gardens, tree planting, habitat restoration, and so on. I hope we can establish a special section of our blog for all this information. So many groups sent information that I cannot thank you all here. But I do want to give special thanks to Corinne Bowman, Allison Deines, Revocatus Edwards, Renée Gunther, Jennifer Hill, Japhet Jonas, Alicia Kennedy, Nsaa-Iya Kihunrwa, Erasto Nvjiko, Shawn Sweeney, and Mike and Karen Weddle.

Tara Golshan and Jasmina Marcheva—you put together wonderful projects from across the United Kingdom, many of them inspired by your workshops. And special thanks to Federico Bogdanowicz. Fede, you invented the marvelous "Professor Roots," complete with magnifying glass, toilet-roll binoculars, and bush outfit. And, in this role, you have got hundreds of children interested in nature.

All around the world I have had help with this book from all twenty-eight JGI offices. But some people have been especially helpful in organizing visits to botanical gardens, organic farms, and so on during the few days I was able to be in each country. In Singapore our executive director Beng Chiak and board member Shawn Lum arranged for me to visit the Bukit Panjang Community Garden, and came with me to the botanic gardens to photograph my Jane Goodall orchid. In Taiwan, executive director Kelly Kok masterminded the visit to the river-cleaning project. In China, executive director Lei Chen Wong helped to organize my visit to the organic farm. And Ilke Pedersen-Beyst told me the wonderful story about getting married inside a hollow oak, and provided the photo. Two people who helped hugely with acquiring information and contacting botanists are Rob Sassor and John Trybus. Much gratitude to all of you.

Joseph Vengersammy, of First in Service Travel—oh my goodness—without your help I could never have gotten to all the places mentioned in the book, met all the people. You have been fantastic in your ability to somehow make impossible schedules work. We have woken you in the middle of the night when flights were suddenly canceled on the other side of the globe—and sometimes you fixed problems before we even knew that they existed. You are wonderful, and I am so very grateful.

It would have been impossible to gather together all the photos we used to illustrate this book without the work of Christin Jones. Christin, you had to track down photographers and pester them to sign release forms, and search through the Internet for historic images. You have done a stellar job, as you did for the last book, and we are very grateful indeed.

And Mary Paris—you have worked miracles to find some of the early photos of me, from the archives. And to enhance the resolution of old pictures, and otherwise get pictures ready for publication. Thank you so much.

Jolie Novak, thank you for jumping in at the last minute and helping us secure and prepare our missing photos. Your generosity and expertise were invaluable.

Then, of course, there are all the photographers themselves who have generously shared their work, waiving fees, searching out their best. A special thanks to Roy Borghouts—you took a whole series of photos when we were searching for an image for the cover, though unfortunately none was selected in the end. I was so sorry about that, but your time was not wasted, for your photos will be used for publicity and on the blog. And Patrick van Veen, you also took photos for the book—thank you so much.

Michael Pollan, I was so absolutely delighted when I heard that you had agreed to write a foreword for this book. I know that this is not an easy task, having been asked to write a good many myself, so I am really terribly grateful. I have so enjoyed and benefited from reading your own books and articles. I remember you saying that to look at the world from the points of view of other species "is a cure for the disease of human self-importance." How apt! And your suggestion that we should see things from "a plant's eye view" seems particularly appropriate for this book.

Tom Mangelsen, you have introduced me to several of America's ecosystems with their varied plants and trees—the prairies, sandhills, the badlands, and the different environments of Yellowstone National Park. You shared your love for the old cottonwood trees and the aspens. Together we have anguished over the impacts on the environment of intensive agriculture. The center pivots pumping up water from ever deeper under the ground, lowering the water table. The draining of wetlands and the leaching of pollutants into the Platte River, already much diminished, the underlying Ogallala Aquifer shrunk and polluted. Over and above this you invited Gail and me to hide away for a couple of days in your cabin to work on this book in between glorious mornings and evenings with the sandhill cranes and snow geese. And, finally, you have always been so generous in letting us use your fabulous photographs. Thank you, thank you.

And huge thanks also to my wonderful friend Michael Aisner for housing and supporting us through the final push to organize our photos in

Boulder. I can think of no better place for such intense work than your extraordinary house. The day we arrived, you showed us the smashed-open door of your car, and the tiny cardboard box that had been inside, now neatly slit open by a black bear. He had gone to all that trouble merely for a couple of lollipops!!!! And many, many thanks to Jeff Orlowski, who printed out countless pictures. Right up to the last minute, Jeff, you helped us during that marathon photo session. And thank you, Chef Linda Hampsten—you volunteered to nurture us at that time with your delicious organic cooking. Just as you did when I was finalizing *Harvest for Hope*—also at Michael's house.

James and "Sue 2" Knowles—I am thinking now of the many days I have spent in the Roger Smith Hotel in New York. Over the years I have worked on three different books in your hotel, including this one. Your generosity is deeply appreciated—I have accomplished so much, spoken with so many plant people, and written so many words in the familiar and friendly suites you spoil me with. I have stayed with you so many times that it truly feels like home.

Many thanks to our excellent literary agent, Debra Goldstein, who believed in this book from the start and worked tirelessly to make sure our contract was secured. Nona Gandelman—you do such a great job as my agent for all my books, helping me to get the best possible deals and finding publishers for editions in various countries. Added to which you brought delicious sustenance—and a bottle of Scotch—when Gail and I were working on the book in Colorado.

Our thanks to Helen Atsma, our extraordinary editor at Grand Central Publishing, who carefully guided this book and lovingly pushed us to make it better. Thank you to Kirsten Reach, Helen's assistant, who has been helping Christin with photos. And a special thanks to Grand Central's Executive Vice President and Publisher, Jamie Raab. This is the fourth book you have published for me, and I know it is not easy for you—I get too enthusiastic, carried away, wanting to fill more and more pages, and you are so patient. Thank you so, so much for your faith in me—it is wonderful to know you also as a friend.

Mary Lewis, Vice-President for Outreach, began working with me in 1991 when she was still employed by Conoco. She joined JGI full-time in 1995, organizing my tours, ensuring that the people I need to see are fitted into the too-busy schedules. She knows everyone and is invaluable in linking people together—a lot of information for this book was acquired in this way. Truly, Mary, without you helping to organize my life, in addition to helping with the organization of JGI, this book might still be unfinished.

Added to that, I could not have a more wonderful friend—kind, generous, and nurturing, welcoming me to the little haven of your house in London when I arrive, exhausted from some crazy tour, and inviting colleagues and potential donors to wonderful home-cooked meals.

Susana Name, who heads up our Office of the Founder (OOF) and works with Mary on my tours. It has been wonderful having you with me on tour, especially when I am in Latin America, not only organizing the events and helping me to meet the plant people but translating—you are my "Spanish voice." And you and your family—Alex, Christian, and Simba the dog—also welcome me into your home.

Dr. Anthony Collins—Tony to me, Anton to many—director of Baboon Research at Gombe, I am especially thankful for all that you have done for me: helping answer many questions about medicinal plants, organizing my visits to the villages around Gombe to visit the coffee program and the traditional healers. Your knowledge about the local trees and plants is quite extraordinary, your wisdom regarding the local people profound. One special memory is when we bumped our way from Kigoma to Mpanda, with Mtiti and some of the TACARE team, so that I could see firsthand the beautiful forest that we are helping to protect. Together we marveled at a magical waterfall and visited a sacred tree where people still leave gifts. For your support and friendship over so many years, I do so thank you.

Almost at the end now. Judy, or "Jiff," as I named you when we were children. What a marvelous sister you are. I can only get down to serious writing when I am at home in The Birches—and I have so little time there, but thanks to you, I have been able to immerse myself in getting this book done because you spoiled me, nurtured me, provided my body with the fuel it needed. Delicious meals, fires in the winter. Thank you, thank you. You, with Pip and her two boys, are keeping alive the spirit of the house that so nurtured our childhoods. And—so very important—there are always dogs, rescued dogs. During my walks with Astro, and more recently Charlie, I did much of the thinking that went into the writing of this book.

Gail Hudson, coauthor, collaborator, and friend—what a true joy it has been to work with you. How endlessly patient and tactful you have been, trying to curtail my passion for writing ever more and more, including ever more photos. Without your input I doubt Grand Central would have agreed to publish the book, so long and unwieldy it would have been. And though we have not agreed on everything, when there was a particular story I really wanted to include, and you suggested cutting, I at once saw why—and then rewrote the piece so that you would say, "Oh, now I see why this is so important!" There is no one else in the world with whom I would want to collaborate. Thus, together, we have given birth to yet another book.

And finally—yes, I have really come to the end!—I want to acknowledge the enormous debt that I owe to the green spirits of the plants themselves. I hope that I and all who have helped with this book have done them justice. We want to celebrate the beauty, complexity, and mystery of their world. That we may save it before it is too late.

Index

Page numbers of photos appear in italics.